Crusoe on Cricket

CRUSOE
ON CRICKET

The Cricket Writings of
R. C. ROBERTSON-GLASGOW

Introduction by Alan Ross

THE PAVILION LIBRARY

First published in Great Britain 1966

Copyright © 1985 Alan Ross Limited

First published in the Pavilion Library in 1985 by
Pavilion Books Limited
196 Shaftesbury Avenue, London WC2H 8JL
in association with Michael Joseph Limited
44 Bedford Square, London WC1B 3DU

ISBN 0 907516 83 1
ISBN 0 907516 70 X paperback

Printed and bound in Great Britain by
Billing & Sons Ltd, Worcester

ACKNOWLEDGEMENT

Acknowledgements are due to the *Observer*,
Messrs Hollis and Carter, Arthur Barker,
Werner Laurie and Dennis Dobson Ltd,
publishers respectively of various sections
of this book in their original form.

Contents

FACTS AND FANCIES

Introduction

It seems to me important, for the pleasure of his contemporaries, for the use of cricket historians and addicts, for future cricket correspondents and for students of good prose generally, that a one-volume edition of Raymond Robertson-Glasgow's writing on cricket should exist. It has not been an easy book to compile, for Crusoe wrote for newspapers for over thirty years and much of his best work has a necessarily ephemeral context. That this should be so, however, is the fate of every journalist; sub-editors usually get at the most telling and vivid images anyway, and those that survive go down into obscurity with the incidents that produced them. In Robertson-Glasgow's case this was the more serious, since, unlike Cardus, he was not really an essayist, nor did he publish any accounts of overseas tours, such as would have been testimony to his evocative skill and over-all tactical shrewdness. In this last respect he was unlucky, for he had planned a book about the 1950–51 MCC tour of Australia, which he was covering for *The Observer*; unfortunately *The Times* correspondent fell ill, Robertson-Glasgow did his job, and his own book, which he had nearly finished, was made obsolete by *The Times* publishing all the match reports he had done for them in a booklet of their own. It was a great disappointment to him and the waste of a lot of work. As a result, his professional brilliance as a daily journalist must be taken largely on trust. About 1953, when I succeeded him on *The Observer*, he felt he had done enough about cricket and turned to other things. He was not very well at the time and he preferred in future to write from the security of his cottage at Pangbourne rather than to report from the field of play. He suffered most of his life from severe and recurrent bouts of depression and in the circumstances the tone and charity of his writing was astonishing.

This present volume, as it stands, contains the cream of the half-dozen or so books that he produced. By 'cream' I mean most of the milk too, for when I came to select I found that there was little, for one reason or another, that seemed to me superfluous or dated. He got as much out of the obscure as out of the famous, and I think he preferred them. He saw cricketers as characters not as robots, and I have found it necessary to jettison

11

less than half out of the two full volumes of Sporting Prints that he collected during his life and on which his fame deservedly rests. There may be occasional repetitions, and sometimes other games creep in, particularly golf, but even when he described the same players twice, at different moments of their careers, he imposed a fresh vision of them.

He was a miniaturist, a master of compression, concise, elegant, witty; the form of much of his writing was dictated by the exigencies of the 700–800 word 'print' but I think in any case that he could say all he wanted in that space. His style was the result equally of a classical education and of a romantic temperament, and he had the real cricketer's indifference to statistics. Where Cardus, in Crusoe's own phrase, was 'master of the rhapsodical style, cutting his sharp epigrams from the most amorphous material' Robertson-Glasgow was the gentle but high-spirited deflater. 'On the great moments and the great cricketers, he has no equal,' Crusoe observed about Cardus, 'but, amid his copiousness, he is eclectic.' He himself was eclectic but not copious. Cardus's materials were the Lancashire and England teams of the twenties and thirties; Crusoe was at his happiest with Oxford and Somerset, with schools and villages. He wrote about Test matches as if they took place in the Parks, as no doubt he wished they did. This does not mean he was disinterested in high drama or the legendary players. He merely recoiled from the boring, the self-centred, the thoroughly ordinary, even when these brought results. Between 1920 and 1950 he still managed to dissect the technique and convey the character of nearly all of those who played out the essential history of their time. No one else did so quite as well.

* * *

I have thought it sensible here to print first an extract from 46 *Not Out*, the autobiography Crusoe published in 1948. This covers the years 1920–24, that is to say the Oxford and Somerset period during which he was, as he calls it, a 'practising cricketer' rather than an 'intervener'. It sets the background and, as it were, establishes the credentials, though this seems scarcely necessary. For the rest of his life Crusoe played at weekends or in the summer holidays. He must, with his high, rollicking action, have been a formidable bowler in 1924, able to get the inswinger to straighten out at a lively pace, and occasionally veer late the other way, and fifteen years or so later he had not lost the knack, though some of the zip. My own appearances with or against him were long after he had given up regular first-class cricket, but I remember at Oxford in 1941, when he played against us before we went to Lord's, being astonished at his pace from the pitch. He was even able, in the Authors *v.* Publishers matches of the early fifties, to get some bounce off the Westminster School wicket at Vincent's Square and anyone who can do that at the age of 50 is no mean bowler.

Next, in order, comes *The Brighter Side of Cricket*, almost in its entirety. This was published in 1933, and was Crusoe's first book. It has always been an especial favourite of mine, not only because it was given to me as a reward for captaining an eccentric but unbeaten preparatory school team, but because it opened my eyes to what cricket was really about, its discipline and grace, its jokey comedy, its rich nostalgias and fantasies. I have read it a score of times and know much of it by heart.

The third section contains a selection from the two volumes of *Cricket Prints* published initially in 1943 and 1948. Most of these appeared in *The Observer* and though some of their subjects are now little more than names they form part of a unique gallery of portraits. They came into being because someone died or retired or emigrated or scored a hundred hundreds, or perhaps just because a space had to be filled. I intended to cut out the more obviously topical, but in the end I could hardly bear to. In any faded old team photograph the humbler have, after all, as much right to their place as the others.

The three last sections, taken from *Rain Stopped Play*, 1948, *Cricket Prints*, 1948, and *All in the Game*, 1952, are, on the whole, more frivolous, written when Crusoe was edging away from the dialectics of the Press box and back towards the village match. I have included nothing from *How to Become a Test Cricketer*, 1962, because there is nothing in it he had not done better before and also because in any case it is obtainable. Nearly everything else in this book has long been out of print. I don't think anything of consequence is missing, nor that any of it is irrelevant.

13

I need say no more here about the writer, at home equally with the great and the insignificant, able as fluently to suggest Tate bowling and Sutcliffe batting, the blacksmith slogging and the curate taking one on the shins. From his prose the smell of linseed oil and ancient pads, of village dressing rooms and of the Long Room at Lord's, come over with equal vividness. It is always a cricketer writing.

But the man was no less remarkable. The thing you noticed about him first, apart from a resemblance to Alastair Sim, was his reverberating laugh. He had, when speaking, a disconcerting habit of thrusting his face right up close to yours, never moving his eyes off you, and then, swaying away out of reach like a boxer, of throwing back his head and roaring. It was a laugh that penetrated all corners of a pavilion and there was no gainsaying it.

He was a fabulous talker, a restless match for Fry and Cardus in invention, anecdote and energy, and he wore his learning very lightly. He was tremendous company, unless you were feeling frail, though his infectious conviviality must often have been an effort. But behind the jovialness and the joking there was a considerateness, a gravity that rarely got into his writing. Above all, he was a man of great sweetness and charm, of abiding loyalties and surprising compassion. With Cardus, he helped to raise cricket reporting from journalism into an art. Those who never saw him bowl or heard his laugh will, I hope, get something of his real flavour from these pages.

ALAN ROSS

46 Not Out

Mostly Cricket

I have never regarded cricket as a branch of religion. I have met, and somehow survived, many of its blindest worshippers. I have staggered, pale and woozly, from the company of those who reject the two-eyed stance as Plymouth Brethren reject all forms of pleasure except money-making. I have never believed that cricket can hold Empires together, or that cricketers chosen to represent their country in distant parts should be told, year after year, that they are Ambassadors. If they are, I can think of some damned odd ones.

The air of holy pomp started from the main temple at Lord's, and it breathed over the Press like a miasma. *'Procul, O Procul Este, Profani!'* We are not as other men. Sometimes I look back at reports of games in which I took part, and I have thought: 'And are these arid periphrases, these formal droolings, these desiccated shibboleths really supposed to represent what was done and how it was done? What has become of that earthy striving, that comic, tragic thing which was our match of cricket?'

University cricket is often written off as a rather advanced schoolboy affair; but the four matches in which I played for Oxford against Cambridge, between 1920 and 1923, produced eight England cricketers, of whom four, A. E. R. Gilligan, A. P. F. Chapman, D. R. Jardine, and G. O. Allen, captained England in Australia. The other four were G. E. C. Wood, J. C. W. MacBryan, G. T. S. Stevens, and C. S. Marriott. Besides these, J. L. Bryan, of Cambridge, was chosen as a member of Gilligan's team in Australia, but was never called on for a Test, and R. H. Bettington, of Oxford, while still an undergraduate, was little behind his fellow-Australian, Arthur Mailey, in skill as a leg-break bowler. Nor will false modesty or fear of 'bad form, old chap' prevent me from saying that Clem Gibson and Norman Partridge from Cambridge, and myself, were all, at various times, good enough as bowlers to have played for England without being laughed at. Anyhow, I have seen several worse than us getting a few wickets in Anglo-Australian matches.

My brother Bobs, who had gone to work in a bank in Toronto,

17

wrote to me in spring of 1920 saying, 'I suppose you ought to get your cricket Blue', and I know I did so suppose. It came on a June evening, in a letter from Frank Gilligan, just as we gathered in the Corpus quad for dinner. Nothing compares with early triumphs. Young success kicks like a mule with a squib under its tail. The years come when friends are not so ready or able to share delight and grief.

Edward Pearce and I went to the pictures that night, in that house where the little manager used to stand at the back of the stalls with imitation diamond-studs in his shirt-front, waiting to restore order, which was almost nightly lost. During the rest of that term, and in the following winter, I liked to walk rather slowly along the High and imagine that other pedestrians were saying: 'Look, that's Robertson-Glasgow, the cricket Blue.' Alfred, Lord Tennyson, they tell us, also liked to be recognized in public. An innocent infatuation. A gift of divination would have diluted my vanity; but I was not yet to know that in four matches against Cambridge I would get only two wickets in 100 overs, for 243 runs. Nor did a batting average of 36 put things right. Few, except myself, cared whether I made runs or not, and, early in that summer of 1920, Frank Gilligan drew me aside in his grave and earnest manner and said: 'I'm not going to let you make runs. You're not strong enough to bat and bowl.' I was pained to think I looked quite so delicate. Besides, I had fancied myself as a batsman.

At the end of April came the Freshmen's match, if match be the word for that trial in which all hope to catch the judge's eye, and none cares which side wins. In their first innings, D. R. Jardine carried his bat for 60. This was the third season in which I had met Jardine. In each of the previous summers I had managed to take his wicket in the Charterhouse v. Winchester match. But in this first innings at Oxford, he made no shadow of a mistake. I had 5 wickets for 23 in 19 overs, mostly with inswingers.

Douglas Jardine, at nineteen years, was the completest young batsman I have seen, both in method and temperament. It was said that while he was still a preparatory schoolboy, at Horris Hill, he had politely but firmly corrected his master on a point of technique and supported his view by a quotation from C. B.

18

Fry's *Batsmanship*. Tall and well-proportioned, he has ever been the perfect example of the orthodox English style. His off-driving, which in Test matches against Australia he was apt to deny himself, was then free and strong, and the bowler who attacked his leg-stump was but wasting himself in vanity. But where Jardine excelled was in his back-stroke. It was professional, near to perfect.

I bowled Jardine for 18 in the second innings, which was abbreviated by the leg-breaks and googlies of R. H. Bettington. Reg Bettington, tall, dark of complexion, and of immense power, had come to Oxford with his brother Jack from Paramatta, New South Wales, Both bowled spinners; Jack at a brisk medium to fast, Reg at normal leg-breaker's pace. When Jack could pitch them, he was almost unplayable; but he was erratic. Both were free-driving batsmen. Both were tough Rugger forwards, but it was Reg who got the Blue, playing against Cambridge in two years out of his four, largely on the strength of his left-footed place-kicking. Jack was the more finished golfer, Reg the more terrific hitter. Here again it was Reg who played against Cambridge. So Jack, who might so easily have played for Oxford at all three games, landed no Blue at all. He wore his disappointment invisibly. He fell gravely ill not long after returning as a civil engineer to Australia. Then he seemed to recover, but death won. He was as fine a fellow as you could want.

Reg Bettington made the ball buzz like a top, and at the moment of delivery there was a sharp snapping sound. There was another and even sharper snapping sound when he asked for lbw or a catch at the wicket. A Bettington appeal brought all Sydney to the Oxford Parks. Six feet and three inches in height, he took a longish run and bowled with a looping trajectory; not flat, like so many of his sort. I had a fine view of his bowling from short slip. His performance was brilliant that summer. Length, flight, spin, and persistence; he had them all; also a faster ball of vicious suddenness. Years later, when his skill at the leg-break had declined, I saw him bowl a fellow-spinner, Richard Tyldesley, with this fast one at Lord's. Poor Dick; he had disentangled the bat-handle from his ample circumference, and stood at the ready, blade in air; but, when he brought it down, the bails had flown.

Greville Stevens bowled leg-breaks and googlies nearly as well as Bettington, and was a distinctly more scientific batsman. Stevens arrived at Oxford with cricket honours already thick upon him. At University College School he had made 466 not out in a House-match. For Middlesex, he had taken 21 wickets at moderate cost in the 1919 County Championship. To crown all, he had played for the Gentlemen against Players at Lord's. As Lionel Hedges said to him: 'Considering these set-backs, you're not a bad fellow!'.

Greville had wit and a salty tongue, which some mistook for conceit. When he had walked out to the field for Oxford in his first match, he said to our captain, Gilligan: 'And shall I field in the place that I've made famous?' That was backward point, where he was a fine catcher. 'Yes,' said Gilligan, 'in the deep at both ends.' Myself, I enjoyed his playful remarks; and I recall with delight Greville's comment on arriving in the dressing-room at Lord's for the Gentlemen v. Players in 1924; looking round at some of his fellow-cricketers, he said: 'This match isn't what it used to be, and I'm rather tired of it.' Not bad, for twenty-three years old.

Tall and fair, with a face that always made the schoolgirls ask for his autograph, he was yet not of athletic build. His run-up to the wicket was rather prancing and awkward, as if he were glad he hadn't to run any further, which, I think, he was; but he delivered the ball with a high arm, and, unlike so many of his kind, he never lost the potency of his leg-break. In the Freshmen's match, he failed as a batsman. I had him caught in his first innings. He had me bowled in my second. He took four wickets in each innings, twice defeating one H. P. Marshall, from Haileybury, who later was to become known to millions as Howard Marshall, broadcaster. On leaving Oxford, Greville Stevens soon deserted serious cricket for business, becoming a prosperous and astute stock-broker. But he played for England, and bowled C. G. Macartney in that memorable Oval match of 1926 when the tide at last turned against Australia, and Harold Larwood became famous, and Wilfred Rhodes ended his England cricket in clouds of glory.

From Tonbridge, with a name as batsman and cover-point,

came Lionel Hedges, bubbling with life and mimicry. Like Stevens, he had been early blooded, having scored 28 and 43 at Canterbury for Kent against Jack Gregory and the Australian Imperial Forces a few days after leaving school. Lionel was at Trinity, which fitted him like a glove. No pleasanter community is to be found in Oxford. Short and strong, he was the best hooker in the side, and at cover-point he was swift to cut off that square single which maddens a bowler. He favoured enormous collars to his cricket shirt and a knotted silk scarf. He was soon into his stride with 86 against Middlesex and 101 not out against Essex. But his nervous temperament was unsatisfied. 'If they don't give me my Blue now,' he said to me, 'I'll make a string of noughts.' He didn't. He played Rugby for the University, at stand-off half, on several occasions, but never against Cambridge. Lionel was full of parlour-tricks, including a ride up and down on a fictional hotel-lift. At the end of the first day's play of the Cambridge match in 1922, he bought a newsvendor's pitch and papers in Trafalgar Square and quickly sold out on 'Oxford's deplorable plight'. Later, he went as a master to Cheltenham, and played some fine innings for Gloucestershire. But he died cruelly early, in 1934, from a virulent form of influenza.

We lost the first match, against Warwickshire. It was cold and wet. I took a stinging catch from that craggy old warrior Charlesworth full on the breast-bone, whence it fell to the grass, at mid-off. I took no wickets, but a very long-run-up to the crease. Stevens had 5 for 35 in the first innings, Bettington 5 for 48 in the second. Willie Quaife, smallest and correctest of great batsmen, batted a very long time for not so very many, and Jardine was bowled by F. S. G. Calthorpe for 0 in the first innings. A bleak start. But I was asked again for the next match, against Middlesex.

'Plum' Warner was in his last season of captaincy, which was soon to be crowned by that tremendous match at Lord's against Surrey, and the winning of the championship. Warner had taken the England team which beat Australia over there in 1911–12 and whose deeds I had rushed to read each morning at school. And here he was in the flesh, bald as an ostrich-egg under his Harlequin cap, slight, small-boned, pale of face, and with nothing but cricket in his conversation.

In my first innings I was bowled by the foxy J. W. Hearne, and I still had the pride to be very annoyed about it. Then, near the end of the first innings, I took my first wicket in first-class cricket, Captain J. M. S. Love for 0. I also had the towering Jack Durston stumped trying some complicated form of attack. After being led by 24 on the first innings, we ran up 349 for 8 declared. We won, by 139 runs; but that was nothing to me compared with bowling Hendren when he was well set at 50. It was a snifter, though I say it, bending in very late from the off. I walked on air, and would certainly have missed any catch that had come in my way.

We followed this victory by beating Essex by 239 runs. The match was doubly notable; first, because Douglas Jardine, in a spell of seven overs and 3 balls took 6 for 6, including the mighty P. Perrin, bowled for 0. Douglas, with a pensive and halting run, bowled what purported to be slow leg-breaks. Secondly, I acquired a nickname which has stuck ever since. Charlie McGahey and A. C. Russell had put on some 50 runs at the start of their second innings when I bowled McGahey with a full pitcher which he later referred to as a yorker. In the bowels of the pavilion, Johnny Douglas, the Essex captain, asked him how he was out, and McGahey answered: 'I was bowled by an old —— I thought was dead two thousand years ago, called Robinson Crusoe.'

I came to know Johnny Douglas well, and I must have stuck in his mind somewhat, because, when he invited me to stay in his flat at Hampstead later in the summer, I left the bath-tap running while having a drink, and an old lady from the flat below came hustling up the stairs to say that her Persian carpet was ruined and what about it. The incomparable John captained England twelve times against Australia, and after winning four victories to one in 1911–12 he lost all five in a row in 1920–21. You knew, and could often hear, what he was thinking on the field. It was battle, and nothing but, when he walked out, a gladiator, from the wicket gate, thick black hair shining and plastered down, rubbing the new ball on his strong forearm, frowning at some imaginary flaw in its make-up; or else went forth to bat, more grimly yet – for his batting was acquired and

22

his bowling was natural – with strong slow gait, feet outwards, tugging his batting gloves on with his teeth, ready for a week, for a lifetime of that fight which was his cricket, and damn the bowlers and blast the crowd. He won the World Amateur Middleweight Boxing Championship in a fight with 'Snowy' Baker that has seldom been equalled. At the age of forty-eight, in 1930, he was drowned. He had gone below deck to save his father, and the ship, nearly severed by a collision, sank at about midnight in a few minutes.

On Wednesday, June 2, 1920, I first met John Daniell, and next day he asked me to play a few matches for Somerset. This was an unorthodox request, as I had no qualification for Somerset, having been born in Edinburgh and living wherever the family, or parts of it, happened to be. Technically, I was qualified for Scotland, but the Scottish selectors have always been rather stuffy about Anglo-Scots, and I was never asked to play for the land of my birth. Not that it matters.

My connection with Somerset was our cousins, the Foxcroft family, of Hinton Charterhouse, of whom Charlie was Member of Parliament for Bath and a High Tory of the utmost spirit and pugnacity. But John Daniell reckoned that this would be good enough. At least I was in the position that no other county could claim me, even supposing they wanted my services. Herein was the mistake made by my friend Leonard Crawley. Being qualified for Durham, he went off to play for Worcestershire, and Durham objected. This little difference led, finally, to a quarrel between George, Lord Harris, Hon. Treasurer to MCC, and Lord Deerhurst, the High Panjandrum of Worcestershire. They met, it was reported, on the pavilion steps at Lord's, and Lord Deerhurst swept off his grey top-hat and offered Lord Harris a short speech of congratulation on his alleged mismanagement of cricket. Stormy tea-cups long ago.

Back to the Oxford Parks. John Daniell had the idea that inswing bowling was muck, and going in first with John Cornish White, he proceeded to the proof of his point, swatting my bowling with scowling ferocity high to the leg-side. At length he hit one even harder than the rest, but rather lower, and Greville Stevens, defending his hopes of posterity, caught it at close square-leg. For us, Ronnie Holdsworth, a batsman of charm and power and a man of much absence of mind, scored 73. In the Somerset second innings Leonard Braund made 67 with his own inimitable and courtly grace, and I took 5 wickets for 20 runs. Needing only 116 to win, we were at first scattered by some grand fast-medium bowling on the part of Philip Foy, a civil engineer on leave from the Argentine. Stevens, with 30 not out, batted us to narrow victory. Soon, after losing to the Army with what amounted to only an 'A' team, we started our tour, against Sussex at Brighton. There, I found time to visit the spot outside Sopers', where the elderly citizen had shouted 'damn the boy' when Bobs pushed me on to his patent-leather toes; and I had a good stare at the cinema in West Street where we used to see the programme round twice, then stagger, half-blind, into the sunlight.

We beat Sussex by 8 runs. Throughout, it was the most even game I have ever played in; Oxford 231 and 214, Sussex 221 and 216. Maurice Tate was the man of the match. Batting at number three, he made 90 and 35, and in our two innings he took 11 wickets for 90 runs. He still bowled at a bare medium pace, and three more years were to pass before, at the age of twenty-eight, he became one of the greatest fast-medium bowlers of all time. He scored runs at high speed, hitting, firm-footed, anything a little over a length, and not minding much about the text-books. But in defence he had a very correct back-stroke.

Greville Stevens and I took all the Sussex wickets except one, and I was much elevated in spirit at bowling their opener, Ted Bowley, in both innings. The other wicket fell to Geoffrey Greig, of Westminster, son of the Bishop of Guildford. I recall his father coming for a Confirmation at my first school, and the excitement of the boys when they saw him adjusting the two pieces of his pastoral staff like a billiard-cue. A. F. Bickmore, from Clifton, scored 59 for us in the first innings. He was a tall and stylish batsman with great power of stroke, and a fine fielder at short-leg, who favoured a large sun-hat. Later in the season he made 104 not out for Kent against Essex. In our second innings, Bickmore's partner, C. H. L. Skeet, made 66. He was a painstaking solid batsman and one of the greatest fielders I ever saw; swift of foot, and with a throw that would have satisfied

Sydney. At the end of August he played for Middlesex in the famous match at Lord's, against Surrey, which decided the Championship, and with Harry Lee put up 208 for the first wicket in Middlesex's second innings. Skeet made 106, Lee 108.

From Brighton we went to the Oval, where Reg Bettington took 13 wickets for 128 runs on a plumb pitch, having Jack Hobbs caught, when well set, at short-leg with a most erosive top-spinner. Skeet made a wonderful catch at cover-point to dismiss Frank Naumann, whose bowling had beaten Cambridge at Lord's the year before. In our first innings, I was top scorer with 48, at number ten. I was not promoted. We left them 313 to win. With the fourth ball of my first over, from the House of Commons end, I had Jack Hobbs caught at mid-off for 0. I thought it was a bump-ball, and was staggered to see him walking out. It was my only wicket in the match, but I didn't mind that. I could live on my one wicket for weeks. H. D. G. Leveson Gower, emerging at the age of forty-seven to captain Surrey, made 54 in their first innings, and saved them in their second with a stubborn 17. He had little power of stroke, but a great heart for the battle. Harrison, a dour and silent cricketer, made 70 not out. F. Parris was one of the umpires in this match. He had a large and bristly moustache which was apt to catch the eye of Tom Webster, the cartoonist.

So we had beaten Middlesex, Essex, Sussex, and almost beaten Surrey. Our pride was squashed by MCC at Lord's. J. W. Hearne and Aubrey Faulkner, two of the great all-rounders of cricket, diddled us out twice. Geoffrey Foster made 143 in the most perfect Fosterian manner, and in him Bettington for once met his master. Patsy Hendren scored 160; and, for the second time in our season, we had to call on Douglas Jardine as bowler. He did not fail. The Press told us we were not so good after all. We took little notice, and sallied forth to the delights of Eastbourne.

Here, each summer Leveson Gower opposed his team to Oxford and Cambridge; a final try-out. Most of the University cricketers were by now safe for Lord's and could indulge any hitherto repressed inclination towards social delights, but there were always a few who knew that this was their last chance to rise and shine on the field, and they, poor fellows, could be observed masking their anxiety with a sticky show of abandon, refusing a liqueur-brandy, or drawing the captain's attention to the fact that they were now going to bed.

'Shrimp' Leveson Gower knew how to handle these entertainments. He had an unrivalled touch with mayors and notables whom he treated with wine and light conversation in his marquee. He buzzed around like a benign little bee, introducing people whom he had never seen before to others whom he would never see again, and, when he felt like a change, he would excuse himself abruptly with the remark: 'Well, I must go and send off a couple of wires now.' Our headquarters was the Grand Hotel, where Mr Gabb presided over the dining-room, like an Archbishop of Canterbury undergoing a bout of head-waiting for a bet. After dinner, in the lounge, the old ladies spread themselves to listen to the music, and it was here that Gerry Weigall, while demonstrating a late cut with a light walking-stick, knocked a Benedictine into some dowager's lap. We won the cricket match through a titanic innings by Bettington, who scored 101 not out in an hour and kept chipping pieces off the wall at the sea end.

The match against Cambridge was a sorry farce. It began with a brisk argument between the captains on the one side and the MCC Committee on the other about the desirable time of starting. Rain continuing to pour down for two days, this diversion soon lost force. We started an indoor match of our own in the Oxford dressing-room, and strong protests were sent up from the reading-room below. These were disregarded. On the third day, after lunch, Jardine and Bickmore opened the innings for Oxford on a wet and weary pitch. Bickmore batted finely for 66, and C. S. Marriott bowled with wonderful accuracy for Cambridge. Thursday was granted as an extra day, and the most interesting sight in that morning's play was the effect of the Cambridge Hawks Ball on the batting of Bettington. I bowled Hubert Ashton with a slowish long-hop which just reached the bottom of the stumps on the first bounce, and a brisk 35 not out by A. E. R. Gilligan, supported by an eccentric 3 not out by the last batsman, Marriott, brought the Cambridge total to 161 for 9; 32 runs behind ours.

So the argument on supremacy was never settled, and continued to be debated off the field for many months. I still think we should have won. Be that as it may, they were two of the best sides that have represented Oxford and Cambridge, and, as I have remarked earlier, but have no shame for repeating, several cricketers from the two teams later played for England.

I played a walking-on part in my first match for Somerset, against Hampshire at Taunton, bowling third change with a mottled ball against that monumental left-hander, Philip Mead. In the second innings he made 176 not out. The Hampshire captain, L. H. (now Lord) Tennyson, and his valet-wicket-keeper, Walter Livesey, had three 0's between them in four innings, the proportion being two to the master and one to the man. Tennyson was caught off Jack White each time. Each year he swore that he would hit Jack for six at Taunton, but the ground is just that little bigger than it looks, and down she used to come into the deep-fielder's hands.

Tennyson missed the poetry of his Laureate grandfather but inherited the constitution and the plain private speech. No stronger or bolder player of the forward stroke was seen in his day. He received the fast bowlers as the oak receives the storm; and, when he fell to them, he went down with no grace or compliancy, but with a sounding, defiant crash. In the next summer, 1921, he fixed his name for ever among storied cricketers, showing his fading companions how to face Gregory and McDonald and, one-handed, smacking them for 63 and 35 in the third Test at Leeds. In all ways of cricket and the world he was and is the perfect English Gascon, a gourmet of the whole feast of life which, for him, has been post-dated by a century and a half. He was cut out for the Regency. Lionel should have been the ancestor; Alfred the descendant.

And so to the return match with Hampshire, at Bournemouth, which was under the dyarchy of bath-chairs and Dan Godfrey. I spent the evening before it exploring with Jack MacBryan. I wonder how many of those who chance to see his name in cricket scores remember what a great player Jack MacB. was? In 1920, he struggled to a Blue at Cambridge. Four years later, he played as opening batsman for England against South Africa, being chosen from a field of openers that included Jack Hobbs, Herbert Sutcliffe, George Gunn, Jack (A. C.) Russell, Andrew

Sandham, and Charles Hallows, all of them rightaway professional topsawyers. MacBryan had been a Prisoner of War with the Germans during much of the Kaiser's war, and had been awarded a spell of solitary confinement for using a soi-disant pudding as a Rugger ball.

That evening, Jack was in one of those moods of *en-tout-cas* preparedness in which a man tends to laugh at the morrow and criticize other people's hats. Soon after leaving the hotel, we were nearly run over by a car which, Jack remarked, was probably in the pay of the Hampshire Committee. At the next corner, the same thing happened. Jack MacB. shouted one of those terms calculated to cause all but the more experienced London taxi-drivers to draw up within a few lengths. There followed an altercation with the charioteer, whose fondness for alcohol was now manifest. Jack drew off his coat, but there the matter rested. As the driver receded, taking what revenge he could out of his gears, Jack turned to me and said: 'Good. Now I'll make a hundred.' And he did.

So did John Daniell; a solid, wearing-down innings, at which he excelled. Sometimes he had fits of thinking he was Jessop, and would be comfortably caught at long-leg. And when he holed out, he was apt to ask why 'that ruddy captain can't keep his fielders where he put 'em'.

We won that match; and I took five Hampshire wickets in their first innings, using the inswerve; and John Daniell told me that no batsman worth a sausage ever got out to inswervers, over-looking, in his disciplinary zeal, his own fate at Oxford two months earlier. Young bowler, don't be put off by the wisdom of the elders! Whichever way you bowl, they'll tell you of a better way. You and you alone will know whether you've bowled like a king or a cow. And, in cricket, the bowlers are the Lords and the batsmen are the Commoners; and you'll find that, as in politics, it's not the Lords who get the Press.

The great Len Braund was then in his last season but one for Somerset. It was twenty years since he had been the greatest all-round cricketer in the world, classic batsman, a destroyer with his leg-breaks, and a slip-fielder who could pick 'em off his toes while discussing the Derby with the wicket-keeper. He was, and is, the wisest judge of cricket I know. He could tell

28

you, as no other, just what to try, against whom, and when. By 1920 he had stopped bowling, except a casual spinner between the fall of wickets, and, for batting, he preferred high noon to the shades of evening. At slip, he was catching the snorters. The easy ones he was apt to leave for the grass.

Now he has passed the three-score-and-ten, but his heart is still seventeen; and he treats his artificial legs as interesting interlopers. He told me how, as he lay in hospital soon after an amputation, he had what he referred to as a natural call, but found the ward temporarily nurse-less. 'So,' he said, 'I got up, got there, and got back. But, as I was doing the last hop or so, the nurse came in, and said: "Mr Braund, what on earth do you think you're trying to do?" And I couldn't help thinking of the time Mr Daniell said the same thing to me when I floored one in the slips. Only he didn't say "on earth".'

H. C. McDonell, who bowled slowish tempters, was in that Hampshire side. He fielded to his own bowling like a red-hot jack-in-the-box, in the attitude of a man trying to catch butterflies in both hands at once. He broke his finger catching-and-bowling Frank Woolley in the first county match I ever saw, at Canterbury, when C. B. Fry made a hundred in each innings and wore a huge white sun-hat. How easy it is to play the House-that-Jack-Built with the cricket generations. It was Fry's vote, though he did not know it or so intend it, which removed W. G. Grace from the England captaincy and team in 1899. And W. G. Grace was being shown a cricket bat by his mother at Thornbury while the Duke of Wellington was still alive; though what the Duke has to do with cricket I'm bothered if I know.

So, the match was over and we'd won. And our stock bowler, Ernest Robson, drank a pint of beer, curled his moustache, lit his pipe, and made as if to offer me a remark; but as usual found himself unequal to it, and walked thoughtfully from the ground.

And, I, being nineteen, rushed away for an evening paper to see what they said about my bowling. They said that the Hampshire batsmen had failed unaccountably against an attack that presented no obvious difficulty.

Unaccountably? No obvious difficulty? Nuts.

There followed a defeat at Lord's by Middlesex, who were on that great spurt to the Championship under 'Plum' Warner. And so to the Weston-super-Mare Festival. Of all county grounds, Clarence Park, Weston-super-Mare, is about the smallest and the most intimate. It was the home pitch of Jim Bridges, Somerset bowler, and there in club matches, he liked to come out strong as a batsman. 'If only they *knew*,' he used to tell me, 'that you and I, Glasgie, are as good batsmen as any in the Somerset side . . . except, possibly, Dah Lyon and Jack MacBryan.' But this knowledge was somehow kept from our captain, who used to say: 'Well, you two clowns can toss for who goes in ten or eleven.' Jim never would toss, but took number ten with an air of injury and neglect. After all, the year before, he'd made 99 not out against Essex on his native sward; mostly by huge high balloons.

The Weston ground in August was a thing of marquees where the right stuff could be found, and deck chairs and wooden chairs under which the spade and bucket could be parked for an hour or two. In those days the pitch was sportive, having sea sand close under the grass, and in the three matches of 1920 only once was a total of 200 reached in 11 completed innings. A short walk away from the ground were the golf-links, where Secretary Bob Riddell held sway. Bob was a left-hand golfer of much skill, and as a host he had no equal. He could produce you golf shoes from nowhere, and a complete change of clothing in rain-storms. There, peace was to be found in the evening, balm for any failure on the cricket field; and in the lounge, Doctor MacBryan, Jack's father, would be sitting, benevolent and conversational, in a drain-pipe collar that kept stiff up to his ears. Something odd always happened at Weston-super-Mare. It was there, in a hotel, that P. G. H. Fender, the Surrey captain, complained to the manager that there wasn't enough room in the bedrooms to swing a cat, and the manager told Percy Fender that he didn't know they'd come down to Weston merely for the cat-swinging.

We lost to Leicestershire in the first match of the Festival. It was a bad batting match, especially for the older gentlemen, our Ernest Robson and their J. H. King, ninety-five years between them, making only 1 run in their 4 innings. King made up for it by doing the hat-trick in our second innings. The third wicket of the feat being also his hundredth of the season. He was surrounded by congratulations; and his face was illuminated by triumph, as I walked to the crease, a possible fourth in hand. But I corrected his exuberance by hitting my first ball out of the ground and over the pavilion at mid-wicket. I added one more, then was feebly caught and bowled by Ewart Astill. In the Leicestershire second innings I took 5 for 33, and caught G. B. F. Rudd, 71, in the deep field with a sound like a bag bursting.

John King, of Leicestershire, left-hand bat and bowler, went on playing for the county till he was fifty-four years old. In 1904, brought into the Player's side at Lord's as a substitute for J. T. Tyldesley, he scored a century in each innings. In his latter years he was a slowish mover between the wickets, and once, being run out at Leicester by many yards while facing the right way for the pavilion, he was told by umpire Reeves to 'keep on running, John, while your legs are loose'. John was very angry about this.

We lost the next match, against Essex, for whom there was playing an enormous man, P. Toone. He was a tremendous thrower, but wild, and once threw the ball from the deep field clean over the wicket-keeper's head against the far screen. He seemed well pleased with this feat. I made 15 not out, out of 99, and 22 out of 160. Hot going, I thought; and in the next match, against Derbyshire, I was promoted to number eight, much to the disgust of Jim Bridges. But as I scored 21, he couldn't say much. We beat Derbyshire by 10 wickets, Jack White, the greatest slow left-hand bowler Somerset ever had, taking 12 for 79. John Daniell scored 102 in the first innings, and was very severe on the off-spinner, Arthur Morton, sweeping him again and again to the leg boundary and reaching his 50 in less than half an hour.

Arthur Morton was a sturdy all-rounder, and later became a first-class umpire. When standing umpire some years after this, he called several no-balls against a certain West Indies fast bowler. The excitable victim, resenting these attentions, revenged himself by running towards the wicket, knocking Morton flat on his face, and shouting: 'Was THAT a no-ball, then?' Apologies were made; Morton straightened his teeth and scraped the grass from his eyebrows, and the game proceeded.

So ended the season 1920. I finished with 55 wickets at 20.90 each, and John Daniell asked me to play again next year, adding the request, 'and for heaven's sake, don't bring that bloody straw-hat'.

Almost nothing, except the sunshine, went right with Oxford cricket in 1921. Technically, this was hard to explain. Of the 1920 team, we had lost only three, F. W. Gilligan, F. A. Waldock, and C. H. L. Skeet. But neither Bettington nor Stevens bowled as skilfully as they had done the summer before, and, as to me, I took on a transitional shape in which I was increasing speed and casting away the habit of the inswing. Probably, I ought to have stayed in the nets and had it all out on my own. Our captain, V. R. Price, was an erratic, occasionally a brilliant, fast bowler, but, somehow, we were never a whole cricket side; just a collection of individuals playing cricket. Against such a side as Cambridge in 1921, this was just asking for defeat. And we had it. They won by an innings and 24 runs.

That Cambridge team was just about the best University eleven that went to Lord's in my memory. They batted thus, in brackets being the runs scored in the only innings that they found necessary: J. L. Bryan (62), C. A. Fiddian-Green (17), G. Ashton (12), H. Ashton (118), A. P. F. Chapman (45), C. T. Ashton (48), M. D. Lyon (9), A. G. Doggart (45), C. H. Gibson (43 not out), R. G. Evans (0 not out), C. S. Marriott did not bat.

Gilbert Ashton was captain. Their opening bowlers were Clem Gibson, of England quality, and R. G. Evans, very accurate and capable of both swerves. To follow, they had 'Father' Marriott, one of the finest slow bowlers who ever played in the 'Varsity match, and Graham Doggart, a sturdy stock bowler who could nip them in awkwardly from the off.

In batting, they had that rare and enviable mixture of the sound and the brilliant. Jack Bryan was sound, and also left-handed. His partner, Charles Fiddian-Green, was the very mirror of orthodoxy, and, further, an all-round games-player of unusual ability, reaching the first-class at cricket, rugby, golf, and hockey. Sartorially, he was the Beau Brummell of the side.

The three Ashtons between them provided all the known strokes of the right-hander. Percy Chapman, on his own, already approached Frank Woolley in all but sheer grace. M. D. Lyon, powerful and aggressive, was soon to become the stay of Somerset; and when these had made their runs, there was Doggart, who was good enough to bat at number three in most 'Varsity teams. To crown all, they won the toss.

In fielding, they were the one team in England that year who could compare with W. W. Armstrong's Australians. At short-leg, Hubert Ashton had no superior. At cover-point, there was Percy Chapman. Some years later, Chapman set a new standard in the gully; but that was when his legs were heavier and his frame set. At cover, in lithe and pliable youth, he was a nonpareil. Nothing stoppable seemed to escape his huge hands and telescopic reach; being left-handed, he could pounce on those balls that swerve away from cover towards third-man, and, still stooping, he would flick them back over the bails.

As a batsman, Chapman was something different from the other very good ones who were – just very good. His great reach, keenness of eye, and exceptional strength of wrist and forearm made him a murderous opponent. In later years, even while he was still captain of England, he had curtailed his full swing of the bat. He learnt cunning and what to leave alone. But, in his Cambridge days he used no cunning, no more than Coeur de Lion would have used it when knocking off some Saracen's head, and he left nothing alone. It was plain, when you bowled to him, that he believed himself able to score off anything, felt himself to be master of the whole armoury of the bowler's attack. And, when you put one past him, he didn't retract from that view or attitude, but thought 'my mistake', not 'your good ball'. On and just outside the off stump he had those delayed strokes that defy description, half cut and half drive, and it didn't matter how good was the length of the ball. He never had the defence of Frank Woolley; very few have had that; but he was a stronger man, far, and you noticed it when fielding at cover-point. Chapman and records somehow don't pair together, but he is the only man who has brought off the 'treble' at Lord's, of a century in the University match, for Gentlemen v. Players, and for England v. Australia.

They dropped him from the England captaincy soon after that century against Australia; and the Australians could hardly be persuaded of their wonderful luck. As a captain, he was the best I have known. He had the flair. He could encourage by a gesture or a look, and he had the whole confidence of the whole side. The critics talk of Archie MacLaren, and Noble, and W. G. Grace as leaders. But results can talk as well; and Chapman captained England in six consecutive victories against Australia. And that's another record. But he had so much that defeats words and the pen; gaiety, freedom, hope, enjoyment. In him was gathered all that makes cricket worth playing.

In the 'Varsity match, Hubert Ashton batted beautifully for his 118, and Douglas Jardine, having Chapman caught and bowling Doggart, surprised both friend and foe. For Oxford, Ward and Hedges made some runs in each innings, Holdsworth some lovely strokes in the first. As in 1920. A. F. Bickmore batted with distinction, and it was sad that his 57 should have been ended by a long-hop. I thought I bowled well, and had Chapman missed at wicket before he had scored, but the wickets wouldn't fall, and Geoffrey Lowndes rebuked me for gesticulating when they nearly did.

Meanwhile, the Australians, with J. M. Gregory and E. A. McDonald as their spearhead of attack, were knocking the dust out of English cricket. Their captain, Warwick W. Armstrong, was now in his forty-third year and weighed at least seventeen stone. He was the nearest thing to W. G. Grace that Australia had produced, both in bulk and ability. He somewhat resembled the Old Man in his method of bowling, rolling the ball from leg for as long as you pleased, with a sort of comfortable assiduity and strainless guile. As a batsman, he had become rather slow of foot, but he still drove with great power, and could stick at need.

As a captain, Armstrong was reckoned among the astutest of tacticians; but it must be admitted that, in 1921, he was not called upon to exercise any exceptional ingenuity, for what Gregory and McDonald left, Arthur Mailey mopped up. Armstrong was not a man of many words, but the few that he uttered were apt to be noticed. He crossed ideas with the MCC at the very start of the tour, demanding a change in the programme to allow the Australians a day's rest before each Test match. This reasonable request caused an uneasy stir in the sanctuary.

The truth was, English cricket was in sore and crusty mood, like an old gentleman who has received a caning. There was another disagreement, humorous enough, if humour were appreciated in the high places of cricket. Armstrong asked that drinks should be served in the dressing-room at Lord's. F. E. (later Sir Francis) Lacey, the Secretary of MCC, said that the bar downstairs was the only and proper place for liquid refreshment. But Armstrong carried his point. These pin-pricks made sore relations, and, when Gregory and McDonald began to make free with the rather timorous remains of England batting, there were not wanting those who said there was something unfair in the bowling. They objected to their old men being knocked about. In result, Armstrong passed as something of an ogre in cricket that summer, and the climax was reached in the Fifth Test, at the Oval, when Armstrong, fielding in front of the pavilion, trapped a wind-swept newspaper under his large boot, and read it. He said that the racing news was more interesting than the cricket provided.

Farmer Jack Gregory was tall, strong, raw-boned, and like one of his native Kangaroos. He bounded up to the wicket in a whirlwind of arms and legs. He was a genial fellow, and enjoyed his cricket like a boy. He batted left-hand, and, free from style or responsibility, attacked with long reach and pendulum, not going out so much for sixes as for strokes that hummed low over the off-side fieldsmen's heads. Undoubtedly he frightened many batsmen from the wicket, but for what is a fast bowler if not for that? I never saw anything unfair in his bowling, and he followed the precept of Sam Woods: 'If the batsman gets above himself, put one past his whiskers now and then.'

Ted McDonald, born in Tasmania, was an artist among fast-bowlers, uncoiling his action with rhythm and controlled power. He was a handsome fellow, with strong and clear-cut features, but saturnine and mahogany-grim; like Carver Doone, he meant to frighten the young men with a look. He had not played in the Australian Imperial Forces team of two years earlier, and his performance against J. W. H. T. Douglas's England team in Australia during 1920–21 was but moderate.

ut, over here in 1921, he showed himself worthy to be compared with the great ones of the past. He had the wicked, thigh-grinding break-back, and the whipping out-swerve. In later years, he used the slow off-break to much effect.

McDonald came back to play in county cricket, for Lancashire, and his magnificence helped to carry his county three times to the Championship. Perhaps he would have done well to remain in his own Australia, for, over here, he found those who were only too ready to play up to his swashbuckling and devil-may-care nature. He loved to be thought the 'tough baby', and he fell into ways of life that somehow foreshadowed tragedy; which came in 1937, when he was killed in a motor accident. I like to remember him as he was at his zenith, for nothing in games is so superb or rare as the great fast bowler in action.

Arthur Mailey tossed me up three voluptuous half-volleys, off which I took 12 runs, then had me stumped a long way from the front door. Arthur was a great bowler, with a teasing flight and acute power of spin. He was witty, quiet and easy-natured, and the seriousness required for Test cricket didn't rise naturally in him. He loved casual matches, where he could appear in old sand shoes and give away please-yourself runs to some local mayor or notable.

I believe his early days had been something of a struggle; anyhow, he had a fondness for dead-end kids, and would sign their autograph-books with running questions about their private lives and ideas, and draw them comic and simian pictures of himself, with button nose and wide space between it and the mouth. I never saw Arthur bustled or bothered. If he got no wickets or plenty, why, there was another innings or match coming along. If he missed a train, well, someone could find a timetable with another one in it. He had a soft and quizzical way of speech. Of all the Australians I have known, he had the surest understanding of the English outlook and temperament, and the keenest awareness of Australian foibles.

There will often be argument as to whether Mailey or Grimmett was the greater bowler. Grimmett, with his persistent length and lower flight, was the more economical. Mailey, liked, and was blessed with, more runs to play with. He would seem to have been collared, then suddenly win with an unplayable leg-break. Of the two, both cricketers of genius, Mailey was the more likely to defeat the great batsman who was well set. Grimmett caused Mailey deep and quiet delight; and Mailey used to relate how Grimmett, a New Zealander, came to him soon after his, Grimmett's, entry into Australian cricket and asked questions about their gyratory art. Mailey told him all he knew. Years later, when Grimmett had won fame, there was some banquet or reunion at which both were present. Grimmett, probably elated by unaccustomed good cheer, for he was a man of abstinence, came up to Mailey and said in that voice like a ventriloquist speaking through a watering-can: 'Arthur, you told me wrong about the Bowzie.' Rather as if Virgil had been accused by Horace of giving misleading information on the number of feet in the Hexameter!

H. L. 'Horseshoe' Collins opened his innings against us with the silent and avuncular Edgar Mayne. Mayne had played over here in the Triangular Tests of 1912, but he took no active part in the 1921 series. Indeed, he only played about 20 innings during the tour. He was a sound batsman, but an indifferent and rather uninterested fielder. A few years later, at the age of forty, he and Ponsford shared in an opening partnership of 456 for Victoria against Queensland, at Melbourne, which still stands as an Australian record for the first wicket. At Oxford, I thought I saw Warwick Armstrong look at Mayne once or twice as if wondering why Ernie hadn't stayed at home in Australia.

Herbie Collins, of New South Wales, famous also as poker-player and racegoer, was a slight but tough man with a free wrist and a beady eye. He would have made a fortune on the old silent films. He was just right for a Stetson hat and woolly doormats for the legs, and he would have been no more than a cat's wink slower than Tom Mix on the draw. As a batsman, he was a deflector, in a style followed, more gracefully, by Alan Kippax. At Manchester, in the Fourth Test, when others fell to Parkin and Parker, he dug in for nearly five hours and scored 40. He was quite a good left-hander bowler: a fact scarcely evident from his 2 wickets for 269 during the tour.

Charlie Macartney scored 77, then played on to his wicket, trying to late-cut a length ball from Greville Stevens. His innings was an hour or so of brilliant net practice. His batting suggested a racket player who makes winners from any position. Length could not curb him, and his defence was lost and included in attack. A month later, he scored that wonderful 345 in three hours and three-quarters against Nottinghamshire at Trent Bridge. He was missed in the slips when 9, but gave no further chance; an astonishing performance. No Australian batsman since him, not even Bradman at his best, has approached Macartney for insolence of attack. He made slaves of bowlers.

In the Australian innings, I took the wickets of Taylor, Andrews, Mailey and Oldfield for 74 runs, and some words of praise from Armstrong that reached my ears made me immoderately pleased. The rest of the season put that right; but his three-year prophecy concerning me was not far from coming true.

The match was drawn. After the Australians had led by 14 on the first innings, we answered with 174 for the loss of Bickmore. Jardine followed 35 in the first innings with 96 not out in the second. But the selectors were mistrustful of novelty, and they gave no place in any Test to Hubert Ashton, Chapman, or Jardine. Ashton, who averaged over 60 for several innings against the Australians, never had another chance, and remains as a memento of official timidity.

John Daniell, remembering my qualifications and, perhaps, forgetting my straw hat, asked me to play for Somerset soon after the University match. I opened with a sparkling 0, b. Tate, at Hastings, where Gilbert Jessop used to knock chips off the Congregational Church and where the distant cliff forms so helpful a pavilion for those who have spent all their money on telescopes. I took three not very grandiose wickets, and travelled on to play Essex at Southend.

I have a weakness for Southend, and in later years, when reporting cricket for the *Morning Post*, I never failed to impress on my employers the importance and brilliance of its Cricket Festival. In August, the homely smell of mankind in the streets was set off by the abundance of whelks, cockles, and stick-jaw rock. Rides were to be had on the miniature railway to the end of the pier and in mechanical boats on the lake below the Palace Hotel. Nowhere else have I found such invigorating air; and morning brought no sense of lassitude or remorse to the nocturnal reveller.

The cricket ground was adorned at one end by a lake, on which prophetic ducks floated, and quacked as nervous batsmen made their way to the crease. Festooned around were private tents, whose occupants said and drank what they liked. One of them belonged to the Mayor, another to the Yachting Club. In both of these the hospitality was warm, and from the latter marine telescopes were sometimes directed on to the cricket.

The Somerset *v.* Essex match at Southend, played towards the end of July 1921, stands out in my memory for its interest and humour. The pitch, like Jezebel, was fast and unaccountable. Soon afterwards, the whole playing surface was relaid, and a new pavilion was erected on the other side of the ground, in front of the ornamental lake. The original pavilion was small and, like the pitch, rather crude. We won the toss, and, after some severe concentration by A. E. S. Rippon (35), some lusty blows by Tom Lowry (28), and some fluent drives by Peter Randall Johnson (38), we collected 163; not good; but not disastrous, on a surface that was already fierce and might soon become wicked.

The Essex innings, apart from a sparkling hour of Claude Ashton (48), centred round the performance of F. Loveday, one of their opening batsmen. This obstacular artist was taking the place of A. C. Russell, who was making 101 in the Fourth Test match, at Manchester, against Australia. Loveday, a thin and resolute man, wore a cap with a large B on its front. I have a fancy, almost a certainty, that, after he had batted for some three hours, John Daniell asked him if he would like to tell us what the letter stood for. Truly, it might have stood for Batsman, as a more determined innings can seldom have been played. Jim Bridges and I, without being fast, often made the ball rise awkwardly from a length. Loveday was of the firm-footed type, and he sometimes became a sort of human kettledrum. But on he batted, nor resting, nor hasting, uncomplaining if not wholly unbowed. John Daniell was very restless throughout, and once, between overs, he hissed in my ear: 'Glasgy, can't you get this ruddy contortionist out?' To add to John's annoyance, a plague of catch-dropping started in the slips. I was hauled out to mid-on, and John, scowling darkly, retired to the deep, where he dismissed H. M. Morris with a grand one-handed catch. Soon afterwards I bowled the everlasting and heroic Loveday, and our captain smiled again. Loveday had made 81 in 3 hours and 30 minutes and Essex headed us by 83 runs.

On such a pitch, this seemed more than half-way to victory. But our batsmen thought otherwise. Daniell, going in first with Rippon, hit strongly. At 10, he was caught over the boundary by Henry Franklin, and recalled after discussion. He added another 32. Meanwhile, Rippon dug in. Though a stylist in execution of the strokes, he loved to make an affair of the act of batting; he did much bat-twirling, in the Jack Hobbs manner, and resorted to Swedish exercises between the overs, and, to the disgust of the bowler, even between balls. He also rubbed his left hand on his behind, which grew ever darker as a result. Lowry and S. G. U. Considine having failed, Rippon was joined by Peter Johnson, an aristocrat among batsmen. Peter, using his height to stand well over the rising ball, batted as only he could, since the days of Lionel Palairet. He made 81 in less than an hour and a half. Tom Young, another stroke-player, joined in with 69 not out. Rippon reached 52 after 3 hours and 20 minutes of strife and bat-twirling, Bridges collected 18 by this way and that, and Essex were left with 222 to win.

From the first over, the ball flew. J. G. Dixon, a carefree cricketer, soon went, and Jack Freeman joined Loveday. Freeman, a very small man like his younger brother, A. P. of Kent, had made 30 in the first innings before being bowled by that accomplished amateur tenor, Monty Hambling. Freeman was a sound and experienced little batsman. He played a few strokes, then I bowled him one which rose sharp from a length, and, unhappily, cut his face badly. This accident cost Essex two wickets, for Loveday, exclaiming, 'I don't like that', went in for a drink, and, soon after his return, he left his bat outside the off-stump to one from Bridges. Poor Freeman bravely tried again, but was almost immediately bowled by Tom Young. Then I had Hubert Ashton lbw, and we were on the right road. It was blocked by Peter Perrin.

Perrin, who was now in his forty-sixth year, batted superbly. A little slow on the foot, he stopped many balls on legs and body, but he showed why he had earned the name of one of the greatest players of faster bowling. The others came and went, but Perrin was unbeaten, if not unhurt, for 62. So we won a remarkable match by 65 runs.

Let us here turn aside and consider one of the great figures in English cricket, farmer John Cornish White. His father, in a comfortable silence that was presumed to represent approval, used to watch him trundling away his slow left-handers at Taunton. Jack inherited his father's tranquillity. I never saw him excited, though sometimes he would go a little redder when an important catch was missed off his bowling, and he would mutter: 'The trouble about that cock is that he's fast asleep.' Most cricketers were 'cocks' to Jack, and he would say of some new batsman who had not troubled the scorer: 'I didn't think *that* cock would last long, Glasgy; he had one of those fancy caps on.'

Jack came from Stogumber when he first played for Somerset in 1909, at the age of sixteen. His beginnings were negligible. He took 1 wicket for 90 runs in three innings. Next year, he did little better, and for the next three summers, Somerset, oscillating around bankruptcy and the bottom of the Championship, did without him. But in 1914 he returned to head their bowling averages with 93 wickets. In 1919 he began that run of uninterrupted success which placed him among the few unquestioned great. In 1921, against Worcestershire at Worcester, he took all 10 wickets in an innings.

He differed from other famous slow left-handers in that he relied very little on spin. Varied flight, guile, persistence, liveliness from the pitch, these were his secrets. He also had the gift of making the ball bounce unusually high for a slow bowler, and he took many wickets by causing the batsmen to play the ball too high on the bat to silly-point, where John Daniell awaited the prey. Many times I stood to White at short slip, and I never saw a bowler who so harassed and teased the batsmen. He would peg down the most aggressive, till by sheer desperation they were driven to their doom. Frank Woolley, being left-handed, was usually White's master; but the most accomplished right-handers, such as Hobbs, Hendren, and Hammond, did not attack him. He bowled, and they played. Hendren used to say that no bowler made him so tired.

White was turned thirty-seven when he first went to Aus-

tralia, and his fair hair was greying at the temples. Few could
have prophesied that he was going out to his triumph. From the
first, the Australian batsmen could not decide whether to play
him back or forward. Young Archie Jackson, that beautiful
player who was to die four years later at the age of twenty-three,
solved the problem; but for the most part the batsmen were
driven into the crease. The climax came in the Fourth Test, at
Adelaide, when, in stifling heat, White bowled 124 overs for 13
wickets and 256 runs, an historic feat of combined endurance and
skill. England won by 12 runs. White had to leave the field to
change his shirt twice during one afternoon, and, at the same
time, to take in a draught of the right stuff. Hendren tells how,
when the last Australian batsman, Don Blackie, came in to face
White, he, that guileful Patsy, standing close to the wicket,
said: 'My word; I wouldn't be in *your* shoes for all the money in
the world.' 'I shall never forget,' said Hendren, 'the look of
pitiable horror that came over Blackie's face when I said this.'
Bravely Blackie defended for a few balls, then was caught by
Larwood at deep mid-wicket.

White was a grand fielder to his own bowling, and a good
slip-fielder to anyone else's. He was less effective farther from
the wicket, as he could throw but little. As a batsman, he had
begun, and looked like finishing, close above the extras; but,
by industry and imitation, he made himself into a counting
player. He used his pads more than most, and I have a fancy that
the umpires whose decisions Jack, as a bowler, accepted with
such equanimity gave him the benefits of many doubts. I never
saw him throw his wicket away. He had the husbandman's dislike of waste. Apart from cricket, he was no games-player, but
he was a cunning cardsman, and one of the best poker-players
in Somerset.

He migrated from Stogumber to Combe Florey. No other
county knows so well how to name its places. I used to drive
with Guy Earle on summer evenings after the cricket from
Taunton to Minehead, through Bishop's Lydeard, Combe
Florey, and Crowcombe. Guy was a mighty hitter, the highest
and farthest of his day, with arms like a grown man's thigh. At
Bristol, in 1923, he hit 111 off Gloucestershire in the August
Bank Holiday match, scoring his first 76 in half an hour and

lifting Charles Parker four times clean over the track that encircled the ground.

But it was the Kent bowlers who most suited his designs, and 'Tich' Freeman most of all. 'Tich' would arrive at Taunton on his way to his annual 200 wickets and Guy would hit him over the river or into the timber-yard. The supposed variety of the leg-break and googly lost all relevance. Guy put his left leg down the pitch and clapped the ball an awful blow. He regarded all bowlers as so much sawdust and any success on their part as a personal insult. Returning to the pavilion after being caught at third-man while trying a six to square-leg, he would cast down his bat with a resounding boom and say: 'I'll wring his . . . little neck.' Within three minutes the thunder-cloud had almost passed, returning in little puffs when Guy would say, as he gazed at the cricket: 'I can't think how anyone ever gets out to that bandy-legged . . .'

At Watts House, near Bishop's Lydeard, Sir Denis Boles used to entertain the Somerset cricketers. It was here, on his private cricket ground, that I was guilty of a social solecism at the tender age of eighteen. Jack White, who was my captain, had put me on to bowl and asked me whether the fielders were to my liking. Casting around my eye, I saw the host standing by the sight-screen in conversation with Burgess, his butler. Without hesitation, I shouted, 'Up a bit, Boles!' The abruptness and titular inaccuracy of this request caused Jack MacBryan to sit down on the grass and laugh. Years afterwards, when I was setting a field, he turned from mid-on and whispered, 'Up a bit, Boles'. Burgess was a very solemn humorist, and, when the head of the family was looking the other way, he used to pretend to trip with a tray full of glasses.

The church at Bishop's Lydeard used to be attended by one of the loudest singers I have ever heard. He was said to be a butcher who had removed himself, or been removed, from the choir after some dispute about his required share in an anthem. His revenge was to try to drown the choir from the front pew. Having considerable power of lung, I was put up as a rival, and I at least succeeded in making him turn round and stare at me with rubicund and surly amazement.

If you wanted to know Taunton, you walked round it with

43

Sam Woods on a summer morning before the match. Sam was Somerset's godfather. He was a lover of life and of nearly all things living. On those walks, he would take you into the back-parlours of little shops and inquire after the youngest son's measles, and whether it had been decided to put Tom into the cornchandling trade. 'Much better let him be a farmer, Missis,' Sam would say, 'and marry a fat wife who can look after his money. For *he* won't, no more than I could, my dear.'

Everyone loved Sam, for the whole world's manliness and generosity seemed to have gathered into his heart. He lived at the George Inn, Mr E. J. Lock, and when not there, might be found at the Club. I believe he decided to do some looking after of me, because he thought I needed it, and also because I opened the bowling sometimes, though not as Sam had opened, continued, and closed it, with speed and invincible hope.

I wish I had seen him in the prime of his bowling, but I only saw him trundling a few down, in waistcoat and watch-chain, at the Oxford nets, when he was fifty-two. He had tremendous shoulders, but was lame in walk owing to rheumatism in the hip. This he attributed to a fall off a camel in Egypt. 'I was in charge of a bunch of those sods,' he said, 'when they stampeded and made for a cactus forest; so off I rolled, and fell a bit wrong.' C. B. Fry told me that Sam, when a young man, was the finest build of an athlete stripped that he ever saw.

Sam came over from Australia to Brighton College when he was fourteen. He was one of a family of thirteen, at Manley Beach, near Sydney. 'At least I *think* we were thirteen,' he would say. For Cambridge against Oxford, he took 36 wickets in four matches, at nine each, and, while still an undergraduate, he played in three Test matches against England for Australia. At rugger he played forward for England, and was a terror in the loose, for he weighed nearly fifteen stone and could run the hundred yards in under eleven seconds. He had neither the wish nor the aptitude for any settled profession. In early youth, he tried a little banking, but was so often absent at cricket when he should have been shovelling sovereigns that he, and his employers, both felt that he should try something else.

As a batsman, he was an attacker, and only G. L. Jessop excited more anticipation in the crowd. Many a time he pulled

Somerset out of the ditch; especially at the Oval, when he would walk out, chin first, to tame the fury of Richardson and Lockwood. In technique, he always advised against deflections to leg. 'You're not Ranji,' he would say, 'so aim at mid-on's nut, and you'll find the ball will go to the square-leg boundary.' I was with him at the Oval when he met little Bobby Abel, who had gone nearly blind. Abel touched Sam on the arm, smiled, and said: 'Oh, Mr Woods, the times you've nearly knocked my head off out in the middle,' and Sam said: 'Ah, Bobby, but the times you carved me off your whiskers to the boundary.'

Sam would hear nothing against W. G. Grace, and loved to tell of the Old Man's hundredth century, 288, for Gloucestershire against Somerset in 1895. W.G. scored at 50 an hour, and gave no chance. 'I had him plumb leg before,' Sam said, 'when he'd made only three or four, and that was the only time I got one past him. I bowled him a shooter when he was in the nineties, and he didn't stop it; he hit it for four to square-leg.' My great-uncle A. P. Wickham was keeping wicket behind Grace, and he told me that W.G. only let five balls pass his bat throughout his innings.

After that match Gloucestershire supporters gave Grace a complimentary dinner. 'He drank something of everything,' Sam said, 'before and during dinner, and afterwards he sent for the whisky. You couldn't make the Old Man drunk. His nut was too large. About midnight, some of us thought we might start for home; but the Old Man said to me: "Shock'ead, get two others, and we'll play rubbers of whist till two in the morning." So we did.'

Sam had his learning from nature, not from books; but a strong memory and a vivid power of corroborative illustration made him a talker who never lacked for an audience. He was convivial; too convivial, some thought; but I could never see that it mattered. Drinking was just part of his life, and it made no difference to his kindness and his humour. He made the younger ones among us stick to beer and early hours—'Whisky and one o'clock in the morning won't suit you, my dear.'

Sam will never be forgotten in Somerset, and they still talk of him as if he were just round the next corner. Not long ago, I met an elderly lady on a railway journey near Taunton. Within five minutes our talk reached Sam. 'Ah,' she said, 'I last met him at a dance when I was eighteen. I had been told that I was not to dance with Sam. But I did.'

*   *   *

1922 was the worst cricket season I ever had. During the Oxford term I was dropped from the side. I came in again on tour, at Leicester, and Douglas Jardine, acting as captain, and having a sense of the situation, said: 'Now then, my boy, either end you like.' I took 6 for 40 in their first innings. In the end, Jardine and H. O. Hopkins had to stand down through injuries, and I played against Cambridge after all. I bowled 43 overs to a humdrum length and took 0 for 97. Much ado about nothing.

One incident of rich humour relieved the dismal scene. It was against Surrey at the Oval. Tom Raikes and I were batting, at numbers ten and nine respectively. Tom was a Freshman from Winchester, a robust and clever bowler, with a be-damned-to-it attitude towards life. It began by my playing a ball to the deep-field at the Pavilion end. We ran our one comfortably, and, when Tom asked if there was another, I said 'yes', and we started for the second. Strange things then happened. As we were about to cross over, Tom suddenly turned round and scuttled back to his wicket. I followed him but thinking this crease overcrowded, I set out for the other (at the Pavilion end). Not to be outdone, Tom did the same. I beat him to it by a head. Meanwhile, the fielders, driven temporarily insane by these goings-on, were having a private game of rounders. At length the ball reached Strudwick, the wicket-keeper, who took off the bails. It was one thing to remove the bails, another to know who was out. We had occupied both ends two or three times each. The umpires, Bill Reeves and Frank Chester, stood impotent with laughter and doubt. But Tom solved the problem by striding away to the pavilion. 'Over' was then called, and, as I prepared to receive the next ball, Bill Hitch, the Surrey fast bowler, said hoarsely at short-leg: 'You know who was out *really*, don't you?' But I didn't. Nor did he.

The Varsity match was like 1921, only more so. Cambridge, with brilliant Hubert Ashton as captain, had lost two fine bowlers, Marriott and Gibson, but they had an admirable attack in G. O. Allen from Eton, P. A. Wright from Wellingborough, and

F. B. R. ('Tishy') Browne, from Eastbourne College. Allen had not yet reached his full pace nor acquired that temperament which can disregard setbacks, but he came fast from the pitch and had a vicious break-back, with Hubert Ashton hovering at short-leg. Browne, tall and strong, had an awkward delivery, almost off the wrong foot, but he was a grand bowler of fast-medium pace, who was lost all too early to the first-class game. Wright was of the old-fashioned sort, medium in pace, with a beautifully easy action and tireless accuracy. A formidable trio.

It has rained in torrents just before the match, but cleared in time for Cambridge to take innings on a slow and soggy pitch. For us, only one bowler touched his true form, Tom Raikes. We could not part Charles Fiddian-Green and Willie Hill-Wood before lunch. They were not exciting; indeed one Oxford supporter rudely described Hill-Wood's batting before lunch as being like a monkey trying to climb an impossibly slippery pole. But their policy was right. At lunch the total was sixty, and no one out.

Soon after the interval, Raikes bowled Fiddian-Green with one of the vastest off-breaks I've ever seen. It pitched nearly off the mown surface. Graham Doggart and Hill-Wood then added 118 quite briskly, till Doggart was bowled by Raikes with a full-pitch. Raikes said he'd tried everything else first. Hill-Wood was caught for 81, made in four hours and three-quarters. Shelmerdine was soon caught at slip off Bettington, but Hubert Ashton and Percy Chapman stayed together till the close of play, when their score was 271 for 4.

On the second morning, Ashton and Chapman batted beautifully. By ten minutes past one the Cambridge score had reached 403 for 4. In a shocking light, Chapman went to his century with a drive off me which Hedges, at cover-point, only heard. Then came the rain, and Ashton, though needing only 10 runs for his second consecutive century against Oxford, declared his innings.

Our innings was opened by Bettington, a temporarily converted hitter, and Frank Barnard, a Freshman from Charterhouse, with a beautiful wrist and style. With little hope of anything better than a draw, they stayed together for an hour, but, by tea-time, they, Holdsworth, and Beverley Lyon had all gone for only 63. Hedges and Stevens then stayed together till the end

47

of the second day, putting on 71. Stevens, the captain, had spent the term in rescue work at number six, and ended with an average of 48. At Lord's he was still suffering from the effects of jaundice.

Early on the third morning Hubert Ashton made a glorious catch at short-leg to dismiss Hedges, and the innings closed for 222. The follow-on was catastrophic. Allen and Wright certainly bowled very well, but our batsmen helped them with some eccentric strokes. As I sat in the Oxford balcony and read our score of 17 for 7 wickets, I could only laugh. Stevens again batted heroically, and I helped him to take the total into the sixties. Tom Raikes added a few lusty whacks, and we staggered to 81. Oxford cricket had hit the bottom of the barometer.

After the 'Varsity match, I played in only two games of first-class rank, both at Cardiff, against Glamorgan. One was for an Oxford and Cambridge team collected by 'Shrimp' Leveson Gower. In this, our gallant captain, aged forty-eight, scored 61 not out at number ten, and I assisted him in a last wicket stand of over 70. He played the slow left-hand leg spinners of Frank Ryan in masterly style, holding the bat loose on the forward stroke, so that 'any snick', as he said, 'is more likely to go along the ground'. He was a very downy batsman. I took 7 for 79 in this match. John Morrison kept wicket. His athletic deeds at soccer, cricket, and golf were current tradition when I was a small boy at Charterhouse. He was the inventor of the water-proof golf skirt as worn by himself, and of a unique implement for sucking up golf balls without stooping. A great character, John Morrison, and for years one of the shrewdest foursome players in the game.

My other match was for Somerset. On this occasion, I had lost my cricket-bag, which had a habit of catching me up just too late. It was a skimpy thing, known in the family as 'the eclair'. 'Essentially a bowler's bag,' as Douglas Jardine once remarked with a meditative air. For all its tenuousness, it yet contained my only pair of cricket boots. I was unable to borrow any on the Cardiff ground, so went out to field in black walking-shoes. This performance so shook John Daniell that he refrained from putting me on to open the bowling with Jim Bridges. Jim scratched his head, and smiled dubiously at my footwear. I was put on first change, and, in my first over, had J. R. Tait, who candidly admitted a likeness to Charlie Chaplin, caught at short-leg. But John remained unconverted, and took me off soon afterwards. Sidney Rippon won the match for us with a superb century. In bidding me goodbye for the season, Daniell said: 'First it's a straw hat, and now you come and bowl in a pair of bloody dancing pumps.' Happy days.

Halfway through the Christmas term of 1922 I was ordered a rest by the doctors. I was sleeping badly and when I began to despise the pleasures of the table, I knew things were out of joint. No name was given to the ailment, which was, in fact, a considerable nervous breakdown. I received several up-and-down physical examinations, and a great many wise nods and 'well – well – wells'. What I needed was bed for six weeks.

This chapter being concerned with cricket, not neurology, I will rest content with the remark that only those who have suffered it know the hell of nervous illness. Twice again was I to be similarly afflicted. This much of good has emerged from it all; first, that I have learnt to regard physical ailments with the contempt that nine-tenths of them deserve; and secondly, that I know the unutterable delight of health found after a long and seemingly hopeless search.

Cut off from work, I went to Jersey, where, after a few weeks, I revived, took to playing badminton, and fancied myself to be in love with the leading lady player. There was also golf at La Moye, with its sand-dunes and sea breezes and friendly club-house. Here I met a man with the only perfectly purple nose I have ever seen. Perhaps he had taken Beachcomber's advice—'How to cure a red nose – drink till it's purple.'

I came back to Oxford for my last summer term with two objects immediately in view, to make myself necessary to the cricket team and, on almost no work at all, to squeeze through the Final School of Literae Humaniores or 'Greats'. So I rose at six each morning for Plato and Aristotle and unintelligible books on Appearance, Reality and the Absolute. My whole being revolted against philosophy and its abhorred terminology. I am still sometimes visited by a noxious dream in which I am about to take the 'Greats' Exam; knowing that I know sweet Fanny Adams, and worried at my ignorance. I squeezed through – just.

In cricket, I knew from the start that I had 'found something'. Instead of just toiling away to a mechanical length, I could make the ball, and sometimes the batsman, hop. This was better than any First in 'Greats', thought I. Further, Oxford were once more a team. This was largely the work of Reg Bettington, the captain. We believed in him. He recaptured his own great skill as a bowler of leg-breaks and googlies, taking 61 wickets for Oxford at 16 each. Also, Greville Stevens returned to something like his old form. Between us, we three accounted for 159 of the 227 wickets that fell. With Tom Raikes as stock bowler, and E. P. Hewetson of Shrewsbury as a shock-troop, our attack was as good as that of most of the first-class counties.

In batting, we were strengthend by the return of Douglas Jardine and H. O. Hopkins. Hopkins, from Adelaide, South Australia, was a sprightly old gentleman in his twenty-eighth year, a quick-footed and neat player with a calm temperament, a pleasant wit, and a leaning towards comic songs in the Frank Crumit manner. Later, he played for Worcestershire with considerable success. He was also an expert at lacrosse.

The stylist of the side was Claude Hilary Taylor, a Freshman from Westminster. He had been coached by that classic batsman, D. J. Knight, and resembled him strongly in method and gesture. He began with 45 against Lancashire, and followed up with 114 against Middlesex, 98 against the Army, and 115 against Sussex at Brighton.

In a very different way, C. H. (John) Knott was equally effective. Coming, like his elder brother, F. H., from Tonbridge, he had failed to strike form in 1921. In 1922 he won his Blue, but, like nearly everyone else, failed against Cambridge. In 1923, he really began. Knott, becoming a schoolmaster at Tonbridge, never played throughout a season for Kent. Had he done so, he might have reached the England side; for he was very good against all types of bowling, and could hit furiously or defend stubbornly. Further, he was a great fieldsman. Five years after he left Oxford he played a wonderful innings of 261 not out, at Eastbourne, for the Harlequins against a representative team of the West Indies, hitting 5 sixes and 29 fours, and seriously disturbing the old ladies and gentlemen at their croquet. In method, he used the short back-lift, like W. M.

Woodfull and Greville Stevens, but his strength of hand and forearm enabled him to hit tremendously hard with no obvious effort. In temperament, he was solid and shrewd.

For entertainment, the batsman of the 1923 side was Beverley H. Lyon, younger brother of M. D. Lyon of Cambridge. He was an adept in all those wristy strokes that 'may or may not', and would surprise the most complacently successful bowler with a high pull to the boundary. In fielding, as in batting, he was fearless and rapid, excelling in the slips, at silly-point, and short-leg. His bowling, when required, was slow, twisty, experimental. In 1922, he had elated his brother, who was keeping wicket for Cambridge, by making a pair of noughts at Lord's. Next year, after playing a brilliant innings of 91 against MCC he made only 14 against Cambridge, but brought off two remarkable catches at short-leg. In later years, he won fame as a daring and original captain of Gloucestershire. He warred against dullness and drawn matches, and in his crusade was always seeking ways of defeating convention and tradition. He was a constant butt of the older critics, but he was among the first to see that county cricket might die from dullness and from the rivalry of sports where results were quicker.

Sometimes he made the mistake of pursuing speed merely for its own sake, but Gloucestershire cricket flourished under Bev Lyon. No doubt he was lucky in having in his side the greatest English cricketer of his day, Walter Hammond, but he knew how to exploit such a possession. He made people talk about Gloucestershire and come to see them play. Nor was he only a master of tactics. He had humour, human understanding, and persuasion. He could handle that temperamental genius, Charles Parker. He knew to a fine exactitude what he could and could not expect from his players, and he clothed a profession and a routine in the finery of rollicking adventure.

Our wicket-keeper at Oxford, as in 1922, was the sturdy Mark Patten, from Winchester, 'Mark Pizzy' as his horse-racing friends called him. No day was too long for him. He was pink of face and very tough. A blow on the head served only to sharpen his skill. He was also a strong and determined batsman, who had seen too much bowling from one side of the stumps to wear much respect for it on the other. He and his fellow Wykehamist,

51

Tom Raikes, shared in some lusty partnerships, and were sometimes known to their intimates as Falstaff and Sir Toby Belch.

After a defeat by Lancashire, we beat Hampshire by 3 wickets. Lionel Tennyson made 74 in their first innings of 258, and was plainly delighted at the feat. I had 4 wickets for 58. We answered with 346, nearly everyone making runs; then Bettington and Stevens shot out Hampshire for 173. Kennedy and Newman bowled beautifully in our second innings, but Stevens's steadiness carried us through.

The Kent match was played in icy weather, and it was no joke fielding to Frank Woolley. He made 107 in their second innings. In the first, I took 6 for 82, sometimes making the ball fly from a pitch that was hard with a top-dressing of rain. Wally Hardinge, an England player against slow and medium bowling, showed an inclination to retire towards square-leg, and soon snicked one off me to Bettington in the slips. George Collins, a useful left-hand bat and right-hand bowler, and an expert at crown-and-anchor, made 47, and the left-handed Ronnie Bryan made 68 not out in his own delightful manner. Business kept him from all but a little county cricket. I can think of no other family that has produced three such left-handers as J. L., R. T., and G. J. Bryan. Of the three, R. T. was the most graceful. At number eight, one W. Ashdown was bowled by me for 0. Later, he scored many runs off me batting at number one. He was a stylist, with the full old-fashioned off-side strokes, and a useful bowler, with a late nip from leg.

For this match, Tom Hayward lent me his huge-collared sweater. Tom was our trainer-coach. Good easy man, Tom was not cut out for work. In the nets, he bowled off-breaks from sixteen or seventeen yards. His verbal instruction was limited to three comments: 'How's that?' 'Hit 'em 'ard,' and 'Oh, what a shot, sir!' The last was reserved for the many occasions when his pupil swept one into the longer and wetter grass, just to see Tom amble after the ball. When pressed to take an innings, he would smile and put the question by. Only once did we persuade him into pads, and then, for about five minutes, he showed enough to remind us of his greatness. His brother Dan was in charge of the rival pavilion at Fenners, Cambridge. Tom fancied himself somewhat as a masseur and kept himself very busy with bandages and liniments when the team went on tour. But he was best of all as a spectator, with his face balanced like a luminous walrus over the wall by the dressing-room steps.

I met Tom once or twice in his retirement at Cambridge. Retirement was, perhaps, not quite the word, as he was supposed to be taking some part in the conducting of the family business. But business was not his line. Over a glass of beer, we went over to the Oxford scene, and I reminded him of how Lionel Hedges used to pull his leg. 'Ah,' said Tom, 'that was all right.' He implied that his present life was all wrong. About a year before the Hitler War I asked for him again, and brother Dan said Tom had taken to staying in bed for breakfast. He died in July 1939. I wonder what he would have made of that second war. I suppose he would have curled his moustache and said 'Ah'.

We lost to Middlesex, after leading them by 101 runs on the first innings, Jack Durston taking 8 for 27 in our second. This was set right by an innings victory over Gloucestershire, whose opening pair were Dipper and the twenty-year old Walter Hammond. I bowled 'Dip' for 3 with what Tom Lowry would have called a 'lallapaloozer', and Bettington had Hammond lbw for 22. In the second innings we ran him out for 15. Already he had signs of greatness about him, but was still impetuous and slap-dash. The innings of the match was 73 by Greville Stevens, played on a wet wicket.

Absent from the match against the Army, which we unexpectedly lost, I was going through the farce of the 'Greats' examination. I wore horn-rimmed spectacles, to induce a sensation of wisdom, but it was no good. I think the Logic paper was the worst. It was 'harder than Bezique'. The only relief was a gigantic negro who kept retiring to the lavatory, surely not in the hope of reading secreted and relevant information.

Between the end of the term and the 'Varsity match, we beat somewhat emasculated teams of Sussex, at Brighton, and Surrey, at the Oval, and lost to MCC at Lord's, and H. D. G. Leveson Gower's team, at Eastbourne; the former by habit, the latter through high living. But we returned to Lord's with buoyant confidence that we should lay Cambridge low. We had much to wipe off the slate.

Our optimism was justified, and we brought off the record win of an innings and 227 runs. A thunderstorm broke in the very early morning after our innings of 422, and Cambridge batted twice during the second (and last) day of the match on a pitch that was at first sodden, then progressively 'sticky'. This storm has often been used to explain the Cambridge defeat; in truth, it did but increase the margin of a victory which we would have won over them on any pitch in nine matches out of ten. We had, in Bettington and Stevens, spin bowling of the first class. Cambridge had no spin bowling at all, nor the sort of batsmen likely to cope with ours. Further, we were the more experienced team. Six of their batsmen came from Eton or Harrow, two schools that have seldom produced batsmen strong in the art of back-play. Style and enterprise they had in plenty, and, in Tom Lowry, of New Zealand, a rugged and dangerous player who had scored 1,000 runs for Cambridge during the term. But a pointer to the standard of their batting was the presence at number three of G. O. Allen who, in those days, was a sound enough player, but no more. Besides, he was their chief bowler.

Here, Cambridge suffered an irremediable blow. Allen, opening the attack from the Pavilion end, bowled a few overs in his best style, then broke down with a recurring injury to his back. He went off for treatment, but not all the Colleges of Surgeons and Physicians can suddenly conquer Nature, and, though he returned to the field, he had to be written off as a counting part of the attack. At the other end, P. A. Wright toiled on with skill and courage, but, as the runs ticked up, the absence of all danger in their change bowling was naked to see.

Greville Stevens, opening the innings with Claude Taylor, was caught at short-leg off a rather negligent stroke. Jardine joined Taylor and soon showed them he was not meaning to allow himself any entertainment on the off side. Far otherwise did Taylor bat. He was 'all elegance, fit to bat before the Queen in her parlour'. Off-drives and leg-glides brought him many boundaries. Claude Ashton, the Cambridge captain, was blamed for not blocking these strokes. But it is easy to be wise from the grandstand. In the nineties, Taylor gave his first chance, a return catch to the bowler. At 109 he popped one into the hands of short-leg. Never before had a Freshman made a century in his first innings of the 'Varsity match.

Beverley Lyon began as if he meant to score a hundred in an hour, but was soon lbw. Hopkins and Knott batted easily enough. At 266 for 6, I joined Knott. I was using a most displeasing bat, like an alloy of teak and tin, and here, at last, was a chance of batting, instead of just filling up the space above the extras. In the intervals of exchanging rude remarks with Tom Lowry, who stood under an appalling homburg hat at short-leg, I moved along to 12. At that point, John Knott was bowled and E. P. Hewetson appeared.

Hewetson's method of batting was simple. Holding his bat very firmly at the very top of the handle, he thrust his left leg towards the pitch of every ball not obviously a long-hop, and swung the bat like a son of Anak. The short ball on the wicket or to the off, he prodded coaxingly towards third man. He was tall, florid, and of great strength, and he feared neither man nor demon. Soon after he came in, Ashton put on Ronnie Aird to bowl at the Pavilion end. Now Aird was, and is, an admirable batsman, but his bowling was the answer to the blacksmith's prayer, straight, pitched up, slowish, and innocent of bias. So Hewetson began with two high curving fours over mid-off and a colossal six on to the lawn-tennis court which then lay to the left of the pavilion. Soon, he smashed his bat, and another was sent out. In 25 minutes he scored 57, and strode away with a face like steaming strawberries. I borrowed his bat. During Hewetson's innings my score rose from 12 to 14, and I was once barracked for failing to let my partner have the bowling. Joined by the jovial Raikes, I decided on haste, and cracked several balls over cover-point's head. At 53 I skied a dolly to mid-off. The innings closed for 422.

During the following night the heat was terrific. At five o'clock in the morning came the long-threatened storm. As the rain swished down, I thought gratefully of Bettington and Stevens, and so to sleep. Stevens, bowling off-spinners, did most of the work in the Cambridge first innings, only Ashton (15) reaching double figures. In the second, Leonard Crawley was promoted to number one. Bettington, blacker than ever in the heat and toil, told me to 'pitch 'em up wide on the off, and I'll skirt about down by the Tavern'. Crawley made a few glorious strokes, then skied one high to Bettington who, having caught it, said: 'That's enough for you ,' and began his last spell, at the Nursery end. By now the pitch was biting fiercely. Allen, Ashton, and Tomlinson each resisted for a time. But Bettington was not to be denied. He took 8 for 66, five clean bowled, and walked rapidly towards the pavilion, snapping his fingers, as if asking for a few more batsmen. He had waited four years for this.

So, my four years of bowling against Cambridge produced 2 wickets, Hubert Ashton and Leonard Crawley. In all matches for Oxford, I took 146 wickets at 21 each, and made 518 runs with an average of 15. In this period, I caught, and missed, my share of slip catches; and talked millions of words.

A week later, I joined the Somerset team against Kent at Maidstone. Three of our best cricketers, J. C. White, M. D. Lyon, and T. C. Lowry, were playing for the Gentlemen against the Players at Lord's, where Lyon made a brilliant 120, Greville Stevens 122. George Louden, the Essex amateur, after having Jack Hobbs lbw for 6, took 5 for 49 in 26.3 overs. Very tall, and with a lovely high action, Louden was a bowler of England quality, but, owing to business, he could play rarely in county cricket.

To return to Maidstone. We lost a good match by 73 runs. I had 6 wickets, including Hardinge twice for the second time that summer. This started me on a run in which I took 39 wickets in 4 matches at just under 14 runs each. Our defeat by Kent was followed by two victories over Sussex. At Eastbourne, we won by 10 wickets. I had 14 for 106. At Taunton, set to make 268 in the fourth innings, we won by 6 wickets, Lowry hammering Tate, Gilligan, and George Cox for 77, and MacBryan making a masterly 116 not out. Here I had 8 wickets for 138 runs. Going to Bristol for the bank-holiday match, we beat Gloucestershire by an innings and 70 runs. M. D. Lyon and Earle both scored a century, and that once-famous spectator, Joe Bottle, roared his impartial advice to both teams. I took 11 for 157. So, with six matches left, I needed only 10 wickets for the hundred.

Three matches at Weston-super-Mare yielded only eight, though I have always reckoned that the ball which bowled

George Challenor, of the West Indies, was worth five wickets — a shooter that also cut in from the leg. Then, at Portsmouth, after getting rid of Kennedy, I had Jack Newman caught at slip, and the thing was done. I have made a good fuss about this performance, but I knew that 1923 would be my last and only chance. Never again was I able to play through a full season, or near it. I also knew that it was my last chance of reaching a Test trial match. I didn't, though I watched the chief selector of that year, 'Shrimp' Leveson Gower, picking his teams for England v. The Rest in the Royal Hotel, Weston-super-Mare. I had earned the right to hope, but no more. Jack MacBryan went up and played for the Rest, and made 80, the highest score in the match.

At the end of that season, I went up to Blackpool and played in a Festival match for Jack Sharp's team against Lionel Tennyson's. Financially, the Festival was a flop, and was played almost in camera. It needed a far richer house to counterbalance the free lunches that the friends of the Committee gave themselves. But the fun was unquenchable. At the start of their innings, the umpires announced that they had been instructed to be 'very generous about lbw decisions'. This was cheerful news in face of a batting order that started with Russell, Sandham, Ted Bowley, P. Mead, and H. L. Dales. George Gunn, sidling up from mid-on, said to one of the umpires: 'and, I suppose, if any one's bowled (rhyming with "scowled") it's just a nusty accident?'

In 1924 Somerset beat Middlesex at Lord's by 37 runs. In their first innings of 128, I had 9 for 38. On the strength of this I was chosen for the Gentlemen v. Players at Lord's. So were White, Lyon, and MacBryan from Somerset. There were a few places still left for the England team that was to sail under A. E. R. Gilligan for Australia, and hope flickered faintly around my fancy. The Players won the toss. Johnny Douglas (Pavilion end) and I opened the bowling to Jack Hobbs and Herbert Sutcliffe. The pitch was very lively. Hobbs was clean beaten by Douglas three times in the first over, and, in answer to Douglas's whirling execrations, said: 'Well bowled, Colonel, well bowled.' My first ball hit Sutcliffe in the midriff. But they batted themselves out of the trough, and Hobbs went on to one of his imcomparable hundreds. Sutcliffe, when 20, was caught off me and his splice by Douglas at backward point. Later, I had J. W. Hearne caught low in the slips by Greville Stevens for 61 and caught and bowled Maurice Tate, for 50, as I stood nearly on his huge feet. 'Why,' he said afterwards, 'you came down the pitch like Abraham.' They made 514, Roy Kilner contributing a very hearty 113. He died four years later. and Yorkshire lost a grand all-rounder, a very true and gay sportsman.

Our batting broke down twice. In our first innings, Johnny Douglas, at number six, was batting away tooth, gloves, and nail, against Tate and Warwickshire's fast bowler, Harry Howell, in an awkward light. I joined him at number eleven. The light grew worse, and Bill Reeves, as he stood umpire at square-leg, and watched some bouncers pass my nose, said in a loud, hoarse whisper, 'Do you want to be killed?' I said I didn't. 'Well then,' he hissed, 'why don't you appeal against the light?' So I did; and in we all went. Johnny Douglas was amazed. 'Well,' he said, as we walked in, 'if that doesn't beat the bloody band; an appeal against the light by a number . . . eleven! Why, I was just getting my eye in.'

I played again for Gentlemen v. Players at Scarborough, and listened to that famous gourmet and hitter and criminologist, C. I. Thornton, discoursing on Madame Fahmy and mutton-fat; and I bowled out Sutcliffe in a sea-mist.

But I had shot one bolt for ever across cricket's door. Till now I had been a practising cricketer. Afterwards, I was but an intervener.

The Brighter Side of Cricket

Puerilities

'O joy! that in our embers
  Is something that doth live
That nature yet remembers
  What was so fugitive!'

In the kaleidoscope of infancy such things as goblins in the dark
corners of the nursery at twilight, a saw-edged Eton collar,
coloured Easter eggs, or the back of the vicar's head in the
Creed, are worthy rivals to cricket. But all of them, cricket as
well, are fugitive, for memory is a fond deceiver, deigning
sometimes on quiet summer evenings to be a friend, yet
readily changing with the east wind or a rainy Monday morning
to an elusive and rebellious servant. So Nature, mindful of the
unequal struggle, has given us eyes as an ally against this rebel.
Hence the proud father, watching his son at the nets drive one
along the ground 'left foot over, body well behind', is carried
gently back to a similar stroke of his own, or more probably to
some glorious 'cow-shot', followed by the inevitable crash
behind and the not less inevitable bray from in front, 'Oh, if you
WILL think you've got a scythe! . . .'

And when, proud father, you have gone home again, revolving
fair visions of another Grace, some second Tate, whose fame
will illumine your declining years, and when you have
perused again the half-term report, the memory of which had
been effaced by your son's skill at cricket, do not, I beg, repine,
do not be amazed!

To repine is useless, for your stern, corrective letter will be
answered by a terse statement that 'we won our match on
Saturday easily'. To be amazed argues sheer stupidity, for your
better judgment should tell you that at this very moment your
son is playing Surrey *v.* Yorkshire, surreptitiously, but with full
analyses, in his exercise-book; in spite of the tragic grandeur of
John of Gaunt who, like other modern John of Gaunts, is
lamenting the passing of the good old days, and in spite of the
undeniable truth that Caesar threw his cavalry (wantonly)
across the river. Or else, having irretrievably confused the
Doldrums with the Gulf Stream, he has issued forth from the

lesson unshaken, and is abusing some wretched ignoramus who oils his splice and thinks Chapman plays for Sussex.

'So don't fatigue yourself, I beg, sir!' or meditate correction. Let fall the reproving pen, and comfort yourself with the thought that Grace and Porson both had their points. Nay more, quinine may quell the incipient cold, aspirin may alleviate the sick-headache, potent is the birch for the genuine sluggard; but no triumph of science, no potion, no nostrum, not even hellebore, fabled herb, can certainly cure that sweet disorder of the youthful mind, *cricketomania*. It can, indeed, be arrested and kept within bounds, but only by the skilled cricketopath.

May I assist you, fond parent, to diagnose the symptoms? Some, no doubt, will ring familiar in your ears. Others need for full development the contagion of other small fellow-patients. Let us take one or two, and examine them.

It is the prerogative of the medical profession to make up Latin prescriptions illegible to all but the chemist—and after all, he, poor man, only pretends to read them as he pours in the paint-water – but *cricketopaths* – that is, devotees of *cricketopathy*, would-be healers of *cricketomania* – flatter themselves that they have invented a Latin diction, limited as yet, to keep pace with the progress of the science, and they affirm that the most universal symptom in this disorder is *cacoethes interrogandi*, or *question-itch*. A well-known cricketopath has made an interesting collection of these, some of which I append:

1. Why did Grace have a beard?
2. Would you rather bat left-handed and bowl right-handed, or bowl left-handed and bat right-handed?
3. How old is Grimmett?
4. If there were no County Championship, how would they know who were the best players?
5. Did Wass know Greek?

The leading text-books on *cricketopathy* lay down that, for this *cacoethes*, any apathy or neglect on the part of the practitioner is dangerous, as the questions will merely be repeated until they become definitely mechanical and purely rhetorical. At which stage no sedative is of any avail. The prescribed medicine is either *responsio verisimilis*, or if that be unobtainable, *plausibilis evasio.*

There is another symptom worthy of recording, no less familiar to the student of this disorder, which is called by some, quite simply, *cacoethes scribendi*, or *writing-itch*; by others, more technically, *punctiuncula caeca*; that is, a kind of blind stabbing with any sharp instrument, a compass, pencil, or even a new nib. A diagram is drawn, containing wides, sixes, obstructed-the-fieldsman-wilfully, no-balls, bowleds, and other human contingencies. Forthwith, in the imagination of the patient, some team, Middlesex haply, or the local village, take the field, and their fate is decided by a series of (clandestine) stabs. If the patient is fond of the team which he is stabbing, he frequently has to create a new diagram containing more sixes and fours. If otherwise, more bowleds and caughts are born. If even this artifice fails to stab the favoured team to victory, the patient opens his eyes to effect critical stabs. But this is a variation of the symptom, and is more properly termed *punctiuncula semicaeca*, or even *punctum mendax*. The scores are then duly registered. Quite recently a cricketopath discovered in the possession of a patient, otherwise quite healthy, a fragmentary indication of this symptom, which read as follows:

J. B. Hobbs, bowled Me   0

ME, not out (at the end of Latin)   .   . 381

I have been assured that there are only two cures for this form of the disorder, and that even they bring only a temporary alleviation. One is *impositio longa*, the other *confiscatio implementorum.*

But, as I have said, it is a sweet disorder. For in boyhood the ball that hits the bottom of the middle stump is not a d——shooter and the groundsman's fault, but a beastly grub, and the action of wayward fate. The loss of a Test Match is just 'a swindle', not the crash of an empire or the harbinger of national decay.

In fact, *cricketomania* is never fatal, at least not to the young.

Gone!

Yes, the lissome days are gone,
When we ran the desperate 1;
When the umpire piped 'How's that? —
Out!' — because he longed to bat;
When those cursed the close of play
Who resent its start today;
When we braved the South-West soaker
Who in age resort to Poker;
When the slight and pliant limb
Sped from cricket to the swim;
Happy hours of oiling splices,
Happier days of eating ices,
Guileless fodder, hardy buns —
Buns were excellent for runs —
When an average of 7
Brought me very near to heaven!
Worlds above one batsman small
Wallowing in his decimal!
Johnny Graham, it was you
Who, one sainted summer through,
Averaged .72;
It is hardly worth referring
To the truth, 'twas 2.
Yet, when we triumphant asses
Laughed, you polished up your glasses,
Smiled your undefeated smile,
And remarked 'Just wait a while',
Till, when radiant day was done,
'Graham, b. R.-Glasgow 1'
Shewed in hieroglyphic plain
How your boast was not in vain!
Does your mind retain the thought
That you shot me out for 0
With a complicated sneak?
Everything it did but speak;
I was telling Peter Brent
Why I'd rather play for Kent,

And my horizontal bat
(Bound with ribbon off a hat),
Swished in agonizing arc,
As men swish in Public Park;
Still I hear your fiendish shout
And your tautologic 'OUT!'
Johnny, whereso'er you be –
Ruling Mesopotamy? –
Telling your unlikely tales,
While your liver runs to nails,
We must somehow meet again,
And the modest flagon drain
To that Neolithic sneak;
To the hours we writhed in Greek,
'Men' and 'Dee' and 'Hoi' and 'Hai',
While the lark trilled to the sky;
Or, we sat like rows of frogs
Through the mysteries of 'Logs',
Blandly plunged, with minds like sieves,
Subjects into Ablatives.
Yes, my Johnny, we must quaff –
You shall pay and I shall laugh –
To the golden days, long gone,
When you made that famous 1!

The Art of Watching

'This way – this way – capital fun – lots of beer – hogsheads, rounds of beef – bullocks; mustard – cart-loads'; this is undoubtedly the way, as Mr Jingle suggested, to watch cricket; the uninvited guest at the baronial sward; quizzing the crab through the cracks in the marquee, eyeing with the glance of prospective ownership those anchovy sandwiches and devilled kidneys and glorious fellows and white trousers and flannel jackets, discoursing to the strangely acquiescent host of fabulous matches in hot climates, calling out, in the intervals of jovial tumblers, to the fielders in terms of 'muff' and 'humbug', and well . . . 'other toasts were drunk'. Some of us have been near it, have hovered on the limbo of this Lucullan paradise, but few have achieved the ultimate apotheosis of the spectator: I knew one man of distinguished profile, who not only did it, but was asked for the next year, but this cannot count, as his host mistook him for an eminent KC.

It is not easy to say what precise form of watching cricket gives a man the greatest pleasure, but I think that perhaps the most deep enjoyment is to be derived from what we may term 'auto-invigilation,' the mental going-over, preferably in bed – with no prospect of fielding till after lunch on the next day – of some rare and long-desired innings; as the soft dews of kindly sleep descend, each stroke is turned over and revelled in, the snicks for four that hummed over slips, those are worth a long chuckle, the late-cut so ripely timed which pulled up by that damsel so fair with the blue parasol – a long think in retrospect here – that off-break to which you covered up so modernly and made the bowler loathe you; you have gained this right of succulent meditation; for you are a bowler, perchance, and at this time tomorrow will be nursing a strained thigh and cursing all umpires, all slip-fielders, and wondering why you ever began this game – but for the sweet nonce you have achieved delight, and with it you sink Lethewards. If there is agony in remorse at failure, what joy can compare to the looking back on the greater moments? What man in the world was as happy as Hobbs that Monday night at Taunton in August of 1925, when pursued by moving-pictures, hunted by furious pens, he won the battle at last, and equalled the record of Grace, the great master? W. S. Gilbert used to sit in the theatre, and cry with laughter at his own humour. Hobbs saw those last runs of his on the screen – spectatorship indeed.

The most uncomfortable form of watching is, surely, when your own opening batsmen (yourself perhaps at number 3) are facing, with all the art that they can muster, those baptismal overs, when the devil is in the bowler, an imp in the pitch, and twenty minutes of gathering dusk to be agonized through. I know a great batsman who, when much is at stake, positively will not watch those overs, but sits in the dressing-room pretending to read a newspaper, while some messenger, a mere bowler, despairing of luring him into the needful sun, keeps him posted of the doubtful moil from over to over: yet, if a wicket fall ten minutes from the close, no captain can persuade him to the sacrifice of a rabbit. His cares drop from him

> 'like the needles shaken from out the gusty pine',

and striding masterfully to the wicket, he treats the crowd to those powerful and elegant strokes which make us wonder why he was worrying: but artistry and nervous tension are for ever inseparable.

If I were to choose one form of watching above all others, it is to stop for a leisured half-hour by some sylvan retreat, some village green where cricket was played before America was one nation, to lean on the railing unseen, while Braces shatters the wicket with devastating round-arm, and the leathern-palmed rustic judges a rocket in the longer grass with an unsung nicety which would have brought all Lord's Pavilion to its feet. For, even if they care, which perhaps they don't, you at least are free from solicitude; interest devoid of anxiety is the ideal spectatorship.

Lastly, there is what we may call Eccentric watching.

Not long since, I read in a newspaper that a lady lawn-tennis player had been pestered with advice on service, stroke-production, and that sort of thing. It was, once more, a case of 'save me from my friends'. At first, it seems, the redundant comments merely came by letter. These, like bills, are quietly and humanely stored away. But the hunter was not the sort of man to lose his quarry so easily. Discarding the impersonal pen, he came and 'would sit near the court, and would cough loudly every time she made a mistake'. A cross-court drive that fell just outside the line was enough to induce this asthmatic display, and a 'sitter' feebly netted would make him almost tubercular. This kind of thing is quite horrifying. Where will it stop? Throughout League history spectators of soccer matches have expressed, unthwarted, their disapproval of indifferent play or uncertain tactics. They are accustomed to greet a missed goal with short, Chaucerian terminology, and a firm decision of the referee has sufficed to produce a torrent of complicated invective. But this liberty of speech is almost unknown to other games. It is

awful to think of this exclamatory adviser, this agonizing
mentor, following Hendren to the wicket at Lord's with dutiful
precision; he takes his stand by the square-leg umpire, and
regales the batsman with cries of 'left foot over, eyes on the line
of the ball, follow through!' Or, if he found it difficult to
persuade the authorities of his necessity on the field, he might
pre-arrange a system of signals. Two blasts on the whistle for
safety-play, a long siren for a late-cut, and a revolver shot for a
full-blooded six.

Even chess-masters might not remain unmolested: the
tormentor will fix his favourite with a glittering eye, and, as he
is about to make a move which will obviously lose him at least a
King's Bishop, will emit a sonorous sigh, and the disaster will be
averted. For more catastrophic mistakes, such as putting the
Queen in jeopardy of a rival pawn, he will play a fantasia on a
bell, or continuously flick his cuff links.

The menace is there, but thank Heaven, the germ of the
plague has been detected on the courts of its infancy.

The Cricketer's Highway

CONTAINING A METRICAL SELECTION OF THE
MORE IMPORTANT LAWS OF CRICKET

LAW I – *The Game*
The game is played between Two sides
  Of just Eleven. This is true
Unless some fellow first decides
  To have Eleven sides of Two.

No side may say 'We'll bat again,'
  Because, as any one can see,
Law I remarks, in language plain,
  'Please take your chance alternately.'

No doubt you think that we have erred
  And are deceived; without delay
We quote this Law – the Fifty-Third –
  Which seems, interpreted, to say:

'A side foreseeing heavy rain,
   Shall have the Option of requiring
The other side to bat again.'
   (A thing they seldom are desiring.)

LAW II – *The Runs*
The key to scoring is 'The Run';
   In ancient days the Scorer notched it
Upon a tree-trunk, which was fun,
   But if he lost his knife, he cotched it. (*Oh!*)

Then came the pen, his task to soften,
   And I must not forget to say
That they who run, and run most often,
   Are always deemed to win the day.

LAW IV – *The Ball*
When twice one hundred runs appear,
   The bowler legally may roar for
Another Ball, not quite so queer –
   This is an excerpt out of Law IV.

LAW VI – *The Wickets*
This problem technically must be
   Referred to when a Hampshire chap
Called Lumpy Stevens cried out, 'Bust me,
   There goes another through that gap!'

Nous avons changé tout cela
   By legislative chains and links.
We bowlers now ne voyons pas
   Those idiosyncratic chinks.

THE GROUNDSMAN – *Equity*
One of the Groundsman's only 'licets' –
   Suspicion clouds his slightest action –
Is lingering upon the wickets
   In silent, hob-nailed petrifaction.

LAW IX – *The Ground*

Except when roseate beginnings
    Of day emerge from Eastern Sea
(Or at commencement of each innings),
    The Ground shall never, never be

Rolled, watered, covered, beaten, mown,
    Or subject unto medication;
This ointment has one fly, I own –
    Fortuitous expectoration.

LAW XLI – *The Fieldsman*

The Fieldsman, by some special grace,
    May stop the ball with any part;
And to receive it in the face
    Argues a most consummate art.

But if, in playful mood, he shall
    Entrap it in his cummerbund,
Five runs are added, and the ball
    Is, *ipso facto*, moribund.

LAW XLII – *The Wicket-keeper*

The Keeper stands behind the stumps;
    He must not incommode the batter
With any cry, like 'Hell!' or 'Hi!'
    Or, 'Do you think I'm getting fatter?'

He must not ooze beyond the bails,
    Consider it an evil omen
If, when each other method fails,
    He flicks them off with his abdomen.

LAW XLIII – *The Umpire*

The Umpire is the only judge of fair and unfair play,
The whatness of the weather and the whenness of the
    day;
And (though he mustn't wager) his position's very
    strong,
For the Umpire, like a governess, is *never* in the
    wrong.

For instance, if the bowler's face displeases him at
    all,
He varies signalling a wide with crying out 'No-
    ball!'
And, like a famous Israelite in Joshua or Kings,
He takes a pride in measuring the Boundaries and
    things.

The Umpire is tyrannical, and when he bellows
    'Play!'
Supposing you or I remark, 'Not, on the whole,
    to-day,'
He doesn't fix another date, but says, 'All right
    then, don't,
For them as wants has won the match, and them as
    doesn't won't.'

If forced to acquiesce you frame a suitable retort,
He, in his simple-mindedness, will parry with 'One
    short!'
So you must make allowances for one who – don't
    forget –
Is human in all other points but one: HE MUST NOT
    BET!

The Oracle

It was a beautiful afternoon in the last days of August, as I rode
slowly past an ivy-mantled church in the outskirts of a certain
village of England; then on down a steep hill with meadows on
either side, revolving in innocent subconsciousness thoughts of
curfews, mute inglorious Miltons, and cool sequestered vales.
I turned back to take one lingering look at the tower beneath
whose shade –

    'Each in his narrow cell for ever laid,
      The rude forefathers of the hamlet sleep,'

and was about to resume my quiet pedalling when I caught

sight of the rude grandsons of the hamlet disporting themselves at cricket on the neighbouring sward. I thought I would beguile the leisured hour in unnoticed spectatorship.

Leaving my bicycle by the road, I walked towards the arena, which was one of those fields where cricket is permitted by the tolerant complaisance of various quadrupeds, whose sole demands are sufficiency of fodder; not much to ask, and an undoubted addition to the sylvan picturesqueness of this remote encounter. After cruising about behind the bowler's arm, a muscular man in jazz braces – and thus aiding him no doubt in the hideous ruin of the batsman's wicket – I was settling down to a pastoral pipe on this lovely August afternoon, when a slow, disgruntled voice issued, apparently, from the trunk of a huge oak tree just by me: 'There 'e goes agen. Fust ball. It stands to reason that when a man 'aving a bat in 'is 'ands don't know as 'ow it were mannifactered for naught but 'itting the ball, 'e will in course of events pay for 'is ignorance. That's Joe Caddle all over.'

No answer came to this peevish homily; only a heavy expectoration followed by a sucking sound. I sat quite silent, hoping for a further bulletin, but none came. Only a blue wreath of smoke was wafted round the oak towards me.

My mind wandered to the ancient Greeks and oracular responses. I thought of the oaks of Dodona. Then there was the smoke too – suggestive of the mephitic vapour of Delphi. But here the comparison ceased. Ancient oracles were delivered in ambiguous verse; now there had been nothing metrical or ambiguous in this Oracle. I determined to investigate the source of the voice. Going round to the other side of the oak I at first saw nothing, but looking down at my feet I beheld, lying quite motionless on a memorable stomach, slowly sucking a huge briar, the Oracle. The temple which contained the Oracle was not ornate. It had all the attractive individuality of rough-hewn ugliness. Its two main pillars were of corduroy; and on a capital of vinous hue there rested a battered but serviceable roof. The Oracle itself was watching the game with a gaze of unblinking scorn from beneath great, shaggy eyebrows. But not the scorn of indifference. It was plain that nothing except the vagaries of the game would claim its attention.

72

However, I thought it would be rather weak to go away empty, like a botanist from an elusive quarry, so I essayed an opening. 'Nice day,' I murmured nervously, 'for cricket. . . .'

I tried again.

'I say, that fellow was bowled all right. No need for an umpire's decision, what?'

I felt, in view of the first oracular comment, that this or nothing would do it. Nor was I deceived. There was a deep prophetic rumble, out of which proceeded the voice:

'Joe Caddle 'asn't got no call for to play cricket. It aren't in 'is line o' bizness. 'E's an 'and-thresher by trade, and there isn't none better, and that's the reason on it.'

Now, although Joseph Caddle was even to the most unpractised eye more essentially a thresher than a cricketer, I felt that the theme of Caddle was becoming hackneyed. After all——

'Joe Caddle,' pursued the Priest of Apollo, 'to my mind wouldn't never——'

I determined to divert the divine flow into some other channel.

'Do you ever play for this district?' I hazarded.

I had scored. The Oracle slowly turned on me an eye; not the usual appraising look of the disgusted bucolic, but an eye, semi-humorous, but withal distrait, as of a man who recalled something rather funny of long ago.

'Yus, I did. I played for 'em; likewise I scored for 'em. But I reckoned I were getting old for the playing, and they reckoned I was a bit oncertain in the scoring. As to the playing, you see, it weren't so much that I lost me art, but me legs and wind didn't some'ow answer, and in running a quick four, f'r instance, I'd as often as not be overtook in the middle o' third run. As to the scoring, I always were a party man, and 'ave always 'eld that a match is played double-like, out in the middle for one, and, moreover, in scorers' 'utch as well; and that, whereas our folk may want for runs out there, there's often summat as can be made out o' byes and other extries by a scorer as knows 'is job. But, mind, when argyment arises with t'other scorer, a man must stand by 'is figures and persevere, in a manner o' speaking. Many's the time in six year o' scoring I've out-argyied old Thomas Penner, scorer o' Blotton, next village t'ourn. 'Seventy-six,' sez I, adding up. 'How comes that there?' sez Thomas; 'I makes 'un seventy-one after three adds.' 'Look at yer extries,' sez I. 'Mayhap you've let slide a wide or two; Johnson's 'e's been bowling mortal wild today; and you knows, Thomas, good scorer as you is, you never 'ave been much on extries.' 'Maybe,' sez 'e; 'maybe,' sucked in proper, and down 'e writes 'em, muttering about the 'eat and being old, and 'ow 'e'll soon 'ave to give up scoring at this rate. But they finds me out at last, and the captain, Mr Knight, squire, lives over yonder, sez as 'ow, if we're to win, which I do say is durned seldom – what with squire not bending at point, and vicar dropping catches, fit to turn a saint in 'is grave, at mid-off – if we're to win, 'e sez, let's win honest. 'Right,' sez I, 'IF you wins,' speaking emphatic-like on the 'if,' 'but don't ever ask ME to darken your score-book agen, 'cos I won't.' 'No,' sez 'e, likewise speaking pretty strong, 'that you never won't ruddy well neither.' And what's more, I 'aven't, and that's uppard o' three years agone, maybe. They once did 'ave me stand umpire when Bob Snatcher 'ad 'is kidneys go wrong, so couldn't stand; but I starts by answer-ing adverse when our folk shouts 'gainst the best man o' Down-weller, village next but one yonder; and 'im dead out, too, if ever a man were, and finishes by giving Squire run out when 'e'd trotted in comfortable and were a-preparing to take next ball. No one 'adnt appealed, not as I 'eard, but I sez 'out,' and out'e'ad to go, scowling 'orrid, and looking back at me like Prussian acid. I 'as a good laugh to meself, thinking over it, and thus gives an eight-ball over, absent-like; opposing captain 'e asks me if I were born in Australia, and Squire 'e gives me the sack from umpire. So 'ere I am, still knowing what good cricket is, but not often noticing any, not from our folk least-ways.'

After his first glance at me the Oracle had delivered this concise autobiography, looking steadfastly at the game, missing nothing. But soon he warmed to his work. Joe Caddle, the original cause of anger and source of discord, had been the last man to bat for the home side, and was now standing behind the wickets with gloves on, watching a deep slip fielder stop with his shins the express deliveries of a small bandy-legged man, with a bow-tie and cap, who did not believe in the conservation of energy. Mr Knight, the squire, at point, stood out against the woods behind in heroic profile, and occasionally kicked the ball, or else was struck on the boot, in the intervals of which he continually disseminated fielders where the last scoring stroke had gone, so that there was a constant general-post and a steady flow of scoring.

'What a brain!' muttered the Oracle, as the fast bowler was at length relieved of his responsibilities, after conceding eighteen byes, two wides, a no-ball, and fifteen runs in four overs. 'Might 'a' been Prime Minister easy, if only 'is father 'adn't seen 'is early talent for cricket.

But the vicar at mid-off was more interesting. His energy was violent, but uninfectious. Wherever the ball was hit he started to run towards it. He was ubiquitous and unconvincing. Quite suddenly a terrific drive hurtled along the ground towards him, awakened the latent activities in his corns, and shot off at a tangent. Undeterred, he did even time towards the longer grass; but a small boy, anticipating his desire, picked the ball from under some trees and threw it quite fifty yards back over his head. Honourably exhausted by this fruitless expedition, and smiling wanly, the vicar resumed his position; only to find that it was 'over,' and every one was waiting for him.

'What sort of a player is the vicar?' I said.

'Player?' replied the Oracle, at last turning round: ''e aren't a player. 'E's a figure'ead; but I will say this for 'im, that, whereas Squire moors 'isself permanent at point, vicar 'e's ready to go anywhere, but prefers mid-off, as 'e says it's there the strokes come 'ottest. Which may be courage, but it aren't policy, neither for 'im nor for the side. Not for 'im, 'cos 'e gets stung up cruel sometimes, nor for the side, 'cos 'e 'asn't never 'eld a catch yet as anybody remembers on. First time 'e plays, Bert Miller, big 'itter o' Downweller, it's a whacking ballooner 'igh up in the sky, and Bert Miller comes running down the pitch pretty quick and 'eavy – can't be much short o' fifteen stone – and then it all 'appens at once. The ball she comes down on points o' vicar's fingers, Bert 'e runs blind with 'is head down, knocks vicar's teeth into the roof of 'is mouth, and bumps 'is own head real and proper. Vicar 'e tries to 'pologize through 'is own teeth gone crooked, but the words come out queer and thick;

and Bert, aggerravated by pain, thinks as 'ow vicar is cussing 'im, and swears blind 'e'll 'ave 'is revenge. We tries to calm 'im down, but Bert sulks all through tea; and durn me if 'e don't 'ave 'is revenge later on when vicar comes in to bat. Bert Miller is fielding close-up slip. Vicar always takes off 'is cap to bat, being I s'pose suprastitious, which aren't religion, but all the same 'e does, and 'e's pretty nigh bald all over the 'ead. Well, the wicket-keep 'e mis'olds a ball, which rolls gently to Bert at slip. Vicar is looking quiet and serene at a daisy on the pitch, wondering, as it might be, 'ow last ball 'ad missed 'is wickets. Bert picks up the ball, and, purtending to return 'er to the bowler, takes accirate aim under'and at vicar's 'ead, which, moreover, the ball 'its with a smartish click, like a cannon at billiards. Vicar 'e says "oh", and sinks slowly to 'is knees with 'is 'ands round 'is 'ead, and then turns round mild and reproachful towards Bert. At this Bert, feeling 'e's acted a bit low, is real genuine sorry, 'elps vicar to 'is legs 'pologizing away like clockwork, and at the end of the over whispers the bowler to send 'im slow 'uns to leg. Vicar scores three 4's, is cheered good and 'earty, then puts a full-pitch gently into the 'ands o' square-leg. But it couldn't 'ave ended better. For Bert was sorry, vicar made 12, and though battered about the 'ead and 'ands, was something of an 'ero for a week or two.'

'An eventful life, a cricketer's,' I suggested.

'Yus,' said the Oracle, sternly contemplating a more than usually fatuous attempt by point to bend. 'It is that, so long as you 'ave them about what are calcilated to cause events. It's the women, too sometimes.'

I demanded an explanation of this dark pronunciation.

'Why, you see, some men 'ave wives; and more than most, John Beadles were married. Seccitary of our team 'e were when I used to play. Strongish chap and a devil fer an 'it if so be 'e caught 'old of 'un proper. But 'is old missus always were dead against him playing. Reckoned 'e wasted 'is time over average-finding and such-like, and I do say that to find 'is average and to tot up runs Squire lets trickle past 'is boots did need a reg'lar knowledge o' figures, and whenever Mrs B. wanted 'im for something partickler, John would say "as 'ow 'is seccitarial dooties drawed 'im away", and that made 'er terrible angry. 'Is cottage, it as you sees over yonder, with 'is back garden going down to them trees be'ind. Well, Mrs B. 'ad always told 'im 'e were no more than a common fool to idle away 'is time at such stuff, and that 'e ought to know better than to get mixed up in a game as went on for hours and no good got out of it. Well, one Saturday the finish came, and John made 'is last big 'it. It 'ad been a close thing on fust innings, with us leading by some dozen or thereabout, and, it being a fine day, captains they decided to play match out to two innings. We skittles 'em out quick enough for once, and goes in to make, as it might be, round about twenty to win. Squire 'e sez, "John, in yer go, and knock 'ell out of 'em in the fust two overs just to take away their morals: mind, no pottering or prodding, John." "Right," sez John, pulls 'is cap down very low, as 'e always did when summat were in need o' doing, and walks out to wickets pretty grim and threatening. Fust ball 'e 'as an almighty, misses 'er, and as nigh as durn it 'as to walk 'ome agen. 'E 'as twelve off that over. Other chap plays an over solid. Then John, victory seeming near to 'im, spits on 'is 'ands, 'itches up 'is pad, grips 'is bat tight, and by chance catches 'er a beauty. Right over bowler she flies, and straight as an arrer through 'is own front-parlour winder. "Six!" we shouts from the side unanimous. "Good old John! one more o' they and we're there." But John 'e acts quick. 'E runs into the pavilion, throws down 'is bat and pad, and, with an awful look, sez, "That's done it, that 'as; for good and for all. I've cracked my own 'earth and 'ome, and I see'd the missus pop up in the opening and shake 'er fist, and me, too, 'aving sworn dead to 'er this morning that I was off this afternoon to do a job o' carpent'ring other end o' village." With which 'e was off to the village like a streak, and never come 'ome till early morning round four o'clock, when Mrs B. was asleep in bed. 'E never played agen; and, as to that partickler match, we 'adn't the face to go on with Mrs B. standing framed in 'er busted winder like a picter of an 'arpy, besides not knowing for sure 'ow the law stood about John leaving 'is wickets irreg'lar.'

'I've often thought,' continued the mighty relic in a ruminating tone, 'when Squire 'as read in church of a Sunday that man always 'eads for trouble as the sparks fly uppard, as 'ow they words must 'a' been written by a chap as 'ad cricket in his mind.

Which calls to mem'ry a rum sort o' match we 'ad one day 'gainst that same village Downweller.'

I had risen reluctantly to continue my journey and take a conscience tea with a frightful aunt, who had sought asylum from the sins of the world near these remote pastures, but the lure of the Oracle prevailed. I sat down again and listened.

'We're good enough friends now, they do say, but things was different then. A League and a Cup presented by Sir Lancinglot 'Anwell, winners' names to be engrave, and the rest o' the bizness. I reckon it were this game of ourn dried up for good the abundance of Sir Lancinglot's 'eart, and now we plays just for love an' honour. Back then there was points and fixed drawings o' stumps, and not 'aving to be late neither – which I do say some reckoned were right and just, but I never see it meself. Well, we was due at Downweller that day, them and us, moreover, running neck an' neck for the Cup. There 'ad been a steady fall o' rain all morning, and the more part on us were for not 'olding the game. 'Owever, we went. Squire 'e couldn't come, 'aving an at 'ome party, and vicar were away on 'oliday which latter p'raps were a pity, in light o' what got said and did later. Our cheerybang 'ad ingine troubles 'alf-way there, and in consekence we was some 'alf-hour late. We goes into the Bull at Downweller, they not 'aving a pavilion, and opens our traps an' stuff. Bill 'Annah, little chap with glarses from the post office, captains us, and, as 'e walks on to the field, the Downweller captain, a rough an' ignorant 'ulk 'e was, marches up to 'Annah full o' rules, and sez: "Ho, so you've come, 'ave you?" "Yus," sez 'Annah; "going to toss?" "No," sez the Downweller chap, "I aren't. You're 'alf an hour late, and by the rules the game is orf and the match ourn." Never consulted, 'e didn't, or wait for reasons. At that Bill 'Annah and us gets wild, and Bill 'e talks a lot to their captain about 'im being lucky we'd come at all in light o' the weather, and, if 'e called 'isself a sport what did 'e think a purple cad was? Soon words was flying indiff'rent, and the end of it were they goes away solid to the Bull and leaves us to do the talk. Well, I never see'd a chap take on like Bill 'Annah, even granting the aggerravation. 'E talked about sending for policemen, and writing to some mayor or other, and breaking winders in the Downweller High Street. 'E didn't cool much, but we purvailed on 'im that, seeing over there was a pitch rolled and wickets set and we thirteen with umpire and scorer, why not play 'mongst ourselves? Which, moreover, we did for round two hour or more, single wicket, ten minutes each, and all the rest field. After this sort o' makeshift, we went across to the Bull to pack up and shake orf the dust of this land of 'eathen. The Downweller chaps were mostly playing darts in the bar. We 'ad to go through there for our stuff, but they took no more notice on us than if we'd been frozen ghosts, and then the thing 'appened. Whether it were chance or did o' purpose is never yet quite got to rights, but, as Bill 'Annah was walking across, a dart 'it 'im from be'ind about 'alf-way up. 'E lets out a screech, and rounds on an elderly party what was standing be'ind 'im 'aving a quiet pint. Turned out after 'e was the boss o' the pub, as liked to pop round from the bar and 'obnob with customers. But Bill 'e 'adn't no reason left – what with the words 'e'd 'ad earlier in the afternoon and then this dart coming on top. 'E knocks the old chap's beer out of 'is 'and, 'oo didn't 'ave no breathing space to defend 'isself before Bill 'ad 'is right ear with one 'and and 'is nose with t'other, and 'ad nigh wrenched 'em both off before we pulls 'im away. I did remark at the time that it was a great pity vicar 'adn't come, 'cos 'e'd 'ave either purvented it ever 'appening by the kind of 'oly calm 'e always 'as about 'im in an argyment, or any'ow 'e might 'ave learn'd some langwidge as 'e could 'ave ever after told folks to avoid. The marvel is we wasn't all in the mix-up, but we got Bill into the cheerybang some'ow, and 'e never spoke a word all the way 'ome; just sat in a steam, looking death and thunder. But that's a pretty time agone now, and it's mostly forgot.'

'Well, I really must be going now,' I said, rising. 'I'm expected to tea more than two miles away in a few minutes.'

The Oracle removed his briar, spat, looked slowly round at me, and delivered in measured tones his only question:

'Before you goes, what sort of a bowler do they say this Voce is? Left-'and, aren't 'e? 'Cos I was left-'and meself – swift.'

First Slip

Full on the boot! Why can't the beggar bend?
　　I hope it sets his beastly corns alight,
And, as he waddles to the other end,
　　He'll tell the Captain all about his sight,
And how the wicket-keeper made a snatch
　　And queered his view, and how I bowled too soon –
As if it wasn't just the sort of catch
　　A child would hold, at midnight, with no moon.
Full on the boot again! The batsmen run
　　Their all-decisive single, swift as deers;
The Umpires pluck the bails, the match is won,
　　But not by us; on my impatient ears
There strikes a voice instinct with self-content,
　　'The light was very bad and growing worse,
The wicket-keeper——' So I turned and rent:
　　'You're far too fat, and fatness is a curse;
You never bend, and if you did, you'd fall;
　　You really never ought to field at slip –
In fact, you never ought to field at all.
　　If some instructor taught you how to skip,
And kept you skipping for a year or so,
　　You might, with fortune favouring, obtain
A minor post in Bertram Mills's show,
　　But never darken Cricket's door again.'

Next Saturday I took an easy catch
Full on the boot, at slip – we lost the match.

Nets

'On Monday last, with rain threatening, and the wind in the
east – that Jarndyce *v.* Jarndyce feeling – I, the greater wading
bird, led down my young wadelings to their baptism, some
flapping their callow wings with eager and lively hope, some
quacking faint but disregarded protest. For twenty minutes we
swam about, then came the rain once more, and evening, and

soon universal darkness buried all.

'And that, my boy, was our first day's practice at the nets.'

Thus, some weeks ago, with aquatic and ornithological metaphor, hitting his favourite quotations a customary crack *en passant*, wrote my old friend S——, who, after preliminary skirmishes, has year by year sent forth his juvenile troops to do battle on the green fields, in sun, hail, rain, wind; the left legs drilled to cover-point, the insidious binocular stance exorcised with tempered abuse, the right foot, that strays too easily to square-leg, goaded into orthodoxy, every move in the field attempted, practised, repractised, bungled, ameliorated, almost perfected – the swift return with flick of wrist, the high swerving ballooner, the cruel kick of the 'half-half-volley' to ankles, till their 'Young skins became as leather'.

And so he writes, in that study well-remembered, surrounded by the flannelled gladiators of his golden age, Sam Woods, Lionel Palairet, the great Doctor towering in bearded majesty – he always favours the heroes of the West – to tell me that he is doing it all over again, cursing the gathering momentum of youthful degeneracy, the soft hands, the dense heads, the all-too-tardy feet, telling me by letter what he once told me so unerringly by verbal precept, anxiously awaiting the first match, yet calm when its inevitable failures come, a noble workman in a noble craft.

*   *   *

In those days the best net to be in was D——'s; for some years there was a hole, by tradition unrepaired, about three feet from the ground, little more than the size of a cricket ball, in the line of extra-cover: to put a drive through it was the Mecca of D——'s pupils: for several reasons; aesthetically it was a greater triumph than finding a dedans guarded by Peter Latham, so small and strait was that hole, and therefore called by some, irreverently, I fear, the 'path to heaven': then, the ball, once through the celestial aperture, came to rest either among sweet-peas, which suitably enraged the gardener, or amid the raspberries, which rewarded the finder: again, it irritated D——, to whom any stroke that lifted the ball an inch was, according to the height of the parabola, a bad stroke.

Good Spartan D——! Long-suffering mentor! Stern and

inflexible purist! None after you has so plumbed the foundations of the game, for ever crying out on the misdirected toe, curtly praising some stray freak of brilliance, never bowling till the bat was raised over the leg-stump, gazing resignedly through short-sighted glasses at your pupil, who scours the red-lipped fruitage for the erring ball, who feebly feigns victory in the search, *iam iam prensans* yet another raspberry, with the ball long since in his right trouser-pocket!

Behind D——'s net, a long carry for a boy, was a bank topped with pines, and beyond them – oh, bliss! – the roof of the school laundry, on to which sometimes, on red-letter mornings, a young Thornton would crash the guileful delivery of D——, and scarcely suppress his shout of triumph as the slates rattled to the earth. One boy there was, a hero ever after to me, though he now renounces such trumpery with elderly disdain, whom I watched hit three consecutive rockets – two from boys, the last from D—— in person – on to that roof, high over the trees against the blue, and D——, almost angry, yet inwardly, I fancy, not wholly displeased, said, 'Dash it, boy, *dash* it! Fetch those balls, and don't grin, confound you!' Yes, he may renounce it, tinsel of infancy, but I can hear the death-rumble of those slates today.

At Greyfriars we were not popularly supposed to be skilful at cricket. That is as may be. But it was not for lack of practice. L——n, noble sward, was netted more accurately than the codfish on the Dogger Bank, and, in the halcyon days, we could burst forth from the sweat of Danish Steelyards and the prison of paradigms to the field where C——, an old professional of immemorial cunning, sparing yet accurate and benevolent in precept, was waiting with an inexhaustible supply of off-breaks pitched to a length: he bowled them without emotion, deviation, or strain, a source of joy and wonder to the unspoilt eye of boyhood; and if he were not obtainable, what matter? Perish the cant which denies value to untutored play! Bradman picked up what passed for a bat, and, unseen of the critical and corrective coach, blossomed into the wonder of the modern world. A coach can guide, but never give: the supple wrist, the intuitive eye, the rhythmic abandon of stroke, these are the gifts of Nature, not the learning of man; and if those untutored nets at

Greyfriars were not always wholly serious, if, after half an hour, the time for experiment set in – monstrous swerves, unearthly googlies, late cuts off half-volleys of a Macartneyesque frivolity – what would you of four boys whose combined ages were scarce more than that of Wilfred Rhodes when he helped England to win back the Ashes and her sliding fame at the Oval in 1926?

Then, in two or three swift-gliding years, came the nets on Green: most beautiful of grounds, with the Hindhead hills in the distance, a glory of varying blue, and M——, true Yorkshireman, bowling away the sunny hours; and with him, the silent G——, left-handed machine, who spun them from leg with horny fingers even on that smooth dureness, and loved to pitch them where the guyropes cast a shadow; dire whim that recalls the figure of honest Lumpy seeking out a fair downhill trend for his shooters on the slopes of Broadhalfpenny Down.

Last, the nets at Oxford, in the Parks: over the High, past the Bodleian, into which there passes a bent old scholar in cap and gown, burdened with books, loving learning more than the sun: a river-party emerges into the light with cushions and laughter and cheering flagons: the smell of the trees in Parks Road, and soon the urchins at cricket under the trees, irrelevant perambulators, and Tom Hayward, reluctantly retrieving *coups-de-vache* from the longer and the wetter grass.

The One-Way Critic

Upon the groaning bench he took his seat –
    Sunlight and shadow on the dew-blessed grass –
He spread the *Daily Moan* beneath his feet,
    Hitched to his eye an astigmatic glass,
Then, like a corn-crake calling to an owl
    That knows no answer, he began to curse,
Remarking, with an unattractive scowl,
    'The state of cricket goes from bad to worse;
Where are the bowlers of my boyhood's prime?
    Where are the batsmen of the pristine years?
Where are the fieldsmen of the former time?'

And, as he spoke, my eyelids filled with tears;
For I, perhaps alone, knew they were dead,
   Mynn an old myth, and Hambledon a name,
And it occurred to me that I had read
   (In classroom) 'All things always are the same';
So, comfort drawing from this maxim, turned
   To the myopic moaner on the seat;
A flame of rage, not pity, in me burned,
   Yet I replied in accents clear and sweet –
'There *were* no bowlers in your boyhood's prime,
   There *were* no batsmen in the pristine years,
There *were* no fieldsmen in that former time' –
   My voice grew firm, my eyes were dry of tears –
'*Your* fathers cursed the bowlers you adored,
   Your fathers damned the batsmen of your choice,
Your fine, ecstatic rapture they deplored,
   Theirs was the ONE-WAY CRITIC'S ageless voice,
And their immortal curse is yours today,
   The croak which kills all airy Cricket Dryads,
Withers the light on tree and grass and spray,
   The strangling fugue of senile jeremiads.'

I ceas'd; and turn'd to Larwood's bounding run,
And Woolley's rapier flashing in the sun.

George on Cricket Reform

George Hickling had invited me to stay. We hadn't met for
ten years. He had been dallying with tea in Ceylon, and I –
well, the lazy life; London in the season, spring fishing on the
Lee, a turn or two of cricket in August.

George and I used to play together before the war, mild
stuff for a gentlemanly club, varied by a more strenuous
encounter with the Surrey shilling crowd on a bank holiday. We
had dined selectively, but well. George is a bachelor. In spite of
the mellowing influence of wine, we had nearly quarrelled.
Causes quite commonplace. Two-eyed stances, and the ethics of
appealing for lbw from square-leg. George and I had always

been good arguers; but a quiet walk on the lawn down to the lazy-flowing Thames, a game of snooker with plenty of cigar-ash on the cloth and volunteering on the black, followed by a succession of soothing nightcaps, had retrieved the situation, and I was looking right through the mirror in my bedroom, through my rather crooked tie and rapidly receding hair, at tomorrow. I was contemplating a punt, a pink-un, a blue sky, and above all, George with the pole, when the victim of my altruistic vision meandered – as only George can meander – through the door.

'As I was saying,' began George, looking at me rather as if I were a leisured bluebottle – a habit of his when attempting to be learned during a Bacchic moment – 'as I was saying——'

'George,' I interrupted, 'I won't let you say. I think we concluded at dinner, so far as two men talking very loud at once can be said to conclude anything, that the forward cut is an obsolete stroke, that six balls are too few and eight too many in an over; and if I remember aright, by way of clinching the argument with a metaphor from a rival field-sport, that a man who serves four double-faults in a game of lawn tennis at Wimbledon feels and looks more of a fool than a bowler who delivers six consecutive wides in the opening over of a match at Lord's – inasmuch as the former has lost a game in two minutes, whereas the latter has not even begun one that may last for three days. Am I right? And may I go to bed?'

'Withdraw,' murmured George, 'or you'll be suspended.' And now that the public meeting had changed to Parliament, I knew the worst. I composed myself in an armchair. 'The honorary member opposite,' continued George incorrigibly, 'has ventured to suggest that a man who bowls six consecutive wides is – well, anyhow, whatever he suggested, I reject it with contempt.'

'Reciprocated,' I muttered.

'Having therefore annihilated these foul attacks on an ancient sport, I beg leave to bring before the House the following motions. I regret to see before me on the benches only two members. I am casting pearls – well, in the first place, I move that the new wickets, as approved without compulsion to use, by the Advisory Committee of the MCC, has so far proved an unmitigated success, a boon to the bowler, a boon to the more shortsighted of the pavilion critics – "They come as a boon and a blessing to men, the wickets, the owl, and the Waverley Pen" – I myself as a bowler——' Here I interrupted: 'Mr Speaker, I crave your intercession——' 'I repeat that I myself, as a bowler, can make more headway than of yore. I congratulate the gentlemen, themselves mainly bowlers, who, by appearing to further the interests of the game, while in reality pursuing their own nefarious ends, framed this most iniquitous legislation. In further proof of my conclusion – that is to say, motion, or rather support of my – I have had it on the best authority that——

* * *

'Anyhow, in the second place, I move that it would be to the interest of the game, not to mention the spectators, if the batsman played with the present very wide bat for the first twenty runs; that he then took off one pad, preferably the left, till he reached forty; that, upon reaching fifty, he played with no pads and a broomstick; and, should even this subterfuge prove inadequate, that he discarded the broomstick for a cane at sixty, and one piece of clothing for every five runs subsequently scored. By this means the century, now so easy of achievement, would become——'

'George,' I said, 'don't be a fool.'

'Mr Speaker, I must once more crave—— In the third place, I beg leave to propose that umpires omit the damnable practice of giving the batsman what is, often satirically, called the benefit of the doubt; transferring that doubt to the advantage of the bowler, if indeed this house wishes that bowling, as an art, as opposed to an act of penance, should continue. I have heard it objected from the Opposition benches that this innovation in etiquette, not of law, would give an even wider scope and more definite sanction to the already sufficiently well-known partiality of the umpire in village cricket. My reply to that, sir, is short. It would make no difference whatever. There never has been any doubt in decisions in village cricket, and there never will be.'

'Fourthly and lastly' – I heard this as at a great distance – 'I propose, not for specific reasons, but on general principles of health, a tea interval of at least half an hour. Mr Gladstone, I believe, masticated each mouthful with thirty-two individual clashings of the teeth.

'In summary, therefore, my proposals are as follows: Any ball that is a ball, a smaller bat, broomsticks and gradual disrobing, kinder umpires, and a more humane tea interval.'

'George,' I said sleepily, as that orator began to sit down on the floor and applaud himself rather feebly, 'that last proposal comes well from one who has profiteered in tea for ten years, but never drunk it for thirty'.

* * *

Two days afterwards George and I turned out for the village. I made eight (three off the elbow), and missed two catches off successive balls at long-leg. George was bowled first ball, got no wickets for thirty-eight, but kept himself on, and invaded the Green Man during the tea interval, whence he re-appeared with some hilarity, just as the visiting team were departing – a courteous captain.

'With reference to cricket politics,' I said after dinner that night, 'what you need, George, is a stable door to bat with, a full-sized soccer ball to hit, a captain who plays you for fun rather than for bowling, your chauffeur to umpire both ends, home and away, and most certainly, George, no interval at all, tea or otherwise.'

'Really,' said George, as he screwed in cleverly off the black; 'you know, I could never have done that at billiards.'

The One-Way Boy

When coaching boys the other day,
Recalling legs that legward stray,
Wearily pleading that it mars
The style, if bats are scimitars;
Persuading bowlers that their length
And rectitude are more than strength,
However jovially applied,
If all it ends in is – a wide.
The father of some cricketer,
A heavy man, approach'd, said, 'Sir,

My boy is *always* caught at slip;
It gives me one gigantic pip:
Now can you give me any reason
Why this should happen *all* the season,
Instead of intermittently,
As it occurs with you or me?'
'Show me the boy,' quoth I, 'sir, please.'
Whereat, scorbutic, ill-at-ease,
Stole from behind his ample father
A boy, obscured till now, or rather
What might have passed for boy, by chance,
But for his cow-like countenance:
Never in any town or rank
Saw I face so *wholly* blank:
No freckle, twinkle: nothing dimply;
It was a facial Sahara, simply.
'Put on those pads,' his father said,
As if conversing with the dead,
'And show the gentleman the stroke,
Concerning which I lately spoke.'
He donned them, filially resign'd.
I gave him guard, to leg inclined,
I bowled him long-hops free from guile,
Full-pitchers you could hit a mile,
Half-volleys straight, half-volleys wide,
Swervers, delicious for the glide:
He never swerved, nor lost his grip,
But snicked the ruddy lot to slip.
Strange wonders have there been in cricket –
Once, in a match, I took a wicket,
Shod in a heel-less evening shoe
(A confidence 'twixt me and you),
Jones bowled a ball through Grace's beard,
And Ranji only Lockwood feared,
But never, since the game began,
Since old men stood while young men ran,
Was such consummate batsmanship
As to hole out, each ball, at slip.
'Take off those pads,' his father said

(Resuming converse with the dead),
'You've shown the gentleman the stroke
By which my heart and mother's broke;
Good day, sir!' and with footsteps slow
He took his tragedy in tow,
The parent first, the portent after,
Leaving me deep in awe and laughter.

An Invitation

The cows, winter lessees of our village oval, mooing mild
protest, have departed to pastures new. Now is their winter of
content become inglorious summer. It is time, therefore, to look
round and take stock, not of *the* season, but of *our* season, to
weigh, not the national gods, but the indigenous, earth-born
giants.

Many obvious questions suggest themselves readily to the
mind. What are our chances of success? Do we progress? Or is
there reaction? Is the popularity of the game waning or waxing
locally? That is to say, will the spectators consist of four old
men telling three small boys, who aren't listening, why bowling
was faster and straighter in their day, or will one of these small
boys, promoted from school to the baker's shop, be upholding
the honour of the second (Wednesday) eleven, and so, by
reason of his first victim – the blacksmith, beguiled by a slow
full-pitch towards dusk – be even less inclined to hearken to the
harmless but mendacious burble of our rustic Nestors? Will
there be a new public bat to supplement the two private ones?
Or will the horny oak be handed by warrior leaving to warrior
going forth to battle? Will the Vicar be allowed to play? If
so, where, with least detriment to the side, will he be fielding?
When, without becoming irrevocably identified with the no-
balls, will he bat? Or will he tactfully confine his activities to a
benign expression of hope that 'You chaps are having a good
season', and the position of honorary bodyguard to the Lady
Squiress, when she presents, with some confusion of names and
numbers, the cups for the best averages (batting and bowling
within a decimal point of each other)? Will our umpire – post-

man on weekdays, Saturday afternoon excepted, shiny-fore-headed sidesman on Sundays – maintain his unswerving loyalty to the only true cause, or will the mellow approach of age tend to induce, in weak moments, a mistaken sense of justice?

Who shall answer such questions? Not I, but the passage of one more summer.

In the greater world of cricket there is change, improvement perhaps, fluctuation. We, of Underwellow, have high hopes that our game will be little altered by the march of time. As a class we despise mathematicians. Not even the police could thwart our tea inverval. Our lbw rule, as I have hinted, is plain. One end you are out, the other end you are in. We admire this system, and are jealous of our traditions.

But if you would know more about us, leave, O county cricketer, leave for some fleeting moments your perfect wicket, your struggle for first innings' lead, your Bridge or Poker that goes on long after the rain has stopped, and the crowd has exhausted its patience and lost its shilling; come and watch us for nothing, and, if you have the heart to do it, come and laugh; if you have the soul, come and play. Has Larwood bowled you with a thunderbolt, third ball, before your eye was set? Come and be bowled first ball by Mr Mugridge, with a fast shooter, before you have taken guard. See Mr Bulberry, our wicket-keeper, in a voluminous position of sedentary alertness, and die. Have you sat for four hours at Lord's, when both your first two batsmen have reached the century? Have you, then, faint almost with the sight of perfection, deafened by the applause that greets the incoming champion, walked the lonesome road to the wicket in fear and dread, only to return at once, broken and sick at heart, with an unavoidable glance at the telegraph – (326 – 2 – 0) – through the pavilion now chastely mute with sidelong curious gaze, to the dressing-room, where, a second before, they had been saying – how well you know it! – that you are not a number three, and never will be, unless you learn to play back?

Come, then, drink deep of the waters of Lethe, come to Underwellow! I will meet you at the station; a four-mile drive through fallen chestnuts and whispering branches. Come on a Friday. We will go out after tea, and inspect the wicket. We will converse with Mr Hurlam, grocer, tobacconist, confectioner, and our secretary into the bargain. I shall tell him who you are: *he* won't remember your failure, not he! With us there is no memory of disaster. He will ask you to play on Saturday. You will play. So will I. I shall go in first. I shall snick a two and be bowled utterly. You will go in, walking, not over a smooth and distant plain, but past a pail of whitening, past a black pad, through thirty yards of long grass, and so to the modest arena. You will wonder, perhaps, why the slip-fielder is so deep; why cover-point is covering mid-off. The wicket-keeper's braces and rugged smile will catch your eye. A horse will pass behind the bowler's arm. You will battle, more strenuously than ever you battled with Kennedy or Grimmett on a sticky wicket, with dandelions, with unsuspected undulations, with the umpire; but, my lad, with all the art, with all the strength you can summon to your aid. You will make 26 out of a total of 42. We will win by three runs, and you will be a hero, and I will bask in your reflected glory. Where, then, will be your 100 against Yorkshire compared with this 26, highest score of the year, against Otterstone, our well-nigh invincible rivals?

Are you enticed? Do I allure you? Very sweet it is, stumps spread-eagled by torpedoesque-shooter, after amassing a solid seven (five of them run with the ball close to mid-on in the longer grass) to retire and recline, careless of mankind, on the back, philosophizing through half-shut eyes at the blue sky, while, in the distance, the lambs 'loud bleat from hilly bourn', or, to begin, owing to the imperious demands of local professions, some Utopian encounter well after tea. To stand in the deep, or rather the deepest, and, unshaken by anticipation of failure, to watch the sun westering behind the trees, whilst overhead the rooks return with clangour to their nests. And who shall say us nay?

Thou, Marylebone, mighty and justly mighty ruler of cricket, wielding a legislative power that reaches the outposts of Empire, rich storehouse of experience, benevolent despot, thy mighty power, thy fiats, have their bounds. Hitherto shalt thou come, and no farther! From us, fallen though we be from our pristine fame – though, a mere shade of the glory that was Hambledon, we no longer dare to challenge 'five of England' – from us thou drawest thy source and thy being! We still have

91

our David Harris, in sheer technique perhaps not simply and severely great like him of yore, yet a David Harris in spirit; Homeric, rejoicing in the mere scent of battle. Still does he delight to 'rind' the knuckles of another Tom Walker, who, with magnificent contempt, rubs his hand in the dust to staunch the flow of blood. Then, as of old, when the game is done, they pledge an eternally rivalrous friendship at the Pelican and Fox, and, as the country bard hath it, 'bind themselves, with pints full twelve, to meet the next Saturday!'

Auntie's Season

Cricket knows varying degrees of seriousness and excellence. But for me the matches of the year are played round Easter-time, in a remote part of Devonshire. No telegraph-board to proclaim your ignominy, no crowd to cheer or deride your public striving. Instead, a large, irregular lawn, bounded on three sides by deep rhododendrons, and on the other by a stone terrace with a sundial from which nobody within the memory of man has ever been able to tell the time. Art, however, flourishes where utility fails, for round it is carved the simple inscription, 'Fear God and honour the King'.

We go there most Easter holidays, and with that fine disregard, common to mankind, of what is only temporarily possessed, we cannot really feel responsible or ashamed when a pane of the conservatory goes the way of all glass, or some treasured rose-bush, extinguished by the desperate outfielder, is sacrificed on the sacred altar of sport. Awkward questions are sometimes asked at lunch, if the crash is more than usually devastating, but Bill, the youngest of the tribe, always says, 'Father can pay', if the head of the family is absent; and, if he is there, puts the blame on Aunt Emily, who has never hit as far in her life, but is so flattered that she meekly takes the blame.

These Easter matches are always called 'Auntie's Season'. She is, of course, a false aunt: no blood relation, but one of those aunts whose generosity has swollen the exchequer of so many generations of schoolboys all the world over, whose descents in term-time have been red-letter days that cheer the mercurial mind of youth through thousands of lines of Ovid and an infinity of scalene triangles. She belongs to that glorious host of

> 'Aunts that understand,
> Good aunts perpetual that remain –
> A landmark, walling in the plain –
> The horizon of our memories –
> Like large and comfortable trees.'

Ever since I can remember she has played cricket. When Hirst was a young man, Aunt Emily's style had reached a mellow rigidity. It is useless to pretend that she is a stylist. She is not a wristy player, and though she may, in the heyday of her prime, have employed the late-cut and even the leg-glide, to-day she never allows herself those liberties. Her bat is always straight. Before the delivery of each ball she lifts it scrupulously over the leg-stump, just as the bowler is in mid-swing, and then down it comes like a pendulum, full face to the enemy. The technique, within its natural limits, is flawless, but of course there are weaknesses in the actual effect, chinks in the armour of execution. Otherwise Bill would never bowl her out, and he has managed that twice in the last three days. A sudden change of pace will sometimes result in a caught-and-bowled – the pendulum swings too soon – and of late years she has shown a distinct dislike for a fastish off-break pitching on the leg-stump. Like all women, and especially aunts, it is difficult to persuade her from the wickets. In our games the wicket-keeper is the arbiter of obstruction, and his decision is considered legally binding. Bill is easy to give out, as he wears shorts. I am next in easiness with long trousers. Joan, the horrid sister, is easy in theory, but terribly difficult in practice. When struck on the leg, she moves it out of the way as quickly as a chameleon imbibing a fly: and, if that artifice convinces none, she resorts to a hopping limp; when the appeal *ad misericordiam* is of no avail, Aunt Emily, if she is bowling, generally tells her to be a brave girl and abide by the decision. But to give out Aunt Emily is next to impossible. In the first place, her skirts are sufficiently old-world to make the point of contact between ball and leg confusing and obscure. The benefit of the doubt, or rather the area of error, is immeasurable. Secondly, the attitude of majestic unconcern, the next best thing to established innocence, which Aunt Emily adopts on these occasions, would unnerve even Chester. It is little short of treason to oust her by any means except clean bowled, caught, or 'retired 20'. Not that she is in any way dishonest. There is no anguished rubbing of the hand. She stands confessed as a candidate for lbw. But the prisoner in the dock is too much for the jury, and the etiquette of these matches, if not the actual law, reads, 'Aunt Emily having been struck on the leg or legs or part of same, she shall be deemed to have played the ball'.

The nearest that she ever came to disaster was last holidays. It was the Second Test. In the first, Aunt Emily and Bill had just scrambled home against Joan and me by two runs, chiefly because Joan, while talking to the gardener at long-leg, had allowed Aunt Emily to run five for a contemptible snick between bat and skirts; and then, rebuked by her captain, had purposely dropped a very easy catch. In the second match, to promote the Empire feeling, the sides were mixed. I was partnered by Aunt Emily, and was keeping wicket. Bill was bowling the opening over. His third delivery was a gross long-hop, which kept very low, and Auntie, shaping for a hook – a great rarity – missed the ball, and was struck sharply on the instep. It was a case which admitted of no ambiguity. 'How's that?' yelled Bill. Aunt Emily, following her custom, completely disregarded the appeal, and prepared to receive the next ball. But Bill, eager for an early victim, was not to be denied. 'How's *that*?' he demanded again, with an impudent emphasis on the demonstrative. The batswoman, unable to evade so obvious a crisis, turned round to me for confirmation. Well, think of it! Would *you* give out an aunt who had never been given out lbw in the annals of cricket, and who had *bathed* you in your infancy? Of course not. Mussolini might. So I said I couldn't see, which wasn't true; the next ball but one shattered her stumps, and all was well. But it was a near thing.

There are only four of us, except on rare occasions when the head of the family joins the rites. When he does, he confines himself to batting, bowling, and sound advice. He is far too lazy to field; and, anyhow, we always regard him as something of an interloper. He is far better gardening and paying for windows. With this restriction of numbers, the composition of the teams varies but little. There is, however, one unalterable rule. Aunt Emily is always picked first, when she is not captain. It is a question, not of politeness or formal courtesy, but of law and routine. No one, not even Woolley, has been chosen in so many consecutive Test matches.

Sometimes I have an awful fear that the house in Devon will be burnt down in the winter, or that someone else will rent it. Surely Providence cannot be so unkind.

Aunt Emily has returned to Kensington. Joan is wasting her time at Bexhill. Bill is being a nuisance somewhere in Surrey; and I have just detected a small boy drawing a picture of F. R. Brown removing Julius Caesar's middle stump in his Latin Grammar.

Memorable Fielding

Perhaps I should have said 'unforgettable'. For there is something in the epithet 'memorable' which implies praise and merit, and my theme is rather of fielding that is wantonly incompetent, culpably negligent, unendurably provocative. Don't meditate, therefore, on the brilliance of Chapman, those breath-bereaving gully catches which have changed the course of Tests, those impudently easy stops at silly-point, which have thrown doubt on the art of bat manufacture – turn aside a moment from these, and reflect – if you are a bowler, with excruciation – on the slip-fielder monotonously struck on the lower shin – and what is his physical pain to your agony of soul? – on mid-ons tethered like large captive balloons to the grass, while the ball drops, a weary poached egg, in front of their everlastingly exasperating stagnancy; and you then wish, patient bowler, that the ball was a hand-grenade, or a haggis, or anything that would burst hastily underneath your static torturer! Or, if your wounded pride forbids such contemplation, think of your own unforgettable moments of fortuitous triumph in the field, when, from second slip perchance, you were 'watching the form' round the gay-pennoned tents of some festal ground – Canterbury, or well-nourished Scarborough – and you awoke from your reverie of a coy ankle to find the ball in your left hand, applause in your ears, pleasurable mystification in your mind; or, if you feel that there is a tinge of conceit in this picture, remember the occasion when you were at cover-point, both batsmen in the crease by the bowler, the wicket-keeper howling like a baulked wolf, and you – oh, shattering memory! – sent the ball high over the bowler's head, careering to the boundary: remember it – and laugh, yes, laugh, clown! Never repine over these singular lapses. To cherish remorse over past failures is the cricketer's ultimate gall, his gloomy Gehenna. Think of men lying awake at night, while around their heads gambol the ghosts of prodigal overthrows, easy caught-and-bowleds never even touched, heavy and humiliating falls. And yet, to a man not hyper-sensitive a modicum of failure in the field can be positively enjoyable. If he be of an unselfish nature he can reflect on the genuine pleasure (if we exclude his own bowlers) which he can give to the players and spectators alike; and, since many unselfish and genial men are inclined to corpulence, his task of gratifying others is rendered the more easy, because, next to a fat man going down forwards on the ice, one must rank – as a spectacle – a fat man going down backwards under a high spinning cricket ball; and the subject of corpulence leads one to the most memorable of all apocryphal feats of fielding, when a famous player snicked a particularly fast ball to a particularly fat wicket-keeper: the batsman was about to congratulate himself on being missed, when the ball flew back past his head, to be caught quite easily by the bowler! Heartbreaking, very.

At the age of seventeen I was privileged to witness the most memorable feat of sustained ineptitude in the field which Providence will ever grant me. The entertainment was given by one whom I must simply call *The Fielder*: partly because he can have had no rival for the palm of paralysis, and partly because mere anonymity cannot deprive him of it. Now *The Fielder* had this advantage over lesser paralytics, in that he owned the very field on which his art was, every Saturday, laid bare to the public. He was far past the time of life when a man can still with safety to himself and profit to his side be concealed between two or more other fielders; yet, by the conditions on which the club played matches on his field, he was entitled to play *when* he wished, and, by a sort of superfluity of egotistical dominance, *where* he wished: and that was cover-point. So, every Saturday afternoon, there he stood, in large brown boots and all the colossal grandeur of top-heavy immobility. There had once been an occasion, many years before, when a young and managing secretary had asked him to field at mid-on. *The Fielder* made no verbal reply, but cast a withering look at the revolutionary, as who should say, 'Cover-point I know, extra-cover-point I have heard of, but what *is* mid-on?'

There were spectators who remembered the game on this ground before *The Fielder* – pre-paralytic days; but they never made any comparisons: there were no similies applicable; metaphor was bankrupt. The figure of *The Fielder* had become inexorably familiar. Exactly why he wore brown boots none knew for certain. Some said that it was his meanness: but that was a senseless libel on one who was, off the field, generous and genial. No, it was just his blooming ignorant independence. That same perversity which moored him to cover-point, induced in him also a fancy for brown boots with white trousers.

His methods of fielding the ball were two: he either kicked it and stopped it, or kicked at it and missed it; both methods resulted in one run for the striker; as a general rule, the batsmen, however, simple-minded, after a few balls, never called when they played to him. His monumental indifference to these repeated liberties was actually more striking than the ineptitude which invited them. He never threw the ball back to the bowler, but kicked it with despotic nonchalance along the ground. The ball was often excoriated and seared by his hobnails; for, if his eye was really in, he could cleverly trap a hard drive under the uplifted sole.

The accompanying chart will be of some service in explaining the customary method of scoring when opposed to *The Fielder:*

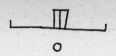

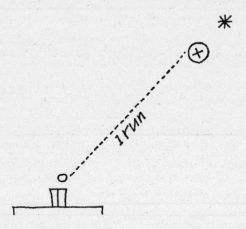

The Fielder is indicated by a cross surrounded by a circle. The asterisk indicates the supplementary or unorthodox cover-point, a sort of satellite or appendix, upon whom *The Fielder*, dimly aware of the reason for his existence, sometimes scowled majestically. You must imagine the rest of the fielders watching these runs with anger, despair, hilarity or resignation, according to their respective temperaments. You must also imagine *The Fielder's* boots. The small circles represent the batsmen, one in the middle of the comedy, the other waiting, as it were, in the wings, for his turn. I hope you understand me now.

There pass before my mind further instances of Memorable Fielding: the first catch that I ever held; years ago: it was a bump-ball, but we always counted them in the Lower Game. Somehow, however, I cannot shift my thoughts from the brown boots, the monstrous *laissez-faire*, the wholly Olympian incompetence of *The Fielder*.

George and Charlie

'And that,' remarked George Hickling, 'is game. Likewise set. I shall not play another. I might lose it; and my creed is to finish on a note of triumph. Failure is in general anti-aesthetic, distasteful to me personally, mars the fitness of things, and saps the confidence.'

'But, George,' I protested, 'I really can't have that. I saw my last drive quite clearly pitch at least a yard inside the base-line. I am ready, even anxious, to overlook your continual foot-faulting, but at open dishonesty, from whatever motive, I make a stand.'

'Pot-hunter,' said George tersely. 'You remind me of those hard-faced women who leave their husbands brooding over the loveless hearth to make the lives of tennis umpires a perennial hell at every town round the coast from Scarborough to Blackpool. I am incapable of deceit.'

'Very well, George, if it gives you any pleasure to win by crooked means, I must leave it at that; but as I said before——'

'My dear fellow, you remind me of some Johnny who wrote about someone somewhere:

"Then, like the echo of a dream,
Harped back upon the threadbare theme."

Give the whole thing a rest.'

'George, I sometimes reckon you as the most arrant cad I know.'

'To me,' George continued suavely, 'you are merely plebeian. You are the one man in the world who never fails to give me a superiority complex. In your presence I always feel like the Scarlet Pimpernel with Monsieur Chauvelin. Whatever you do or say, I just smile down from lazy eyelids and metaphorically flick a speck of dust from the irreproachable Mechlin lace at my wrists. But we must cease this useless wrangle. I must devote my vast talents to winning a prize of ten pounds.'

'And how do you propose to do that?'

'By cutting a coupon out of your paper, agreeing to abide by the editor's decision in all its damning finality, signing my name, and filling in the first twelve counties in order of merit.'

'But, George, whence this rush of ambition and lust for gold?'

'Leave out the ambition, dear boy, and you have me. It's a snip, a certainty, a cinch. I have an infallible system. I have worked it out in the silent watches.'

'Explain.'

'First, I have consulted the weather forecast for the whole year in the *Daily Post*. The black mountain ranges which rise to a peak between August 24 and August 31 indicate a period of drought. That means a week's steady rain. Right. I shall then study the form on August 24. Continual depressions from Greenland will envelop us during the ensuing week. Not a ball will be bowled. Much money will change hands in many pavilions. The twelve counties will remain *in statu quo* on August 31. My forecast will be accurate. I shall win ten pounds or an equally divided part of same. Probably the latter.'

'Very ingenious, George. But you must leave the plot to hatch for half an hour, and come down to the village to buy that bat you were talking about.'

'I should hate to buy a bat, my dear man, and I don't believe there is a bat in Shotterley – over and above the two that are handed round on Saturday afternoons. When you invited me to stay, my first thoughts were of diversion, and I consulted a motorists' guide. It described Shotterley as "a hamlet within striking distance of Waverley Abbey, partially restored; Guildford Castle, a ruin; and Frensham, famous for its ponds". It is a sheer local pride to talk about bats. No, it's either Guildford Castle or your whisky, and on the whole——'

'But, George, you benighted flat-fish, there is an excellent athletic outfitter of great renown in Shotterley. He harbours every known requisite, and has even been known to replace broken goal-posts at blow-football. His name is Charlie.'

'It can't be just that only.'

'Yes, it is. He may have had a surname once, but it's been absorbed. The shop is Charlie, and Charlie is the shop. And if you think that you are going to use my bat on Saturday you're wrong. It's not that sort of bat.'

'Of course, if you refuse to accommodate me, I shall just waive my innings, and don't tell me that it is better than waving my bat, as a pun gives me heartburn. No, I'm not going to buy a bat in this burgh, old man; besides, I'm worn out by arguing with you at tennis. Let's compromise. Arbitration is the keynote of modern existence. Think of Geneva. Bring that table and two deck-chairs over. I'll fetch the doings from within, and, as you love him so dearly, you may, when we are peacefully settled, discourse for a short space on Charlie, while the smoke curls up, and the cicada scrapes whatever he does scrape, and the sun begins to wester——'

'Look here, George; you didn't always prattle in this ghastly manner. What is it?'

'Nature, my dear host, just nature, expanded by Wilhelmina Stitch, and a blow on the head in infancy.'

* * *

'And now,' said George, lowering the decanter to the table and himself into a deck-chair with equal circumspection, 'proceed with narrative.'

'Listen, then, you superannuated dealer in tea, to his history. He is a quaint character, is Charlie, and a man of many resources. Ten years ago he came to Shotterley and set up business as a saddler and trunk dealer. As far as I know, he never sold any saddles; probably, as he said, because there were already as many saddles in Hampshire as there were horses, when he started, and saddles "don't die, whereas horses do".'

'Pessimism,' remarked George, 'allied to illogicality.'

'As to the other side of the business, it was a little, but not much, more prosperous. He occasionally worked off a canvas suitcase at Whitsuntide, but otherwise there was a marked stagnancy. Pretty soon Charlie sold the business, started his present shop, and is now a man of tolerable means.'

'A brigand, of course,' interrupted George. 'Monopoly of croquet balls, and all that.'

'I was going on to say, George, that he was once a cricketer himself. He unfolded the past to me one evening, led on by a pint of dark and the settlement of a two-year account. It would seem that in the heyday of his manhood he played for a village between Rottingdean and Newhaven. He bowled round the wicket, fast, with a short run.'

'I know what you mean,' murmured George.

'He said the wicket looked good in the distance, but when you got close to it it had a double slope, up and down, and from side to side.'

'I see; a sort of whited sepulchre.'

'I asked him how much it really did slope, and he admitted that a man fielding in the deep one end could see nothing below the batsman's waist, and that if a northerly wind was helping the slope, an off-drive could be made to skirt round in front of cover and finish between mid-on and mid-wicket. But he had only seen this achieved twice, and both times the man had been run out.'

'It savours of Braid's Advanced Golf. Tell me more. Tell me more.'

'Charlie was a gardener in those days, to an old buffer who was crazy on bulbs. Every morning, in the season, heavy consignments used to arrive from Holland; and the old fellow was practically chained down while they were opened. Once they had been unravelled he spent hours crooning over them. Like the lady in the poem, who brooded over the Pot of Basil: couldn't be wrenched away. Meals floated up and down the kitchen lift unheeded. Well, Charlie was entrusted with the care of some of these bulbs. He said he'd rather have worn the Crown Jewels at night in Chicago.

'One day the old buffer had to go away for a whole morning on business, Charlie being left in charge of the bulbery. It was a hot day and he was taking an easy about noon, when a fellow he had met once or twice in "The Running Footman" bulged his face over the hedge and suggested a pint. Charlie said, "Can't be done: bulbs." Other fellow said, "Bulbs is nothing. Come along!" So Charlie went.'

'What sort of man was this seducer?'

'Charlie said he had a black beard, the eyes of a ferret, and the soul of a rat. But of course he was prejudiced by what happened after.'

'Sounds like a Chinese general. Go on.'

'To cut the matter short, Charlie came back to find a complete gaggle of the most valuable bulbs lifted. The old buffer gave him the sack, and then cried himself to sleep. Charlie got another job after in some livery stables. Of course he could prove nothing, and the actual robber was never discovered. A year passed, and one fine Saturday in late May Charlie was playing cricket against a neighbouring village. I wish, George, you would go and buy that bat, as the story falls well from Charlie's lips. His eye even now sparkles with——'

'Proceed and away with redundance.'

'The match, as far as Charlie was concerned, was running an uneventful course. He had made some dozen runs, mostly as he says, off the back of the bat. He had bowled a few overs, but without result, and ten minutes from time, was standing in the very deep field, talking to a friend, when a high catch came towards him. He is not a great catcher in the general way, but Providence took charge and Charlie held it. Had he missed it, the glorious sequel would no doubt never have occurred. At the fall of this wicket there was some delay; at last the batsman appeared. And here, anyhow, George, I must try to give you, as near as possible, Charlie's own narrative. I have heard it quite often, and I think I know it by heart.'

'I glances towards the pavilion, and sees a face coming out with a black beard fixed on it. Blackbeard walks to the wicket. I remembered then they'd only fielded ten, and it seems Blackbeard 'ad arrived close after tea, 'oping no doubt, like the coward 'e was, that 'e wouldn't be batting that evening. Well, they'd run one while the ball was in the air, and the other 'ad the strike. I turns to Fred Banning, as I was talking to and says, "So long, Fred, maybe I'll be wanted to bowl now." I walks up to the skipper, Bert Traggett, and says, "Bert, give us a go top end next over. One'll be enough." "Why so?" says Bert, "Jack's bowling steady enough." "Yes," says I, "but it's not steadiness as is needed just now." "All right," says Bert, "but don't give nothing away, Charlie." "That's all right," says I, "I shall be bowling pretty straight, Bert." Blackbeard never notices I was going to bowl, 'aving me cap tight down over me eyes, and 'im took up with 'ow to stay in five minutes. Good Lord, if 'ed only known 'ow much more another man was took up with the same thing. Over is called, and I passes quietly by Blackbeard on his blind side, while 'e takes guard. I measures me run, just five paces, and gets ready to bowl from the down-'ill end. "Play," says the umpire; and then Blackbeard sees me. I knew he was struck all sideways, but there wasn't nothing to be done. Ev'ry man really lives just once, I reckon, as I did then. The more so when I saw 'e only 'ad a pad on the right leg. Fust ball, sir, I 'its 'im on the part nearest the square-leg umpire, and appeals. "Not out" of course. Next ball I 'as 'is cap off, and the wicket-keeper dusts it up and gives it 'im back. Third ball I never 'ave quite got to rights, but it did seem to pass between 'is beard and 'is neck. Fourth ball, 'e just waves 'is bat about it, random-like, and it whistles over 'is middle stump. Fifth ball 'its 'im a crack over 'is left shin, sort of 'ollow kind of noise, like tree-tapping. I 'as to say something then, so I says, "Sorry, old man, but I thought it was the wooden leg as 'ad the pad on it." 'E was near finished now, so the sixth ball I 'as 'im in the stomach, to put 'im out of 'is misery, and the ball drops very slowly on to the off-stump. Batsman my end 'e protests, and says, "It's not cricket," and I says, "No, but it's out; and any'ow," I says, "it's always the same with me; I bowls 'em where I don't mean, and 'its the batsman where 'e don't like, and what's more," I says, "that'll learn 'im to pinch a chap's bulbs and lose 'im 'is ruddy job." And so the match ended. It began poor, but finished pretty good.'

'To-morrow,' said George, 'we will go to buy a bat from Charlie. Meanwhile, let us discuss the future of English cricket.'

Rollo Gallacher's Benefit

'And don't forget, Rollo, don't forget, my beautiful quarter-wit, that we shall expect you at Bishop's Coombe for the last match on Saturday: the rest of the week doesn't matter; but on the Saturday we always play Colonel Cochrane's Eleven, and dear father keeps his yearly run for the occasion – 10.20 from Paddington. You will be met——'

'But, I say, you know; listen, Joan; I haven't played cricket since——'

But Joan Harries was no more. The swing-doors of the Savoy

swung, and Rollo Gallacher, her gay affianced, was left, like a classic lover before him, preparing to say many things. He opened and shut his mouth twice, but the performance was soundless. He passed into the evening air and the roar of the Strand traffic.

'Ev'nin' paiper, sir? *Stawr, Standurd*, sir? Record at Lord's, sir!'

'Curse you, your boots and your battered bowler! Blast your papers! Blast records! Blast Lord's! and Blast Cricket!'

*   *   *

Rollo Gallacher had obtained his name in the customary manner, from his mother and father. His father, long since dead, had been descended from a Gallacher who, among others carefully selected, had been sent out by the most pig-headed of all Stuart Kings to repeople those northern districts of Ireland which the constant attention of marauding Englishmen had rendered fairly void. This ancestor had continued the good work of deceiving the natives, and had left a comfortable sum to his sons, who, not behindhand in piracy, went on from generation to generation multiplying the shekels and being importuned for loans by the denuded victims. Of them all, Rollo's father had died the richest, baffled only once in his life, when his Suffolk wife had insisted on the name Rollo, prating vaguely of some fabulous ancestor, who, she averred, had 'wound his horn in the valley of Roncesvalles', though she could never explain why. So Rollo, as a child, had been left with an adoring mother and the prospect of most of the money in Antrim; considering these set-backs, he was as fine a lad as any one, except a few schoolmasters, could wish to see. From a private school in Sussex, where he had left his name behind on every desk except the headmaster's, a reputation as the worst cricketer in the school and the toughest all-in wrestler in the scrum, two saw-edged Eton collars, and a pair of rusty roller skates with no straps, he had, after a long series of pitched battles with Caesar and his accessory Labienus, arrived in the bottom form at Greyfriars: there, like a man who has for some reason walked from London to York, he took a prolonged siesta. At length the irresistible forces of time and nature drove him, somewhat dazed but still cheerful, through two more forms, till he found himself one

May morning on the first day of the Summer term, confronted with Mr Pringle as form-master. Rollo was now sixteen and a half. Mr Pringle was fifty-three and a quarter. Rollo disliked Mr Pringle and cricket. Mr Pringle was passionately devoted to them both. They were the complete antipathetics.

Pringle had that perfected gift of facile sarcasm which makes the pupil handle ink-pots and lexicons lovingly, to the verge of poising them. But on Rollo his choicest arrows pinged harmlessly. Direct abuse he understood and loved, but his form-master was above all that: he never stormed, never called his boys pigs individually and robbers in the aggregate, but, when Rollo, in all good faith, indicated on the pendant Atlas the Sea of Azov as the Lake of Gennesaret, Pringle smiled his feline smile, and purred, 'No, Gallacher, certainly no; as usual, you have allowed a suspicion of inaccuracy to cloud your judgment. The Lake in question is quite elsewhere. Some two weeks ago a comfortable steamer left England under the auspices of the Athenian Society to tour Greece, the Cyclades, and the Near East. A pity, Gallacher, a great pity, that you were not numbered among the passengers; for then you could have corrected your erroneous view by personal inspection. Ten maps of the Holy Land, please, Gallacher, in different coloured crayons, by this time tomorrow. Thank you.'

Gall to the heart of Rollo was Mr Pringle, but the cricket was very wormwood. He felt about cricket much as Lamb did about boys: in its own way very good, but not a proper game for grown people. In fact, Rollo was a heretic, almost a martyr. But he had attracted, at the age of sixteen, a jovial band of fellow sufferers who, though the gliding river was calling them to plunge into its cool current, and though corpulent haystacks seemed to wheeze, 'Here I am; get behind me with a packet of Gold Flake', yet allowed themselves two or three times a week to form a high-spirited Soviet on the most remote ground of nine, where they dissolved into a quorum of two venal umpires, some casual groups masquerading as fielders, and a few intermittent batsmen. The rest of the Game, who were not dieting on ices at Shop, formed a Gallery, whose comments rang round the 240 square yards of the field, and sometimes affronted the ears of Pringle who, clad in an oleograph blazer

(Joseph's Coat), was putting a series of rhetorical questions about left legs and right elbows to the young and still guileless.

In the drama enacted on this distant stage there was a variety of Acts, symbolic of the pervading theme. Two examples will suffice:

Act I

Personæ – A Bowler and an Umpire. *Time* – 3.30 pm

UMPIRE: Over!

BOWLER: How do you know?

UMPIRE: I counted.

BOWLER: Then count again. (*Finishes the over.*)

Act II

Personæ – A Bowler, a Batsman, and an Umpire.
Time – 4.30 pm

BOWLER: How *was* that?

UMPIRE: Out.

BATSMAN: You weren't looking.

UMPIRE: I know.

BATSMAN: Well, then. (*Complete innings.*)

On Gala days these Dramas were supplanted by Variety. Fancy Dress and the Nervo-Knox spirit obligatory. Gallacher's most famous role was the Pantomime Dame, based on Wilkie Bard, with white stockings, elastic-sided boots, and jewelled skirt. He found that, so clothed, lbw was next door to impossible.

One morning, during the Latin hour, Pringle, after a fatuous attempt by Rollo to transmute an adverb into a noun, remarked in his most silky tones, 'So, Gallacher, your craving for fame at the Alhambra has so far debilitated your intellect as to destroy your discernment of the simpler parts of speech. When you were born, it seems, the habitual supplement of a head was overlooked.'

'Ruddy fool,' growled his victim.

'What's that, Gallacher? Did you blossom into speech?'

'I said "Wonderful," sir.'

'And you are right. It is a modern miracle.'

The pupil's ensuing comment was luckily absorbed in a chorus of laughter from the faithful knot of pro-Pringle sycophants.

*　　*　　*

From Greyfriars, Rollo drifted into his late father's affairs, London extension, and five more years brought him happy oblivion of Pringle, the Lake of Gennesaret and Cricket; but also, one winter evening at a dance, Joan Harries.

Her father was one of those wealthy landed gentlemen who, when young, trickle into Sandhurst, and thence into the Army. Long passed are those trickling days, alas! This was done partly because their fathers had achieved it, and partly to learn from the Sergeant-Major those few Saxon expletives which had been no more than hinted at in the Army Fifth Form. These terms Lieutenant Harries had carried in his head to the Boer War, and kept them warm on Paul Kruger and other taciturn Dutchmen. Soon after the day when Cronje was snookered at Paardeberg, he left the Army, inherited the property, forgot some of his more chromatic oaths, and, in due course, married a lady of charm and tact, who while seeming to acquiesce in her husband's ideas on household economy, invariably executed her own; except on one point, the cricket ground. There Colonel Harries – he had seen a greater War since the Kruger-cursing days – reigned indivisibly supreme, weeding the pitch on a small mat through October and November, maledicting the groundsman, who never listened, and making, when summer came, an annual series of '0 not-outs', punctuated by an occasional stately 1, which pleased the Colonel but ruined his average. Three sons were followed by a girl, and this was the Joan Harries upon whose toes Rollo Gallacher had been lingering during the last tango.

'What an awful floor!' murmured Rollo.

'Those,' replied Joan, 'are my feet.'

And thenceforward things went from strength to strength. Rollo loved Joan, and she, with that penetrating intuition peculiar to her sex, saw something in Rollo beyond his genial irresponsibility, which had permanently eluded the pince-nez of Mr Pringle. By April they were engaged. Slowish, but definite. And, up to this awful moment in mid-July, when Joan had subpoenaed her Corydon as witness in Harries *v*. Cochrane before two umpires, Rollo had never seen a cricketophobe in the flesh.

* * *

The Cricket Week at Bishop's Coombe had reached its climax when Rollo Gallacher arrived; an inopportune moment, he felt, as he saw the trim pavilion with the Union Jack and the Harries Ensign, 'Aut tentes aut vadas ad avernum', gaily fluttering atop. But when Burgess, the butler, emerged from a French window in full Ganymede marching order, and disappeared inside a marquee by the side of the ground, his heart, without actually singing for joy, yet revived a peg or two; and when Joan walked over to him and discussed the prospects of battle, he felt a little less like an invalid with no arms sent in to face Grimmett for ten minutes before lunch.

'Hullo,' said Rollo, 'what news of the Army? What of tactics and subtle strategy? Is all well with the commander-in-chief?'

'Far from it, my dear recruit; they are counting the wounded and burying the dead. We have lost four matches and halved one, and that by the intervention of Burgess, who, as umpire, kept his place of butler and the Harries flag flying by giving our last man, Colonel Harries, in, when the rest of the world thought otherwise. Briefly put, we must defeat the enemy today or——'

'Die,' said Rollo; and he moved over to join the gaily-clad throng who were after each other's shins in front of the pavilion, with fast off-breaks, except the two Captains, Hannibal Cochrane and Fabius Maximus Cunctator Harries, who stood on the wicket in likely places, as if they rather suspected the smooth-shaven turf of meditating a mutiny. Not one player on either side, except Rollo, regarded the match as anything but a struggle *à l'outrance* – lbw one end, safety the other; of the non-combatants probably only Burgess was faithful to the true cause, and even he, being a man prone to bookmaking, might play false.

No cricket match deserves a detailed account. Running commentary is a modern heresy. But in Cochrane *v*. Harries there were two obvious crises. The home platoon, batting first, had made 85, largely off the edge, when Harries (number 11)

109

joined Gallacher (number 10); the latter was dreamily contemplating the carnage of the late performer's wicket. The weather was perfect. Similar scenes, more vociferously greeted, at Greyfriars, floated into his mind, when a loud bellow of 'Middle and leg!' brought him round. Burgess, with a few masonic signs, performed the rites, and the Colonel stood, for the last time that week, at bay. The first two balls would have hit a fourth stump, had there been one on either side: the third hit the bat with a dull crash and rolled behind point. Rollo smiled and nodded – a friendly nod, as who should say, 'Well done, old mushroom!' – but the Colonel, never a nodder, started running: Rollo, anxious, like us all, to avoid dismissal before receiving a ball, stood firm. Already the Colonel was on him; point seemed to be juggling with several balls: 'Out of my way, sir! Let me pass! Make way, sir! Damn it, man, run! Leave your crease this instant!' But Rollo fathomed the scheme, and at length point, disgorging the leather, ran the striker out by a full twenty-two yards.

The Colonel marched, choking, pavilionwards. Sympathetic fieldsmen gathered round Rollo, as he too turned to go, and mentioned the rashness of the call, referred to the heat of the sun, and its reaction on advancing years. But Rollo knew that the Colonel would be waiting. He was, and unburdened his soul lyrically: 'Great heavens!' he cried; 'you young blackguard! You stand there nodding and grinning, and seduce me, sir, yes, *seduce* me from my crease, and leave me high, and eternally, blast it, dry!'

Rollo rolled a few apologetic words into the verbal spate, and passed, slightly shaken, into the care of Burgess. An interval, miscalled tea, brought balm to most. Within the marquee

'They soothed their cares and purged their hearts of toil.'

As the Colonel, yet breathing out threats and slaughter, was about to resume the field, Joan cornered Rollo, and told him that only a human vacuum would run-out his future father-in-law.

'Well,' said Rollo, 'only a galvanized avalanche in a stiff collar and 1890 tie would play a ball to point and then start on a marathon.'

'Hurry up, sir, get into your place there, Gallacher: short leg, and no nonsense!' It was the call to arms, what the early Romans rightly called Tumultus.

Two hours later the enemy score stood at 82, and the last survivors were fronting the foe and toeing the line. Without Rollo, the side would have been out for some 70. He had missed two catches: one was a sitter; the other would have been, if the umpire had been less conversational. Rollo had also used his legs continuously as a croquet-hoop. Fabius was speechless. Then came the second crisis. An elderly man was bowling high leg-breaks, evidently for the first time. Three to tie. Four to win. The fourth delivery of this pioneer was even slower, higher, and more succulent than the preceding three, all of which, truly struck, had been fielded by mid-on with the feet and blasphemy. But this one was an oblation, Corban, a parabolic present to the blind. Crack! All eyes on the leg boundary, and then, gradually, with pain but triumph, Rollo exhumed the ball from his gastric regions, smiling that slow, lazy smile which had brought him fame on the Greyfriars fields in the old Alhambra days.

The case of Harries *v.* Cochrane was no longer *sub judice.*

* * *

'I do believe,' said Rollo that evening, 'in fact, Joan, I am certain that my brilliance at short-leg today has saved us the trouble of an elopement. Who would have thought that anything good could come from cricket?'

'Quarter-wit,' said Joan.

O. E. Jugg: A Memoir

I received a letter – not long since – from a friend, who told me that O. E. Jugg, our mutual acquaintance, and a minor cricketer of, to some, imperishable memory, had retired finally from the game: that after careful thought he had decided to pay his final tribute to the sward, to give away his pads, to oil his dear bat no longer, and to grace as spectator, the sun-blessed scene which for so long he had adorned with many strokes previously considered foreign to the art of batsmanship.

'Jugg' (he writes) 'thinks that the humour of the thing, which was ineffable, is perhaps at last played out, and has given me leave either to publish abroad or to commit to everlasting silence that queer art of his which you and I have so long enjoyed together. So, if you will deflect your thoughts for a space from the more terrestrial interests of Bradman, and English bowlers toiling on Melbourne's macadam, to the celestial but more recondite charms of Jugg, I will revive your memory of what we both know, supply, from my more intimate friendship, data peculiar to myself, and thus enable you to give to the world a crystallized Cameo of this unique man.

'It is only right' (he continues) 'that the public, in order to appreciate Jugg as a cricketer, should be aware of Jugg as a man: in no game is character more evident: a domestic whim is so frequently paralleled by an idiosyncrasy at the crease: when Jugg was in difficulties as a batsman, when he was prodding at length leg-breaks with that irritable and fruitless stab of his, you could verily see him poking his study fire: both actions were invariably the heralds of disaster, the signs of impending catastrophe. The one led to a simple catch at short slip: the other to a slow but certain sinking of the flames.

'No man more visibly carried his hearth on to the pitch. At home, and equally when padded, his futility could be relied upon; he was consistently inept, and never spoiled it with some spasmodic or irrelevant brilliance: he was ineffectual, but with that quiet, steady, admirable incompetence which commands respect: he knows it, and is, to a quaint degree, proud of it; and he knows that I am telling you of it, to pass it all on to others.

'Fate has always inflicted upon him loads which would weigh your common man to the ground: to Jugg they are incentives, almost inspirations. He barks his shins on the coal-scuttle, and, after an interlude of quiet blasphemy, murmurs, "Je recule pour mieux sauter", and doesn't give a fig that the words are not apposite.

'He is fond of the quotation, for it is one of two that he has committed to memory: and he used it once when his middle-stump had been flattened first ball, regardless of the fact that he would have to recoil till the next Saturday, and even then, being number eleven, might never have the chance to make a better leap. He was proud of going in last, and would say that he was going to watch the ball, "as if on that alone hung the issue of the day". He enjoyed "riding in on the roller", as he called it, and never was man less depressed by the insulting alacrity of the ground staff at the fall of the ninth wicket. He regarded himself as the last hurdle – no facile vault, either – a sort of licensed liaison which, he would assert, came between the "humanity of the approved batsmen and the mechanical fortuitousness of the meretricious extras", an extraordinary phrase which he claimed as his own, but convinced none. He was a man of lovable excuses. He would buy a dozen Valet blades in mistake for Gillette, and say that they were much the same thing, which they never will be, and in like mood he would defend himself when he had run out a batsman on his own side by asserting that the other fellow would almost certainly have run him out in a few more balls.

'He never really knew where he had put anything: he would mislay the twine with which he had meant to bind his pipe, and, after fussing around for a long time, would resort finally to a sombre little roll of plaster which he invariably managed to keep at the bottom of his golf bag. Similarly, he would find that there were two right-hand gloves in his cricket bag – one so new that it hurt his nails, one of such depraved senility that it protected nothing and hindered his off-strokes: so, when he thought that no one was looking, he would plunge into other bags, and, making a desolation, would call it peace.

'He has particularly asked me not to spare his style. You remember him – who would forget that stance? – at the wicket: the "W. G." cock of the toe; the delicate curve of his rotundity; the many-coloured sash vainly trying to quell the rebellious billow of the shirt behind; the cap so jauntily awry – a touch of Hobbs here – as if he needed but a few graceful glides for the century; that late cut, so very late that it was merely posthumous; that questioning glance at the umpire when, amid a cloud of blanco, the stern Rhadamanth adjudged him leg before. He was ever the same with umpires: he heard them but he heeded not! And then his fielding: square-leg he loved above all; and enjoyed nothing more than a stout arbiter, behind whom he could retire diplomatically from the more painful hits, and with

113

whom he would share his wheezy mirth, quips on the bowler's run, comments on swerve and spin, chuckling obloquy of his captain.

'Yes, O. E. Jugg has retired from cricket, and you will comb the world in vain for a substitute.'

Envoi

So, then, cricket has a brighter and a gentler side, in spite of Ashes lost or won, and yearly averages gravely scrutinized. Cricket is desecrated by futile levity, but elevated by a certain high-spirited detachment: between the extremes of indifference and over-anxiety there lies a proper mean. The ideal cricketer has in him the implacable, and, no less, the airily resilient: he is something of a Sarah Battle, yet as often he has the mind of Puck. 'Don't be ruffled by your occupation,' said Mr Skimpole to the urgent dun, 'don't be ruffled by your occupation. We can separate you from your office; we can separate the individual from the pursuit.' So, with cricketers, it is when they are ruffled, when they are embittered by disappointment, overawed by a false idea of the game's values, goaded by criticism or puffed up by praise, that they cannot separate themselves from their pursuit. And when laughter goes out of a game, it is drudgery indeed.

Can cricket be defined? You can see it, in perfect miniature, in the small, howling schoolboy, rushing from work some midsummer day, where an irritable master, who would fain perhaps himself be watching at Lord's, has been trying to sup-plant with Corn Laws or Equinoxes the crowded imagery of the cricket-stuffed mind – rushing from work to bat like Sutcliffe or bowl like Verity – noble imitation! Then to dream away the night in some fairy Test Match, where he has been chosen to bat first, and is just taking guard, when the morning bell clangs out the close of play!

Consider cricket in full length. It is the perfect mirror of character, the true reflection of nature. If we are cricketers, great or humble, household words, or one only among the great unnumbered, the game means to us something primordially human, something that lives next door to the elements of life: it brings with it the rare smell of mown grass, pleasant breezes in the face, panoramas of rolling meadows and green hedges, or – in more serious moments – noble pavilions towering to the blue sky, seas of faces. Let your mind dwell for a space upon this storied game, and there will glide in, almost unbidden, a host of images which you treasure more highly than any picture painted by the brush of man: some great player, walking with easy confidence to the wicket, whom you love to see coming, love to see exercising his consummate art, and, most of all, love to defeat, yes, even to pass his bat, though the ball misses the wicket; for you've beaten him, and he knows it, and looks at you – a familiar look, perhaps, which tells you that you won't do it again. . . . It will bring to you memories of village matches with desperate finishes towards sunset – perhaps the game hasn't started till after tea – lbw decisions whose patent iniquity made you cry out to Heaven, while the umpire turns an unrepentant back; catches that hissed past the slip-fielder like bullets, and which, if held, might have won the match – so you think, fond bowler! though the culprit will swear that you bowled before he was ready. You will remember days when you batted like a fool, and made thirty; when you resisted, nobly in your small way, the bowler's every thrust and resource for an hour, and then fell at last for some ten or dozen, so paltry in print, so treasured in retrospect! Days when you bowled but ill, when the pitch seemed thirty yards, and yet you got your five wickets; days when you bowled like a king, and got no wickets at all – and the world judged you accordingly.

And then, when you are alone, and you lean back in your chair and comfortably close your eyes, there will pass before you a procession of shadowy recollections, the years that are no more, memories of boyhood's bowling, the lithe run-up, the lissome swing; treasure them, for they are you, you before you knew that legs are strained, backs rheumatic, cricket clubs often overdrawn; it was you, living in a paradise that you thought would last for ever. There is no greater moment in a cricketer's life than the first overhand ball that takes a wicket, the first off-drive, crisp and luscious, that is at the boundary almost before cover-point has turned; after what strivings, what surreptitious imitations of the great, what bitter disappointments! I remember bowling perpetual phantom overs in Lower Regent Street, to the imminent peril of testy old club-men and the helpless dismay of a governess; and then the long summer evenings at school: the two concrete pitches with solid wooden wickets which boomed out the batsman's knell under the impact of the whizzing 'stringer', marvellous rope balls, which, when pounded into shapelessness by weeks of honest service, would suddenly out-Freeman Freeman with a leg-break of paralysing unexpectedness! Fleeting, irrevocable days of glorious experiment, of desire to do everything with the ball that human fingers can encompass – days when umpires were hopelessly corrupt. . . .

It is such things as these, triumphs welcomed with humility, failures breeding discipline of spirit, which day by day go to the making of each new generation of cricketers; to fit players for the noblest game in the world, a game so great yet so humbling, in which merit often goes unrewarded, in which perfect fitness of mind and body alone lead to the possibility of success, in which so very few can justly say

> 'I do what many dream of all their lives,
> – Dream? Strive to do and agonize to do,
> And fail in doing.'

And yet we love the striving and the agonizing, and revel in the very failure of the doing.

The Bowler's Epitaph

To Cricket's shrine I offer'd, day by day,
Pace, length, and spin, swervers that 'ran away';
For Cricket I threw Tennis down the drain,
Abjur'd my mashie – abjuration vain;
For England's game I bowl'd on English muds,
Bowl'd, to a field of never-bending duds;
Heard, while the catches dropp'd, the river's call,
The pop of Bass, the punt-pole's sleepy fall;
Beheld, each Over, Slip's unpleasing face,
And wonder'd why Short-leg was not in place;
Till God, who saw me tried too sorely, gave
The resting-place I ask'd – a Bowler's grave;
O thou, whom chance leads to this nameless stone –
Come with a baffl'd trundler, or alone;
By Wides, No-balls, by Extra-Covers stout,
By lbw's, miscalled NOT OUT,
One last APPEAL. Let fall a kindred tear
O'er Bowler's dust. A broken heart lies here.

Cricket Prints

J. B. Hobbs — *Surrey*

Hobbs was the greatest English batsman that I've seen and tried to remove. He was the most perfectly equipped by art and temperament for any style of innings on any sort of wicket against any quality of opposition. He was thirty-seven years of age when I first had the pleasure of bowling to him. Misleading suggestions are sometimes heard that a cricketer, after the age of thirty, is tottering on the brink of decline. This is humbug; not only in a Pickwickian sense. Tom Hayward was in his thirty-sixth year when, in 1906, he scored 3,518 runs in first-class cricket, which still stands as a record.

The early Hobbs, before the last war, may have had all the brilliance and daring, but he would be a rash man who denied that his meridian of skill was shown about the years 1919–26. In the 1924–25 tour to Australia, under A. E. R. Gilligan, he and Herbert Sutcliffe formed an opening pair which many regard as the greatest the game has seen. Back in England for summer 1925, Hobbs scored 16 centuries. Of these, two were made in one match, against Somerset at Taunton. By them he equalled, then passed, Dr Grace's record of 126 centuries. In the next summer he and Sutcliffe made the memorable stand on a difficult wicket against Australia at the Oval in the Fifth Test, the first match of six running in which A. P. F. Chapman led England to victory. Sutcliffe made 161, Hobbs exactly 100; then had his bails flicked off by a beauty from J. M. Gregory. But, apart from the runs, Hobbs showed himself the master tactician. He foxed A. J. Richardson, who was bowling off-spinners, and the Australian captain into thinking he was in difficulties. He was not. So, while the pitch remained difficult, he contrived to keep on and, for the most part, to keep the strike against the spin bowler whom he least feared.

At Taunton, the year before, on a hot August Saturday, I saw him nervous for the only time that I can remember. There was a large crowd, as crowds go in the West; a news-reel cinematograph was perched on the reluctant roof of the little pavilion. The match was 'news'. For Hobbs had made his 125th century some time before, and had been followed round by ill-luck and most of the cricket correspondents. We batted first –

more waiting! and fared poorly. Then the struggle began. He was anxious; the strokes were calculating, even stuffy; he was twice nearly lbw, once at each end. At about 30 he gave a chance to wide mid-on, which went wrong. But throughout these embarrassments his instinctive excellence of method saved him from those faults of execution which another man in the same circumstances would, fatally, have committed. At the close of play he was in the early 90s. Then – a Sunday, for more waiting. But nice for the Somerset gate.

On the Monday morning J. J. Bridges and I were the bowlers. I bowled a no-ball in the first over, which Hobbs hit to the square-leg boundary. Someone afterwards suggested that the no-ball was bowled on purpose! It wasn't. Hobbs never needed any presents at the wicket. In Bridges's second over Hobbs scored a single to leg that gave him what he has told me was the toughest century of the lot! His second hundred was a beauty, care-free and brilliant of stroke, and he began with a four past cover that I can still see.

I have seen Hobbs described as a frail man. Actually he had strength of thigh and forearm far above the average, a strength which was concealed in the art of method and grace of movement. His footwork was, as nearly as is humanly possible, perfect. In every stroke he moved into the line of the ball with so little effort that he could bat for hours without over-taxing energy of mind or body. I never saw him unbalanced in a forward stretch, or 'hopping' on a back-stroke. The interplay between judgment and execution was wonderful to see and baffling to attack. He covered his wicket much in defence. So did 'W.G.', according to one of his greatest admirers and opponents, S. M. J. Woods.

There was no one stroke of which you could say that it was less strong than another. You will hear someone remark – 'What a glorious square-cut Headley has!' or, 'Do you remember Hendren hooking?' You will not hear that of Hobbs. All his strokes, that is, all the strokes in the game, were equally strong and easy; they were of an even perfection. He would hook bumpers off his nose; and, as to leg-breakers, which can find out the faults of the best, he mastered them all in turn, from the South Africans on their matting, when he was young, to Mailey,

Grimmett, and Freeman, when he was in early middle-age.

To crown all, he had the gift of smiling quietly at failure and triumph alike.

H. Sutcliffe — *Yorkshire*

Herbert Sutcliffe is the serenest batsman I have known. Whatever may have passed under that calm brow – anger, joy, disagreement, surprise, relief, triumph – no outward sign was betrayed on the field of play. He was understood, over two thousand years in advance, by the Greek philosophers. They called this character megalo-psychic. It is the sort of man who would rather miss a train than run for it, and so be seen in disorder and heard breathing heavily.

He sets himself the highest available standard of batting and deportment. His physical discipline equals his mental; shown in the cool, clear eye and the muscularity of frame. If he is bowled, he appears to regard the event less as a human miscalculation than some temporary, and reprehensible, lapse of natural laws. There has been a blunder, to which he is unwillingly privy and liable. The effects of this blunder will be entered, with other blunders, in a score-book, and the world may read of it in due time. He does not regret that it has occurred, for he is never sorry for himself; but he is sorry that Nature should have forgotten herself. To the later comers to the ground he would, so to speak, announce: 'Mr Sutcliffe regrets he's unable to bat today, being, ludicrously enough, already out.' Yet he is not proud. He leaves pride to little cricketers. There is nothing little in Sutcliffe. He is great. Great in idea and great in effect.

In the matter of round numbers he has scored over 50,000 runs in twenty-one years at an average of 52. In Test matches against Australia his average stands at nearly 67 for 2,741 runs – easily the highest average among English batsmen. On his first appearance against Australia, at Sydney, he played an innings of 115. He took part with Holmes (P.) in the world's record first-wicket stand of 555 for Yorkshire at Leyton in 1932. These are but a few of the feats in a career of resounding triumph.

When I first saw him, in 1919, he was a debonair and powerful stylist. He didn't look Yorkshire; even less a Yorkshire Number One. He looked, rather, as if he had remembered and caught something of an earlier and not indigenous grace of manner. Pudsey was his home, but his style was not Pudsey. He had easy offside strokes and a disdainful hook. I would not say that with the years he lost this manner, but it was increasingly seldom seen in its fullness. Two visits within five years to help Hobbs for England against Australia must mark any batsman of Sutcliffe's will and intelligence. It became hard to discern which predominated, the pleasure of batting or the trick of staying in.

As you bowled opening overs to the later Sutcliffe you noticed the entire development of every defensive art: the depressingly straight bat, the astute use of pads (as with Hobbs), the sharp detection of which outswinger could be left; above all, the consistently safe playing down of a rising or turning ball on leg stump, or thighs. This last art you will, I think, find only in the best players; Makepeace, Holmes (P.), Hutton, D. R. Jardine, Sandham, and Hobbs as a matter of course, spring to the mind's eye. Professionals generally acquire it more readily than amateurs, whose early coaching often tends to a neglect of the onside strokes.

Sutcliffe added a defensive stroke of his own; not exactly pretty, nor easily imitable. It was often played to a rising ball on about the line of the off stump. The bat started straight, on a restricted forward stroke; then with a swivel or overturn of the wrists he caused the ball to lie 'dead' a few yards down the pitch, or where a silly-point would have stood if such a liberty had been taken; as if Sutcliffe had thought: 'Ball, you irk me. There. Be strangled, and lie quiet.'

He has always been capable of scoring at a great speed, especially from fast bowling. His hook is imperious. Some remark that this stroke has often been his downfall. They forget the many hundreds of runs that it has brought him, from balls which make lesser batsmen dodge and murmur of danger. I hope we shall soon see his batting again.

W. R. Hammond — *Gloucestershire*

W. R. Hammond is the sort of cricketer that any schoolboy might wish to be. Schoolboys are very good judges of most things and people. They think and look straight on, unapprenticed to prejudice.

It might be interesting, and it would be unprofitable, to argue Hammond's place as a batsman in the ranks of all the great, or to compare his ability with that of famous contemporaries. It has been tried, and it ends in futility. To me he is, quite simply, the greatest cricketer who began in the last twenty years, and that, too, by a long distance. In the word 'cricketer' I count not only batting, bowling, and fielding. In these combined arts there is not one, not Bradman, not Constantine, who could stand a full and unbiased comparison with Hammond as he showed himself in the decade from 1925 to 1935; when he would make a hundred or two against Australia, then bowl down their first three wickets, then make with ease a slip-catch which others would not merely miss but would not even have rated as a miss. But I count also those things which cannot be translated into words, far less into print, but belong to the brain and the heart. I mean the effect on a match of his presence alone; the influence on a bowler's feelings of the sight of Hammond taking guard at about 11.50 a.m., when lunch seemed far and boundary near.

Such abstractions belong as surely to a batsman's greatness as do his technical ability and his power to make the numbers rattle on the board. It is something to have seen Hammond walk out to the Australians from the pavilion at Lord's; a ship in full sail. There is a pride in possessing such a player. There was an anxiety for his success, not only from party reasons but because his failure would be an affront to sense, a slap in the face to Nature. Surely he would do it today. And none that saw it will forget his batting on a June Saturday in 1938. He gave one chance in an innings of 240, and that split a fieldsman's finger.

As a batsman he has it all; and with double the strength of most players; strength scientifically applied. In his prime his hitting, mostly straight and through the covers, was of a combined power and grace that I have never seen in any other man. I can't think that human agency could do more to a ball. To field to him at cover-point was a sort of ordeal by fire. You would take a ball, perhaps, with as much give as possible and in the middle of the hands, then wring them. I have heard the criticism that he is not a good hooker. I never noticed the deficiency when I bowled him a straight long-hop. It is nearer the truth to say that his method and strength enabled him to play straight, or nearly straight, many short balls which other batsmen find easier to hook.

I have seen him in trouble to leg-break bowling, but not often. Far oftener I have seen a leg-breaker preparing footwork for a dodge from violent death. I have known him lose his wicket through what looked like a sudden failure of concentration, generally to fast bowling. And I believe that from the first, when he was a free and sometimes abandoned hitter, he had to learn and hardly acquire concentration. It was not born in him. For his method, when he is allowed to play as he wishes, and his conversation, both show that he regards fun as the first reason for cricket. He got as far as acquiring the iron temperament of Test matches for the neccessary period. But he never wholly enjoyed that mood, and it never sat comfortably on him. You should see him in a Festival.

As you would expect in such a player, he has generosity and humour, especially in his judgments of other cricketers, given quietly and with a twinkling eye. I chanced to meet him soon after close of play, when he'd been cut by a rising ball in the Old Trafford Test against West Indies in 1933. 'Well,' he said, 'we began it, you know; and now you can see just a bit of what it was like. Just the luck of the game.'

Hammond is not only a great cricketer.

F. E. Woolley — *Kent*

Frank Woolley was easy to watch, difficult to bowl to, and impossible to write about. When you bowled to him there weren't enough fielders; when you wrote about him there weren't enough words. In describing a great innings by

Woolley, and few of them were not great in artistry, you had to go careful with your adjectives and stack them in little rows, like pats of butter or razor-blades. In the first over of his innings, perhaps, there had been an exquisite off-drive, followed by a perfect cut, then an effortless leg-glide. In the second over the same sort of thing happened; and your superlatives had already gone. The best thing to do was to presume that your readers knew how Frank Woolley batted and use no adjectives at all.

I have never met a bowler who 'fancied himself' against Woolley, nor heard one who said, with conviction, 'Woolley doesn't like an off-break on the middle stump or a fast bumper on the leg stump.' I never heard Woolley confess that he preferred or disliked any bowler whatsoever. But then he is a very quiet man. I have a belief that he was particularly fond of them fast and short. They went that much more quickly to the boundary.

It has been said that he was not a good starter. Like other great batsmen, he would sometimes miss in the first minutes. But equally he could kill two bowlers in the first six overs of any match. His own innings might be only about 50 or so, but he had fathered the centuries that followed. Only a few years ago, when he was some forty-seven years old, I saw him 'murder' Voce and Butler, the Nottinghamshire bowlers, in the first overs of a match at Canterbury. They were pitching a little, only a little, too short, and they extracted an exhibition of cutting and hooking which was . . . but we have refused the use of adjectives.

Merely from a personal aspect, I never knew so difficult a target as Woolley. His great reach, and the power of his pendulum, made a fool of length. Balls that you felt had a right to tax him he would hit airily over your head. He was immensely discouraging. The only policy was to keep pitching the ball up, and hope. He could never be properly described as being 'set', since he did not go through the habitual processes of becoming set. There was no visible growth of confidence or evident strengthening of stroke. He jumped to his meridian. He might hit the first ball of the match, a good ball too, if left to itself, crack to the boundary over mid-on; then, when he had made 60 or more, he might snick a short one past slip in a sudden freak of fallibility, a whim of humanity.

Sometimes he is compared with other famous left-handers, such as the late F. G. J. Ford. But these comparisons seem to be concerned only with attack. It is often forgotten, I think, that Woolley's defence was as sure and correct as that of Mead or Bardsley. Of its kind it was just as wonderful to see, on a sticky wicket, as was his attack. It had a corresponding ease and grace, without toil or trouble. For this reason I think that Woolley will rank as the greatest of all left-handers so far seen in the game. None has made so many runs while giving so much delight.

For many years Woolley was a great part of the Canterbury Festival. Myself, I preferred to watch him or play against him on some ground not in Kent. Praise and pride in home-grown skill are natural and right; but at Canterbury, in the later years, these had degenerated into a blind adulation that applauded his strokes with a very tiresome lack of discrimination. They had made a 'raree' show of a great batsman.

No one, when county cricket is resumed, will fill the place of Frank Woolley. I have tried to avoid metaphor and rhapsody; but there was all summer in a stroke by Woolley, and he batted as it is sometimes shown in dreams.

E. Hendren — *Middlesex*

Cricket, sometimes a rather solemn and calculating old bloke, will never forget Elias ('Patsy') Hendren. He played around cricket, and pulled at it, and called it names, and provoked it, and loved it. When he stopped playing for Middlesex, cricket must have missed its imp, its laughing familiar, as Lord's missed its hero. Hendren has been called a clown; but he was more like the 'Fool' who called Lear 'nuncy' and tried to keep the old man from going mad by a stream of talk that poured unmixed from the elemental humours of the earth.

But, besides that humour, that natural outlet of balanced faculties, he had dignity and judgment. He never, as it were, insulted his own colossal skill. He would burst that balloon, pomposity, and upend the façade of hypocrisy and show. He liked slapstick, but he knew when and at whom to throw the pie. His short, square build, busy movements, and low-geared run were made for comedy.

I think that he most enjoyed doing something outrageous when the scene was all majesty and strain. Perhaps it was the crisis of some Test match. He saw the serious doctors bending anxiously over the patient. He saw rows of faces in the crowd like flock upon flock of sheep, absorbing the wonted pabulum, relieved by some incredible ass in a horned handkerchief, who was plainly doomed to bore whole families for whole weeks with bleating stories of the wonderful play. He saw the pavilion members, righteously conscious of privileged accommodation, some affecting knowledge, others sobriety; next to them, the gentlemen of the Press, poising the knowing pencil, forging a paragraph from a no-ball, making a sermon of a cut. And his demon whispered to him: 'Hendren, for heaven's sake do something funny.' And he'd do it.

Hendren made 170 centuries, and his average was close on 51; yet to the end he was a nervous starter; and it was, surely, the character of boyhood, which he never quite threw off, that caused him such visible emotion over the first run of each innings. He liked to score it by a push to leg, or, better still, by a queer huddled little prod towards extra-cover, in the making of which he seemed to be nurturing into difficult life something very tender and rare.

As the innings lengthened, so his stance grew more upright, and he seemed to achieve in his strong forward strokes a height and reach not in fact possessed. His style, like that of most short, strong men, was practical rather than beautiful; but it was strictly correct. He excelled in the hook off fast bowling, and I cannot remember any batsman who played it more boldly, or with such a fierce and violent relish. Those who saw him batting against the fast bowlers in the West Indies say that his hooking there has never been equalled in this generation of batsmen. The spectators, who sometimes turned the trees into clusters of human plums, would cheer wildly and shout 'Patsy!' then fall, still applauding, from their perch! They christened a motor-bus 'Patsy' in affectionate admiration of his skill.

It was the fashion at one time, soon after the last war, to say that Hendren hadn't the 'Test temperament'. The truth was that he did not make many runs in Tests for the simple reason that he wasn't often selected to play in them. This idiotic mistake was later rectified, and he played a great part, both in runs and by example, in the winning of the series under A. P. F. Chapman in the 1928–29 Australian tour.

My own earliest memory of Hendren is a superb innings of 50 that he played for Middlesex, almost in the dark, in the Parks at Oxford. As night fell, I happened to bowl him with an inswinger: and the memory of his kindly congratulation to a struggler of eighteen remains with me.

M. Leyland — *Yorkshire*

'Even at this moment the Sergeant is dishing out rations.' The Sergeant is Maurice Leyland, and these words are from another cricketer. Earlier he had remarked: 'He is quite unruffled, and we consider his aloofness a sort of genius.' And these words brought back to me Leyland standing absolutely still at the crease; not a shift of the foot, not a movement of shoulder or head; while O'Reilly started his odd, walloping, ducking run to the wicket. Leyland's mind, like his body, was still; no fretting, no impatience. He just stood, quietly dishing out defiance.

Leyland in a tight Test match reminded me of the famous four-squarers of ancient or romantic times. He was Horatius on the tottering bridge; Hector, who alone stood between Troy and destruction. He was born to rescue. But he is more dangerous than those who are just stubborn and grim. He has something of D'Artagnan in him; there is a gaiety besides the simplicity and strength; seen in the slight list of the cap, and in a certain jauntiness and optimism of gait.

But solidity is what you most notice in his batting; a breadth of defence most dispiriting to the bowler. His muscular strength is great, and those forearms were well made to destroy a long-hop or baste a half-volley.

In recent years an England Eleven never read well without

Leyland's name. If something went wrong early none could so well repair the damage; and it was in the losing matches that you most clearly saw his greatness. He has never said 'Come in, then,' to the knock of defeat; even when the eleventh man joined him and there were 300 more runs to make on a doubtful pitch. His only concession to Fate would be to take guard again and to stare rather more fixedly at the bowler. When runs came easily on a perfect pitch in the sun, and life flowed gaily as the sparkling Thames, you might not particularly notice him. His element was foul weather. He would disappear into the haze of Bramall Lane, where a sterner sort of game was being played under the name of cricket, and entrench himself among the sawdust and smoke and off-breaks and appeals, and do his raw, tough work in silence.

He played an innings of 137 at Melbourne on his first appearance for England. But his great year was 1934, when the Australians won back the 'Ashes' here. He made three centuries in the Test series, and, when all around him was falling, insisted on a century in the disastrous match at the Oval.

He regards his left-hand bowling as something of a humorous feat, sending down broad off-breaks with a broader smile; but he has taken more wickets than you would think, and has baffled the best with his strange twiddlings. I think his ambition is to shove Verity out of the analysis.

His attitude to the bowler may, with slight change, be taken from a letter of Dr Johnson: 'Any violence offered me I shall do my best to repel. I shall not be deterred by the menaces of a ruffian. Your rage I defy. Your abilities are not so formidable. I pay regard not to what you shall say, but to what you shall prove.'

D. R. Jardine — *Surrey*

It was no joke for a bowler when D. R. Jardine came in at number five for Surrey on a perfect Oval wicket – Hobbs, Sandham, Ducat, Shepherd, Jardine. He used to say: 'The position is peculiar. Either you hustle to a sticky wicket with your pads crooked, or else you go in when there are already so many runs on the board that it doesn't matter whether you make nothing or a hundred!'

Jardine stopped playing first-class cricket at the age of thirty-three; that is, in his prime. He had never played regularly. By then he had been twice to Australia. Twice running he had headed the batting averages. He had captained England abroad and at home, and had played a classic century against the fierceness of Constantine and Martindale at Old Trafford in 1933. But when summer 1934 came round, and the Australians were here again, he was in the Press Box. Rightly or wrongly, he had differed with the Marylebone oligarchy; and he was lost to English cricket when he was much needed. I remember a spectator at Leeds, where Bradman batted on and on, calling up to the Press Box: 'We want you out there, Jardine.' And, upon my word, we did. For the captain was gone, Larwood was injured and out of it. English cricket was at its lowest ebb since the disasters of 1920 and 1921.

Few great batsmen can have matured so early. At the age of fourteen he looked like a county batsman in miniature, and I am sure that at seventeen he could have walked from the Winchester eleven into a Test side and done reasonably well. Among amateurs of his time he was the supreme example of orthodoxy, but what placed him above the others was the strength of his back-play, which equalled that of the best professionals. His skill was to a great degree inherited, his father, M. R. Jardine, having made a century for Oxford *v.* Cambridge and played many fine innings for Middlesex. To this was added natural intelligence and coaching of the very finest order, first at Horris Hill, where he enjoyed the influence and precept of the famous Evans family, then at Winchester, where his skill was polished by such notable cricketers as E. Rockley Wilson and H. S. Altham.

His own model and hero was C. B. Fry; and in many ways Jardine resembled him; in the method of his back-stroke – the right leg well over, the left away from the stumps, the stance boldly upright; in concentration, and in the powerful will to improve; and in a certain combativeness of character, which not only made him a most stubborn fighter in a crisis but led him into first place in one of cricket's most perplexing controversies.

But the time to see Jardine batting was in a care-free net on a summer evening in the Oxford Parks; and many of these we had together. Here he would show every stroke in the game, all played with grace and power, and with an abandon which he hardly ever allowed himself in a set match. And that was the one weakness in all this strength, that the stringency of an occasion was reflected in a corresponding restriction of his art, which was in itself so effortless and fluent. Something of iron in his temperament would not let him play free and full in the greater matches. It is said that the best innings he played in Australia was one of 140, in 1928, against New South Wales. Bradman has told me that it was one of the finest displays of stroke-play that he has ever seen. But, in general, as the task grew greater, the strokes grew fewer. He remained a terrific problem for the bowler to solve; but my point is that he had it in him to kill a bowler, yet was so often content to wage a long battle on fairly level terms.

As a captain I should rank him very high. He was thorough and observant. His preparations and his study of individual methods were exhaustive. None knew more exactly what he meant to do nor could express his thoughts more pointedly if some plan misfired. He took far more pains than many knew to weigh the abilities and inclinations of his own team. He had the true Scottish dislike of waste in material or words; but his cursing, at its best, was Elizabethan in scope and variety. His wit could be both deep and broad, as when, after batting for many slow hours in a Test in Australia, he apologized to an Australian for playing 'like an old spinster defending her honour'.

So much for Jardine as a cricketer. Old acquaintance may perhaps allow me the liberty of remarking that, if he has some-times been a fierce enemy, he has also been a wonderful friend.

A. Sandham — *Surrey*

Andrew Sandham was a first fiddle who, for most of his time, played second in the orchestra, Or, if you like, he was the magician Hobbs's assistant; sharing in the show and most necessary to it; far removed from the 'anonymous bloke' whose hand is sometimes seen in the wings throwing in a hoop or some property of illusion; regarded with esteem and affection not only by the master but by the discerning audience. Yet, because of the unalterable injustice of circumstance, he was generally standing just on the shadow side of the spotlight while the applause at last died away and the spectators chattered of the greatness they had seen.

In almost any other county but Surrey he would have been the hero, the cynosure. I know that he was capable of such a position; I am not quite sure if he was desirous of it. His style of batting, like his talk, was quiet, neat, crisp. Like most smallish men, he was very nimble of foot. His judgment of a ball and his grasp of infinitely various situations were sure and sensible. He was quick-witted, and a natural intelligence drew the full profit from experience and from a close observation of one of the greatest batsmen that the game has known. His style was correct without being stifled by the restrictions of correctness; for under the inscrutable and polished exterior there were merriments and fancies, which often found expression in a remarkably gay late-cut or a hook off the eyebrows, which was like the joker's answer to the blundering big man's rudeness. He was a courageous batsman, the courage being inherent and deep, not aggressive and obvious. He would make little reference to a success won by this quality, regarding it less as a triumph won than as a task accomplished.

Maybe I have said too little of his method of batting, by which he scored 107 centuries in first-class cricket and retired with 41,284 runs to his credit, at an average of nearly 45. But the sum total of Sandham, as with all those whom we may call the 'quiet great', was compiled by an inseparable combination of skill and character. He has a restraint, a dignity, a self-respect, and self-discipline which you will find in the best of the English professional games players; and I *mean* games; not just diversions, entertainments. He is, if you like, old-fashioned; that is, he has always been primarily the servant of his art and his team, only secondarily the entertainer of the public. He did not rise suddenly, but served an exacting apprenticeship to cricket; he was willing to think of himself as a learner to the end, and for that reason he has become one of the game's most eminent teachers. He is an embodiment of those qualities which cricket, for all the scoffing of pink intellectual cynics, can teach better than any game – self-control, manners, and endeavour; the opposite of those defects which so often pass for true touch in modern sport – flamboyance of behaviour, noise, arrogance, visible annoyance or self-satisfaction, catchpenny bravado.

He did not need to learn that unselfishness which his subsidiary position would, in any case, have helped to induce. One instance of it, out of many, I recall. It was in the second innings of Surrey against Somerset at Taunton in 1925. Hobbs, having equalled Dr Grace's record of 126 centuries, had set out, with a care-free brilliance, to pass it. Sandham, too, was in wonderful form, but there were not enough runs needed for victory to allow of a century each. So Sandham saw to it that his great partner should have opportunity put in his way, and the record was passed.

It is right that one record should stand to his name, the highest innings, 219, played by an English batsman for a county against the Australians. For he gave all that he could to cricket, and took from it less than he deserved.

G. Gunn — *Nottinghamshire*

Cricket is still scratching its head about George Gunn, Senior; and it will not readily recover from him. Technically, he was a genius. Aware and capable of orthodoxy, he mostly preferred to laugh at the book of words.

He mocked equally the rules of batting and the Rules of Cricket. He was silently and exquisitely amused at cricket's precise measurements and its neat pomps. Why twenty-two yards? Why not an acre or so? wherein a man might stroll about with bat and pads and play any ball jerked along by unseen agency, backhand or forehand, cutting half-volleys square to the boundary and driving long-hops for a single over mid-off's head. Why not? And, in these genial wanderings, he should have come upon Edward Lear, looking, as usual, perfectly spherical and wearing a runcible hat; and there should have been a single-wicket match of no time, no dimensions, no result; then an argument, over a glass of ale, on whether Aunt Jobiska was exactly right in her view that a Pobble is better without his toes, as everyone knows. Then they should have pledged a return match, to be played three weeks earlier, with Lewis Carroll as umpire.

As the great Frank Crumit might sing, 'He robbed the world of fancy'. In his late twenties, some six years before the last war, he found himself in Australia, trying to recover that health which so often, unhappily, eluded him. The England cricketers were also there, and their batting wasn't going right. Gunn was called from his restful meanderings to a violent struggle on the Sydney arena. He played an innings of 119; his first appearance for England against Australia. More recently, at the age of fifty, he and Andrew Sandham, touring with MCC, scored 322 for the first wicket against Jamaica, at Kingston.

There were some odd happenings on that trip. Gunn, at an age when it is often found convenient to prop the feet on the mantelpiece and discourse on cricket's decline, went out to open the innings in a Test match against some very fast and very awkward bowling. In the intervals of taking the ball anywhere between the left armpit and the left thigh, he played beautiful strokes in an innings of just under 50. 'How did you like it?' a fellow-player asked him on his return. 'All right,' was the answer, with a wry smile, 'but I'd sooner play a hand of solo.'

On the same tour he was fielding in a solar topee near the leg-side crowd. A tremendous skier was hit, I think by Constantine. Gunn, after skirting around on his bearings, stood quite still under the ball. In his left hand he held his topee at full stretch, to suggest an infringement of Law 41; with his right he made the catch. It is said that this performance bewildered Wilfred Rhodes, who was riven between wonder and disapproval. 'Ay,' he said, in that confidential, husky, Yorkshire voice: 'Ay, a grand catch; but George shouldn't have done that.' Ah, Wilfred, you, if any, must know there were no shoulds and shouldn'ts with George Gunn.

I happened to be playing on the same side as Gunn in a match soon after the last war. It was a North-Western Festival. Experimental. They called it, I believe, North *v.* South; though it might have been China *v.* Japan, for all anyone seemed to know or care. There were queer occurrences both on and off the field. Gunn and another player opened our innings, and I noticed that the batsmen, before the start, were in earnest colloquy with the umpires. At the interval I asked Gunn what they'd been saying. 'Oh,' he replied, 'they were telling us there were to be no lbw's in this match; and I was saying "Thanks very much; and if we have middle wicket knocked out, it's just a *nusty* incident, and we knock her in again and go on." '

The faster bowlers will remember Gunn best. He loved to walk sideways towards them, like a grimly playful crab, till they seemed nearly to meet in mid-pitch. A flash of the bat, and the ball would be flicked away to third-man or glanced to long-leg. Of him alone I should say that words cannot describe his moods of batting. One hour you might find him plodding along like any old sedate number one; the next, he would be playing strokes for which the word 'brilliant' is just ridiculous. His view was that cricket is made for man. Perhaps it was a sunny morning, and he wanted to sit in a deck-chair by his family or friends. Very well. The pitch was true. Nottingham had plenty of batting. And, about noon there Gunn was, sitting in a deck-chair, watching the others at the wicket. He stood no nonsense from the game.

I see that, apart from his 62 centuries, an average of 26.71 stands against his name. 'How very funny,' I can hear him say. 'Why not 267.1, or 2.671, or 2671?' In genius, in pleasure given and enjoyed, the last figure is about the truth.

J. W. Hearne — *Middlesex*

J. W. Hearne was the batsman's batsman; even as, in high art, according to those who are thought to know, Spenser was the poet's poet, Del Sarto the painter's painter, and Bach the musician's musician.

I don't mean that Hearne was the best model for young or old, though, personally, I should have been pleased, in dreams, to have batted like that. He could be both more and less than orthodox. He could, when it interested him, which was rarely, bat like any young gentleman newly stepped from the text-books who is redolent of the rectitude of left and right feet and is instructed in the manoeuvres of conscious propriety. This sort of thing, I fancy, he found rather unexciting. But, instead of seeking variety in the fervours of high driving, pulling, and downright swatting, he preferred the quieter eccentricities. He would play a half-volley for two or three off the back foot between point and cover-point; a long-hop he might deflect, rather than hook, to square-leg, a stroke which silently but evidently asked the bowler to take more trouble, if you please, and not to waste our time with frivolities when the batsman and the discerning public, if any, expect a duel on level terms.

Hearne could and, more often than some know, did score at a fast pace, usually on a bowler's pitch, when the heroes of force and speed were, as they say, all Elephants and Castles. I remember an innings he played for the Champion County of 1920, Middlesex, against the Rest of England on a beast of a sticky wicket at the Oval. Frank Woolley, in those days still among the best slow left-hand spinners in the game, was doing much as he liked with the ball and the batsmen; except Hearne, and Hearne made a century. In defence he showed resource and craft; then, about once in two overs, he would sweep the ball off the stumps crack against the boundary. It was an innings that could not be forgotten, containing the perfect blend of sensible risk and sure vigilance. Those who played with him for Middlesex will tell of other such innings by Hearne, and the men of Yorkshire had reason to regard him with respect.

He neither possessed nor valued those obvious qualities which please spectators. His art was not for those who drop into a pavilion or out of a tavern for an odd hour's watching. As profitably might some elated senator have gate-crashed the more didactic periods of Mr Gladstone. Sometimes in his later time, he overdid tranquillity; and the onlooker would allow impatience to obscure justice of criticism. For, even in these moods, if he was somewhat tedious to watch, what then was he like to bowl to?

He was indeed a difficult target. If he can be said to have offered one weakness, it was a tendency to overwork the back-stroke to a well-pitched-up ball on or just outside the off-stump, arousing and sometimes fulfilling the hope of a catch at wicket or slip. But the fortress was very tough.

He had a quiet and, if I may stretch an adjective, a dapper concentration peculiarly his own. His batting, like his appearance, was trim and cool. There were no disarrangements; no plunging and narrow recoveries. He saved energy, as he amassed runs, by avoiding the clumsy and irrelevant. So smooth and contained was his method that few spectators, with all respect to them and their shillings, could know how wonderful was the art presented to them.

Of the great batsmen I have seen, J. W. Hearne was the farthest removed from showmanship. He avoided pranks and waving of bats or caps. He did not decorate his craft; but he had a wit whose depth and breadth embraced many people and most things.

E. H. Bowley — *Sussex*

Ted Bowley, of Sussex, always looked to me like a number three batsman playing at number one. His ideas and execution were free and airy. He liked to begin with a square-cut or a hook for four. There were no wrestlings with theory or toiling extrications from the valley of mistrust. Nature was the tutor and the friend of his batting. He was too impatient sometimes, perhaps; too much the pure stroke player, who would rather force a length ball for a couple past cover-point than kill it gloomily a few yards from the bat. And so he made more mistakes than some opening batsmen of far less ability; but they were mistakes that were worth it; sacrifices to freedom; casualties in the battle against dullness.

He was interesting to watch, but ten times more so to bowl to. He had a powerful back-stroke, with a long pendulum, which he used more often than any other batsman I know; so often, that you felt he must overdo it, and so tried to have him with an outswinger pitched a little farther up than was convenient for such a stroke. It might succeed; but, far oftener, he would change his idea in a flash, and drive the ball past cover off the front foot. But the back-stroke was his glory; and here he excelled because his footwork was quick enough to 'give air' to the ball. I never saw a batsman who played this stroke with his bat and elbow so high, meeting a rising ball, which others would leave, with tremendous force, and hammering it straight or to the off boundary. Again, he would lean back and cut square from the off stump balls which others were content to stop. These were his favourite strokes, and they were enough to place him apart from the general run of batsmen. But in all else his equipment was full and correct. He was a notably fine player to slow bowling, partly because of his speed of foot and his naturally offensive method, partly because he knew so much about slow wiles, with which he himself harassed many a good player and broke many a stubborn partnership.

So much for technique. It exactly reflected the character of the man: open, witty, and generous. Perhaps I may be forgiven for confessing that, after Somerset, I next loved the Sussex grounds, and our matches against their cricketers. I felt the same about them as a very young friend of mine feels about afternoon tea-parties without grown-ups: 'I like them,' he says, 'they suit me.' Horsham is small and beautiful, and it used to have a pitch which, in a dry summer, could make a batsman mind his whiskers. The chemists hadn't got at it. Eastbourne is a very proper place for cricket, where the schoolboys brought their bananas and autograph-books and blunt pencils in their season.

But Brighton was the best. Was it the sea-fret that sharpened the turf there and, in a never-to-be-explained manner, helped the often derided swerver? But it had, for me at least, a mysterious pleasure, a secret none can utter. I have always loved cricket by the sea. And, in the train to Brighton, there were faces that made you ponder on the munificent variety of Providence. They alone were worth the journey. And the town itself exhaled an air of abandon, some inheritance from the

Regency, as if it contained and encouraged a world of men taking a holiday from work, reason, and their wives.

Of such things is cricket made.

A. P. F. Chapman — *Kent*

There is a certain sort of ball, of a good length on or near the off stump, from which even great batsmen are not inclined to score. True, they don't get out from it either. It's a dull scene. There is the ball; there is the stroke; and there is the neat little dot in the analysis. But at least the bowler draws comfort from knowing that he can produce a 'quietener'. He is on level terms sometimes. I never had this feeling when bowling to Percy Chapman. He had a discouraging habit, visible, too, in Frank Woolley, of hitting a good-length ball square or later to the off boundary when it should have been in the wicket-keeper's hands.

In his prime, that is, roughly, from 1920 to 1930, he was not to be kept quiet. He made more mistakes than Woolley, but, like him, he kept the attack; and he hit the ball even harder, if with more obvious effort. Now, that is greatness of a kind; and Chapman had a certain greatness as a batsman, a fielder, and a captain.

As weight increased and his feet answered more slowly, his batting and his confidence declined; but for some years after the last war they were magnificent. Tall, strong, and lithe, he was a left-handed hitter with orthodox defence, much of which was rendered unnecessary by a vast reach and an ability to drive good-length balls over the head of mid-off, bowler, and mid-on. His cover-driving, too, was immensely strong. In 1922 he made 102 not out for Cambridge against Oxford at Lord's, reaching his century with a drive off me that 'went through' so fine a cover-point as L. P. Hedges. Soon afterwards he made 160 for the Gentlemen against the Players. But for sheer hitting, probably the greatest innings of his career was one of 260 for Kent against Lancashire at Maidstone. Again and again he hooked and cut McDonald's fastest to the boundary. It was murder in the G. L. Jessop manner.

His captaincy, like his batting, was natural. It was founded on quick perceptions, a wide knowledge of human nature, and a happiness of disposition which native shrewdness never allowed to deteriorate into mere geniality. He knew his men as perhaps no other captain of modern times has known them. To a bowler, I can say from experience, his knowledge of the game gave the fullest opportunity, as his love of it gave the fullest desire, to do well. He was only twenty-five, and unversed in county captaincy, when he was made England's captain in the final Australian Test, on which the 'Ashes' depended. With such players as Hobbs and Rhodes under him, who had won Tests when he was reading of them at his first school, he yet relied on his own observations and made his own decisions. It was a great victory in a double sense.

He took some of his team to Australia two years later. No stronger combination has ever left England. Hobbs and Sutcliffe to open the batting, Hammond, Jardine, Leyland, Hendren, and Chapman to follow. Tate and Larwood began the bowling, backed up by Jack White, with a type of slow left-hand admirably suited to Australian pitches but seldom seen in the game. A great team with a great captain. Four matches were won in a row; the fifth, in Chapman's absence and with several players injured, was lost. In the England summer of 1930 Chapman added another victory, at Nottingham, his sixth against Australia in succession. At Lord's Bradman took control. Australia won, though Chapman nearly saved the match with an innings of 121. Two drawn matches followed.

Then, when all depended on the Oval Test, the selectors chose another captain, R. E. S. Wyatt. The Australians, when first they heard the news, did not believe it. Little further comment is needed. It was a miserably misguided decision. Wyatt was sound enough; but Chapman was brilliant; and he knew the men.

As a fielder he was among the greatest. In recent years he has stood at gully, where he has made wonderful saves and catches. But I best remember him at cover-point for Cambridge, where his large left hand would seize a fast swerving ball and return it to the wicket-keeper with a flick of the wrist.

How much Kent owed to his captaincy the players would tell

you. He brought breadth and humour to what was in danger of becoming narrow and parochial. He was an enemy of pomposity, and tradition without performance did not appeal to him. My own idea of a cricket match is to bowl on a fast pitch with damp on top and to have Chapman, as captain, in the gully.

C. P. Mead — *Hampshire*

'Hants wickets fall. But Mead still batting.' Such, in brief, was the history of Philip Mead. There have, doubtless, been greater left-handed batsmen; certainly, there have been more attractive. None could have been further removed from what is, almost unutterably, called a 'glamour-boy'. But what other batsman has there been whose broad back a bowler has so rejoiced to see receding to the pavilion at long and weary last? I should say none in this generation.

He was number four. Perhaps two wickets had fallen cheaply; and there the cheapness would end. He emerged from the pavilion with a strong, rolling gait; like a longshoreman with a purpose. He pervaded a cricket pitch. He occupied it and encamped on it. He erected a tent with a system of infallible pegging, then posted inexorable sentries. He took guard with the air of a guest who, having been offered a weekend by his host, obstinately decides to reside for six months. Having settled his whereabouts with the umpire, he wiggled the toe of his left boot for some fifteen seconds inside the crease, pulled the peak of a cap that seemed all peak, wiggled again, pulled again, then gave a comprehensive stare around him, as if to satisfy himself that no fielder, aware of the task ahead, had brought out a stick of dynamite. Then he leaned forward and looked at you down the pitch, quite still. His bat looked almost laughably broad.

I have known him start poorly, but very seldom. You had to try for a fastish break-back on the off-stump; a leg-break to the left-hander. For his part, he liked to start with a comfortable push to leg; an amiable and natural desire that needed thwarting. He could play all the strokes, without frill or fancy; but, in general, he avoided adventure because he could prosper without it. His off-drive was exceptionally strong.

Risers didn't seem to hurt or harass him; there was, often, a heavy sweater, and some very solid Mead behind it. In defence, he sometimes used a stroke peculiar to himself, correcting an intended forward stroke to a sudden half-cock, which stunned the ball dead in front of his bat. His solid method gave a false impression of slow scoring. Two occasions come to my mind when he was utterly beaten. Once at Taunton, when he ran down the pitch to play, not hit, a ball from J. C. White, and was bowled yards from home. Another time at Weston-super-Mare, when W. T. Greswell made a ball swing in from Mead's leg, pitch on the middle-and-off, and knock out the middle stump. Almost the stick of dynamite.

But mostly I think of Mead just batting on; a most fearful, interesting, and delightful opponent.

J. Daniell — *Somerset*

At the end of the 1920 season John Daniell, our captain, said to me: 'Well, come again next year and bowl some of your in-swingers; and for God's sake burn that straw hat.' There was a good deal of laughing in the Somerset side, and not a little cursing. The captain excelled at this, and nobody minded. It was part of the show, and would have been missed. Besides, he had good reason, for he was shepherd of a strange flock.

Like all men of character, he had strong prejudices. He believed that inswingers were heaven's gift for hitting, and, if assailed by them, he would have a terrific swat, whatever the state of the game. As often as not this would end in a skied catch to long-leg or deep square-leg; but that made no difference to the theory. The same assault would be committed next time.

He believed also in Homburg hats, and my chief memory of these games is Daniell standing with such a hat on the back of his head, very close at silly-point to Jack White's bowling, scowling severely at the batsmen, making terrific stops, and sometimes wonderful catches; or, perhaps, once in a while having a half-volley driven straight through him, when he would look at White, and some fearful observation would stir unexpressed on his lips.

As a batsman he was best in an awkward situation, for his defence was very fine, and his attack was strong enough to look after itself. He excelled against the off-breakers on a difficult pitch. Forward play was the foundation of his method, and none that I remember showed better that these off-breaks can often be smothered and played dead with a half-forward stroke. At the same time he never missed a chance of hitting the over-pitched off-break. He had a great duel with Morton, of Derbyshire, one day on a wet pitch at Weston, all sawdust, and off-spinners, and about once in two overs he would hit hard to mid-wicket for four or six. It was the best century I saw that season. He had a strong contempt for the obsession of back-play on fast wickets. This habit was increasing in the early 1920s, and, together with exaggerated pad-play, was already beginning to injure batting as a spectacle. I think that in some respects his batting improved with years, as the ability to hit violently was retarded. At any rate, he made a century in each innings at the age of forty-six, which argues a bed-rock correctness of method.

His exhortations to bowlers were memorable. They would begin, as we walked on to the field: 'Can you bowl these beggars out?' After twenty minutes or so, if success were still but a dream, he'd say: 'Can't you bowl these beggars out?' Still no change. And then: 'Oh, I believe I could bowl that beggar out.' There was a magnificent combativeness in his attitude to the opposing batsmen. If they played with what is known as 'commendable care', he would contemplate them from silly-point with a pitying gaze, as if the remainder of their sunless days could most suitably be passed in a wheel-chair or rest-home for the stricken and palsied. I believe that he stared some self-conscious batsmen from the wicket. They felt that they were a false pretence, and that further tenure was useless.

He was a great leader. You bowled or batted or fielded your best for him. He praised by look more than word; and I have thought sometimes that we and our swerves must have seemed pretty dull stuff to one who had begun under Sam Woods and learnt batting against Tom Richardson and C. J. Kortright.

There was no really fast bowling in these years. Sometimes he told us so. But the young don't believe that sort of thing.

J. W. H. T. Douglas — *Essex*

J. W. H. T. Douglas was by nature a bowler, by force of character a batsman. He was what is called a 'forearm' player; the
flashing drive and all those indefinable strokes that send the ball
anywhere between third man and cover-point were not possible
to that method. Such players miss some beauty of stroke, but
they also avoid much risk. Woodfull, the Australian, was of that
sort.

Yet Douglas was not dull, except to the blind, because when
he went in to bat he had so obviously arranged himself for a
battle. His figure was very strong, yet springy, as befitted a
boxer. As he walked to the wicket, capless, with shining black
hair, he looked almost jaunty but for the intention and hostility
in his gait. He looked as if he meant to come back from the fight
victorious or not at all; 'with his shield or on it'. After taking
guard, he did much entrenching with the toe of his boot, and
often bit his gloves into position, an action which he seemed to
repeat as often as he took renewed grip of any awkward
situation.

He was best to fast, rising bowling, standing right over the
line of the ball. To leg-breaks and googlies he was less im-
pressive, and must be considered to have come off second in
many duels with the Australian, Arthur Mailey. He had determined to conquer this weakness, and in the MCC tour to
Australia in 1920, when he was captain, he said to a fellow-
player: 'Watch me when I'm batting against Mailey, and tell
me what I do wrong.' When he was barracked for stubborn
batting, his obstinacy increased, and once, when some wags in
the crowd chanted 'The Dead March in Saul', he stopped play
and sat on his bat, refusing to resume till the concert was over.
A delightful scene.

As a bowler he was quite indomitable and nearly tireless. He
launched a tremendous attack in the opening overs. He could
make the ball swerve either way very late in its flight and come
off the pitch wickedly fast. Also, he bowled very straight,
without waste. When he just missed the stumps he would wave
his arms, and often testify above and below. There was nothing
theatrical about it. They were the instinctive gestures of

abundant keenness and pugnacity. In the Gentlemen *v.* Players, at Lord's in 1924, he bowled a wonderful opening over from the Pavilion end to Hobbs. I think Hobbs played at all six balls and only touched one. The very wickets seemed to shrink. Douglas was beyond speech, arms akimbo. Hobbs, tapping the pitch in his thoughtful way, said: 'Well bowled, Colonel; well bowled.'

Not long ago a book on cricket was published in which Douglas was said to have been harsh and tyrannical as a captain. This is a misrepresentation of act. To the slacker and the 'trimmer' he was often merciless. But his wrath was short-lived, and he enjoyed the terse and humorous answer. He was something less than a man who could not stand up to the breeze.

I shall remember him for his kindness and for the inspiration of his example; for a short innings that he played in a foul light at Lord's against Maurice Tate and Howell, the fast bowler. I watched him from the other end as he took most of the bowling on his splice and gloves. In due course I appealed against the light, with success; and he cursed me as if I had interrupted some care-free partnership in a school house-match! Then he laughed, and muttered: 'A number eleven appealing against the light. Marvellous!'

He was drowned in a collision at sea, at the age of forty-eight. Almost certainly he could have saved himself; but he went down to save his father, and wasn't seen again.

His skill was great; but his courage, strength, and enthusiasm were greater. His philosophy was simple – 'Fight on!'

C. W. L. Parker — *Gloucestershire*

On a sticky wicket Charles Parker, the slow left-hander of Gloucestershire, was the greatest bowler I have seen; for, then, there was no man whom he could not make to look like a child batting with a pencil.

His flight may have been less difficult to judge than that of Blythe or Rhodes or J. C. White, but there was no running out to squash the break. It came just too fast and too low; and the spin was so acute that he would hit the off-stump with a ball that had pitched just outside the leg.

He wasted nothing; to every ball some stroke had to be offered; and there was Walter Hammond roaming, predatory, at very short slip. In such a mood, against Yorkshire, Parker once hit the stumps with five consecutive balls, but the second was a no-ball.

On fast pitches he was just very good indeed. It could not be otherwise with that beautiful action, all ease and hidden danger. Only two bowlers, Rhodes and A. P. Freeman, have taken more wickets. He took over 200 in 1922, 1924, 1925, 1926, and, at the age of forty-five, in 1931; and it cannot all have been done by sun after rain. Yet the silly saying went that Parker could not bowl on a plumb pitch; as if so great an artist were a sort of one-pitch man, like some elder who must occupy but one certain chair in the room, and, if that be taken, cannot sit down at all.

And so he played in only one Test match, against Australia, at Manchester in 1921. He took 2 for 32 in the sole innings of 175; 28 overs, 16 maidens; Macartney bowled for 13; Pellew caught for 17. He went in an aeroplane to another, but, so he used to say, 'they signalled that the pitch was dry, and I flew away again'.

In temperament he was an ironical as the fate that held him down. Slim and angular, he was a sad-eyed executioner. He was never easily convinced that things were good, and I have seen him read a bowling analysis, in which he had taken eight wickets, as if the whole thing were an undoubted forgery. Under stress, he spoke sharply and to the point; and once, when mid-off and mid-on, neither of them athletes, turned to pursue a straight drive off his bowling, he said: 'There go my greyhounds.'

His first match was against Lancashire, in 1905, and with his second ball he took the wicket of R. H. Spooner. But not till 1920 did he take 100 wickets in a season, and he was thirty-eight when he began to deal in 200 aggregates. In all, he took 3,274 wickets at 19.48 each.

He came late into only a partial kingdom. But he was a king indeed.

Lord Tennyson — *Hampshire*

In the gathering twilight of one May evening at Oxford, Lord Tennyson, then captain of the Hampshire cricket team, judging, rightly, that the University number eleven had exceeded himself and his time-quota, went on to bowl at the north, or croquet lawn, end. He retired a long, long way behind the wicket, then pivoted abruptly, grinding his right heel.

To the batsman, musing alone about half-way between bowler and wicket-keeper, it seemed that his antagonist, having intended to make some speech to the crowd, had suddenly changed his mind. To the same batsman, musing alone some twenty years later, the idea strongly returns that the bowler, like Mr Luffey, 'applied the ball to his right eye for several seconds'. Be that as it may, the first ball was an appallingly fast wide on the off; the second flew over the middle stump, and disappointment was expressed.

As a batsman Lord Tennyson was a most dangerous opponent, especially to fast and fast-medium bowling. He has been described as a hitter, which is less than half the truth; for, either in defence or attack, he could use a forward-stroke which, for sheer decision and orthodoxy, I have never seen excelled. His back-play was less convincing, and his footwork was somewhat too heavy for a full answer to accomplished spin-bowlers, but that forward stroke was, like the man, tough and determined. On a fast pitch you would more easily pass or overcome some of the best professional batsmen, because they might sometimes be persuaded into an inopportune back-stroke; Tennyson, hardly ever.

After a brief career at Cambridge University he tapped fame on the shoulder with an innings of 110 on his first appearance in first-class cricket for MCC *v*. Oxford at Lord's. At Lord's again, eight years later, when the England batsmen, except Frank Woolley, withered before the artillery of Gregory and McDonald, his courage and forward-stroke gave the answer in a second innings of 74 not out. At Leeds, for the Third Test, he was made captain. Hobbs having retired with appendicitis, Tennyson split his hand fielding. Grimly elated by catastrophe, he scored 63 at number nine, making many strokes with one hand against the fast bowlers. A severe attack of gout might have brought him to the century. The match and the rubber were lost, but it was Tennyson that was remembered.

The drama of Leeds was followed by the comedy of Manchester. Rain having spoilt the first day and the crowd having exchanged remarks with the police, Tennyson declared the innings closed at 5.50 p.m. Warwick Armstrong 'strongly demurred'. They retired to the pavilion to argue; Law 55 was read: and the England innings was continued. Whereupon Armstrong, weakened perhaps by the strain of dialectic, broke Law 14 by bowling two consecutive overs. The match, like the talking, was never finished. At the Oval, where Armstrong retired into the deep and read a passing newspaper, Tennyson played an innings of 51.

For all these triumphs I like to think of him most as standing at mid-off for Hampshire, throwing a burly shadow and, from time to time, a disparaging observation to some friend at the crease. Nowhere was his geniality more enjoyed than in the West Indies, where once, in the close season, a spectator was heard to ask with pleasing ambiguity: 'Is the lord coming next time?'

He belongs more properly to the Regency. He would have questioned Brummell's cravat, flattened the hardest nuts at faro, and made 100 in a single-wicket match after a thirty-six-hour spell at Almack's.

I asked him once about his Laureate grandfather, and he said he just remembered a beard peering over his bed.

A. E. R. Gilligan — *Sussex*

Arthur Gilligan ran up to bowl like the winner from scratch covering the last twenty yards in the Powderhall Handicap. He seemed to run nearly as fast as he bowled, and for a few years in the early 1920s that was very fast indeed. Then came a severe blow over the heart when batting, and, when he went to Australia in winter 1924 as England's captain, he was but a shadow of the man who, a few months before, had taken 6 for

7 in South Africa's innings of 30 at Edgbaston.

At Dulwich, as a schoolboy, he not only excelled in cricket but was a runner and hurdler of great ability. After service in the 1914–18 war, he opened the bowling for Cambridge in 1919, and, against Oxford in the second innings, his pace and accuracy were remarkable. Only D. J. Knight was his full equal, and it was a duel worthy of a Test match.

A few days earlier, he and J. H. Naumann had put on 177 for the last Cambridge wicket against his own county of Sussex. He was a tough, rough batsman, strong in the drive, and best against the faster bowlers.

In 1922 he took over the Sussex captaincy. In the same summer Maurice Tate suddenly jumped from useful to great, and in 1923 the Gilligan-Tate opening attack was, on a fast wicket, something that no other county could quite equal. Both bowled to hit the stumps, using slips rather than a close leg field.

Beyond this, Gilligan was a wonderful mid-off, of almost acrobatic agility and unflinching courage. Here, too, he would return with a nod and a laugh those despairing gestures and frantic signals of Tate, who had once more burnt the stumps with beauty.

He may not have been a great captain – you must keep winning to be that – but he was a great leader, because he knew how the game ought to be played and saw that his cricketers knew it too. Under Gilligan Sussex cricket was reborn. He gave and received unbounded enjoyment; and, apart from the technical skill, this was done by bringing to the first-class game exactly the same things that make worthwhile a club, or village, or school match.

With him there were no sharpnesses, no petty restraints, no mathematical cricket. He won or lost plumb straight. Thus he lost in Australia, and earned from some critics a name for weakness. But, to those who played with or against him, he remains the kind of cricketer that a man might wish to be.

G. T. S. Stevens — *Middlesex*

G. T. S. Stevens was one of the best all-round cricketers that the modern game has produced; but business seized him early. Had the fortune of life made him a professional, he would surely have had his 1,000 runs and 100 wickets in every season from 1920 to 1939. Instead, after 1923, he made occasional appearances for Middlesex, the Gentlemen, and England, with some Saturdays for Hampstead thrown in.

He would emerge from the City to bowl out Macartney or to make 100 off Maurice Tate; and, the other day, a young cricketer asked me about Stevens as we once used to ask about the Dohertys or John Roberts. So hungrily do the generations tread each other down. Happily, I was able to tell him.

Stevens was an infant prodigy who lived up to it. He played for the Gentlemen at Lord's when he was still a boy at University College School, and he looked like the hero in a school story who makes 100 against the visiting team for Marylebone. In those days he was a hitter with a good defence, and a leg-break bowler with a prancing run and a high action. He made leg-breaks and googlies look the only natural way of bowling, whereas most of his kind seem to be unfolding some difficult and rather disreputable rite. Not since J. N. Crawford had so early ripe a cricketer burst upon the game.

At Oxford he won his Blue early and, with R. H. Bettington, taxed the very best batsmen that came to the Parks. His ability, too, as a close leg side fielder was severely tried by the opening bowler's weakness for inswingers. In the gully, also, he brought off remarkable catches.

In 1922, as captain, he was called upon to play a series of saving innings at number six. Again and again he turned disaster into moderate respectability, and at Lord's a second innings Oxford score of 17 for 7 somehow, owing to Stevens's defence, reached 81 in the end. A sad story. Next season, on a wet pitch at Lord's, he was called upon to bowl off-breaks only. He did so, and he and Bettington sent Cambridge back twice in a day for an aggregate of 195. In 1923 he made a century against the Players at Lord's. It was not without fault, and was overshadowed by a brilliant 100 by M. D. Lyon.

Neither of these two young players went to Australia in the winter of 1924.

By now Stevens was at the height of his powers. As a bowler, he had the most difficult googly to detect of any of his kind, and, unlike so many, he never lost the leg spin. In batting, he used a short back-lift, rather in the Woodfull manner, but great power of wrist and forearm enabled him to drive with unexpected fierceness, often over mid-off's head.

In 1926 he played against Australia twice. At Manchester, in a drawn match, he took the wickets of Bardsley, Andrews, and A. J. Richardson. In the famous victory at the Oval he bowled Macartney and Oldfield. His scores were 24, 17, and 22. This, at the age of twenty-five, was the beginning and end of his England cricket.

It might have been a tremendous story; for he had true genius.

T. B. Mitchell — *Derbyshire*

If the cricketers of A.D. 2000 have any time to read of their forerunners, it is not likely that T. B. Mitchell, the little Derbyshire leg-break bowler, will long detain their interest or much excite their wonder. They will find that he played twice for England at home, once in Australia, that from 1929 to 1938 he took his 100 wickets a season. Good enough, they will say, but not so good as so-and-so and so-and-so, and they will turn the page.

But Tom Mitchell is one of the great bowlers, an artist of spin and deception, a master of flight and variety. But he only does it when he feels like it. He is not interested in a cold level of efficiency. He cannot, so to speak, sit down to it every day, as Maurice Tate or 'Tich' Freeman or Jack White sat down to it. His brain, shrewd and calculating, is of the North; but his temperament is torrid, of the far South. He calls a spade a spade and something more, and I have sometimes thought that he wouldn't mind having a something-more spade to give a good wanging to the pitch, or the umpire, or the batsman, or his own captain.

Yet mostly he argues with intangible enemies, with leg-breaks that have spun just too much, catches that have defied instructions, puffs of wind that have interfered with his own private theories of ballistics. There is something of Donald Duck about him. No cricketer so conveys to the spectators the perplexities and frustration of man at the mercy of malignant fate. He has much in common with that golfer who missed short putts because of the uproar of the butterflies in the adjoining meadows. He is the comedian of tragedy.

His overs are rapid and impatient. Very short of leg, strangely long in body, with sleeves flapping, he pivots into the attack, and astonishes the batsman with a sharp burst of leg-breaks, top-spinners, googlies, and old-fashioned off-breaks. A ghastly long-hop is hooked whizzingly past short-leg's head. He stands, arms akimbo, reproving the invisible, then flicks up the returned ball from boot to hand. Next ball, he emits a shattering appeal, and his very spectacles flash disagreement with the answer. But, on his red-letter days, when all the tricks are going right, he is the master; and then he looks as if he might break into song or execute a rhumba.

As a batsman he is often good for two or three boundaries, but likes to play most of his strokes somewhere in the middle of the pitch. His fielding, especially at cover-point, is often brilliant. He has taken all 10 wickets in an innings at Leicester, in 1935. He took valuable wickets at Brisbane, in the Fourth Test, when D. R. Jardine's side won back the 'Ashes'. But, most of all, he has taken pomposity and convention by their noses and tweaked them sharply.

A. Mitchell — *Yorkshire*

In a north country tavern a few years ago Maurice Leyland was discussing cricket and cricket reporting with an eminent writer, famous for style and fancy, when Mitchell (A.) joined himself to the party and, after listening gravely for a few minutes, abruptly remarked: 'Mr ———, I don't like tha writing; it's too flowery.' Whereat Leyland, displeased with this captious and personal turn in the conversation, retorted: 'And that's more than anyone would say of tha batting, Arthur.'

In this humorous rebuke lies the story of those many York-shire cricketers who have won matches but no place in the headlines, batsmen of a rather low but consistently hostile temperature, men blessed, or cursed, with an ineradicable love of the crease. Among these, Arthur Mitchell, with 44 centuries to his name, takes a high and enduring place.

But, lost somewhere in this able and saturnine batsman there lies a tremendous hitter, with long and powerful stroke; lost because he grew into part of the Yorkshire machine. Publicans are popularly credited with red faces, bakers are supposed to walk about with flour in their hair; in the same way Arthur Mitchell bears about with him, and will never lose, the marks of his apprenticeship to Yorkshire. It was severe.

His promise was grimly and briefly approved in 1922, and, four years later, he was allowed sixteen innings for the county, averaging 32.7. In 1927 he did less well. But in 1928 he topped the 1,000, and began further to assert himself by wearing his cap at an angle which could not have been wholly approved by Wilfred Rhodes. In 1930 he scored five centuries, averaging 51.5, and in 1933 he strung four hundreds in a row, three of them during the Scarborough Festival, exceeded 2,000 runs, and went, that winter, to India with MCC under D. R. Jardine.

He had emerged into a tough, angular batsman who might, if he remembered his boyhood, suddenly hit an enormous six; and he contemplated the bowler with a solemn and unforgiving stare.

As a fielder he is brilliant anywhere, but has specialized in the silly positions, leg and off. He has the prehensile hand and the telescopic arm.

I have seen him bowl a few overs very steadily, like a dutiful horse. He is fond of imparting to common truths the air of mystery and novelty, and he once said to me: 'To write on cricket tha wants to watch it.' A curious reflection.

L. G. Crawley — *Essex*

At the age of fifteen Leonard Crawley had that flourishing sandy moustache which has been poised menacingly over many a golf ball and fiercely proposed down the pitch to many a confounded bowler. It can be seen in House groups of the First Great War period at Harrow, famous nurse of cricket and Crawleys, who have cut a notch on almost every game that demands a strong wrist and a keen eye.

This Crawley, as he should, made his century against Eton, and failed by only two runs to make another for Cambridge against Oxford, and so to draw level with his uncle. Thereafter, he played from time to time for Essex, adding to natural ability and a magnificent sense of attack the shrewdness born of experience and a power of concentration that was almost audible.

He became that rarest of birds, an opening batsman whose idea of setting the scorers in motion was to drive the first ball of the innings smack against the sight-screen. At Leyton, once, he forced Maurice Tate, then in his prime, to set deep-fields, and his century, one of the finest played in this generation, beat the clock and Sussex. But his cricket appearances became fewer. The driving and the dank sandshoes, flickering at deep third man and mid-on, were soon nearly a memory. He removed the former, sometimes the latter, to St Andrews and Sunningdale.

As a golfer he started lower and finished higher, at any rate in print and record. For Cambridge he played tenth in a team of ten, and lost to an Oxford player who drove with an iron. His hitting was terrific, but the ball, as he used to say, 'refused to use the fairway'. Very well, it must be taught. So, with an industry not exceeded by Henry Cotton, and such as would drive the mere golfer to nervous atrophy and even the grave, he set out for control and fame.

Soon he won the English close championship and the Putter of the Oxford and Cambridge Society. His driving lost, as it could afford to do, some ten yards in length, but the ball had learnt discipline. His iron-play was of a length seldom seen and of an accuracy reasonably approaching to that of the best professionals; his putting as good as the next man's. Only his judgment of distance remained uncertain. He has never quite gauged his own strength and, even in his most brilliant rounds, he is capable of hitting an iron-shot high over the green when his opponent has sneaked to the confines with a full brassey.

His greatest match was for Great Britain against America

in the Walker Cup singles, played away from home. He was set against the then almost invincible George Voigt, and beat him on the thirty-sixth green by holing a downhill putt of some six yards. But Medal play is his choice and his excellence. He does not fear the phantom, and has emerged unbowed from many a tussle with old St Andrews, which revenged itself, in the last Walker Cup match before this war, by encouraging that great American golfer, Mr Fischer, into an unanswerable sequence of threes. Crawley had a round of 72 and no hope.

Yet, with all his iron-shots and medals, I think Crawley was the greater man when he banged the length-ball back past Tate's large boots.

H. Larwood — *Nottinghamshire*

In cricket between the wars the two most magnificent sights that I have seen were Hammond batting and Larwood bowling. In skill, or style, or numbers others may be argued as equals or superiors; but in both these cricketers I have found something heroic, something of immortal fire, which conquers argument. Perhaps it is mere envy, the hopeless desire to bat like the one or to bowl like the other.

Very short was Larwood's bowling life; I mean the Larwood who blew like a gale and bent the flower of Australia; for there was a fastish bowler of the same name and aspect who later bowled for Nottinghamshire very well, as they say, with a much shorter run; well enough to play for England, perhaps. But the real Larwood lived and flourished for only eight years.

Half-way through the summer of 1925, at the age of twenty, he was raised from the second to the first eleven of Nottinghamshire, and he took 73 wickets at 18 each; with long arms in proportion to medium height, and tremendous strength of back.

In 1926 he arrived. It was the last hour of the first day of the Oval Test, the decider with Australia. England had made only 280. Then Larwood had Bardsley caught at the wicket for 2, and bowled Andrews for 3. In the second innings, Australia needing 415 to win, he soon had Woodfull and

Macartney grandly caught in the slips by Geary, and the spine of the batting was broken.

In 1928 he went to Australia under A. P. F. Chapman. In the First Test, after scoring 70, he had Woodfull out for 0, caught at third slip by his captain, one of the most wonderful catches ever seen; then he bowled Ponsford and Kelleway. After the first two Tests he fell away somewhat, and his virtue was still in sudden penetration rather than in sustained excellence. Always, whether for Nottinghamshire or England, he needed and received careful nursing.

He played only three of the five Tests here in 1930, and his 4 wickets cost 73 runs each. Then came the second visit to Australia, and the uproar, and the triumph. Long ago the noise has died; but the greatness of Larwood lives on, though we in England were never again to see it in its fullness. It was the giants who fell before him; Woodfull for 0 in the Second Test; 10 wickets for 124; Bradman and McCabe in the Third Test; Bradman twice and Ponsford in the Fourth; Bradman and Woodfull in the Fifth; and an innings of 98 thrown in, ended with a catch by Ironmonger, who caught but little. In those Tests he took 33 wickets for 19 each. And it was the end.

Once, in a county match, when Larwood was in the middle of that glorious run-up, the batsman raised his hand and stopped him. Perhaps the dull reason was simply that he wasn't ready. I think, rather, that the batsman, a humble enough performer, was seized with that last love of life which must have urged victims of old to address some trivial and delaying remark to the executioner. A few seconds later the blow fell, and the bails whizzed past the wicket-keeper.

R. J. O. Meyer — *Somerset*

R. J. O. Meyer left English cricket in the middle 1920s as a fast-medium paced bowler with a late swerve from leg and a fine free action; also, he was a batsman who, at number eight or nine, liked to raise the covers with those strokes peculiar to rackets players and golfers. At Cambridge, from 1924 to 1926, he was an opening bowler, of an ability comparable to that of C. H. Gibson and G. O. Allen. But he was strangely unlucky against Oxford, and even the more attentive critics do like a bowler who takes wickets.

'Nothing,' adds a contemporary report, 'remarkable was seen in the batting of Meyer during these three 'Varsity matches,' overlooking, I think, a pleasant inclination to drive balls of good length into the deep and to cut yorkers past backward point. Soon, it may be added, nothing at all, remarkable or otherwise, was seen of Meyer in English cricket, for, after a spell with Hertfordshire, in the Minor Counties Competition, he went to India. From there came occasional news that his great natural abilities were earning their reward in the Pentangular and other mathematical cricket tournaments. Then he came home and settled as a schoolmaster in Somerset.

Meanwhile, a new cricketer, R. J. O. Meyer II, had been evolved, subtly arranged, in bowling, to flout the adage 'old age must come', and, in batting, to achieve a higher place in the order than those which are on nodding terms with the extras. The wilder delights had been pruned; strong power of scoring remained, but had been reinforced by watchful back-play, and an extraordinarily vicious hook. Over all there lay a veneer of respectability, hitherto lacking. This method brought, in 1936, an innings of 202 not out against Lancashire, which was one of the best exhibitions of batting seen that season.

The new style of bowling, with both spins at slow-medium to medium pace, and other recondite variations, was one which the older critics had long cited as the best, if not the only, way to bowl. Its author admitted that, highly as he thought of it, it had one great disadvantage – the need of twelve or thirteen fielders. 'It works,' he said in his philosophic way, 'but, like the earlier models of the motor-cycle, it needs a lot of attention.'

It was a loss for Somerset, and cricket, that this most experimental of all modern cricketers should rarely be able to play except in August. One month or so is not long enough to work out all the theories. But he had time to show a rare and remarkable artistry which must place him high among the all-rounders of the present day.

H. Verity — *Yorkshire*

Some think that Verity is not a great bowler. They are wrong.

I have heard such adjectives as 'good' and 'mechanical' applied to him. The first is merely inadequate; the second is true in so far that he is the nearly perfect bowling machine, directed by one of the acutest brains that the game can have known, and kept in motion, against the best batsmen, by an indomitable purpose.

His prevailing pace is slow-medium, though sometimes he likes to whisk down a yorker or inswinger that may be nearly fast. Only on broken, dusty, wet, or sticky pitches does he bowl at a genuinely slow pace, and then not all the time.

For exhaustive comparisons I have neither the space nor the sufficient reason. But, for those who like to measure cricketers with each other as if they were triangles or trout, a little arithmetic may be of interest.

Verity has played in first-class cricket for ten seasons, 1930–39, starting for Yorkshire, a little late, at the age of twenty-five. A decade is, perhaps, the shortest period over which a bowler's performance can be nicely judged. By then he has met most weathers and conditions, and if he be, like Verity, an England bowler, nearly all the world's batsmen who matter. Over these ten years, for Yorkshire and England, Verity's bowling record is: 1,956 wickets at 14.87 each. Remember, too, that he has been bowling for the most part on pitches whose over-preparation evoked some two years ago special advice from MCC.

And now, just for a little meditation, I add the records, as given by *Wisden*, of eight other famous English slow or slow-medium left-hand bowlers: – (i) J. Briggs (Lancashire) – 22 years – 2,200 wickets – at 16.10 each. (ii) R. Peel (Yorkshire) – 18 years – 1,754 wickets – at 16.21 each. (iii) W. Rhodes (Yorkshire) – 29 years – 4,188 wickets – at 16.71 each. (iv) C. Blythe (Kent) – 16 years – 2,506 wickets – at 16.81 each. (v) J. C. White (Somerset) – 25 years – 2,358 wickets – at 18.56 each. (vi) C. W. L. Parker (Gloucestershire) – 29 years – 3,274 wickets – at 19.48 each. (vii) G. Dennett (Gloucestershire) – 20 years – 2,147 wickets – at 19.82 each (viii) F. E. Woolley (Kent) – 29 years 2,068 wickets – at 19.86 each.

Not all these years constitute full seasons, but those are the figures. Draw from them what conclusions you will. Whatever they be, Verity's present bowling average stands at over one unit better than that of J. Briggs, and at almost exactly five units better than that of F. E. Woolley, and he has taken wickets at an average of nearly 196 a season.

He is a scholarly bowler; graduating, to judge by his inquiring attitudes, in science and experimental philosophy rather than in any romantic Faculty. He is tall, and much stronger than his pace needs. His run-up, longer than in most of his kind, has a measured delicacy that you would expect from this fastidious and nearly prim craftsman. Only his delivery has a grace which mathematics can't explain.

I have seen him, in certain company, become rather bored with his bowling and their batting, which is something of a weakness. A fellow-bowler in Yorkshire says that, to get the best from Verity, you must tell him that everything depends on him; which argues the vanity of the artist.

In his battles with Bradman he has lost more than he has won; but he remains Bradman's Cricket Enemy No. 1. He has twice taken all 10 wickets for Yorkshire at Leeds; on the latter occasion, against Nottinghamshire, for 10 runs in 19.4 overs. Well, well!

As a batsman he looks like Sutcliffe gone stale. That is, pretty good.

L. E. G. Ames — *Kent*

Since the game began cricketers have argued about wicketkeepers. Ninety per cent of the arguments have a partisan and territorial origin, and are therefore suspect, if not negligible. A Yorkshireman, for instance, will not admit, at least verbally, the superiority of any Southerner. The older among them can still be sometimes heard to mutter that David Hunter was a better wicket-keeper than Dick Lilley. They may be right; but if they were wrong they wouldn't care!

But I shall boldly say that, since the prime of G. Duckworth, of Lancashire, about 1926–32, L. E. G. Ames, of Kent, has been England's best wicket-keeper, and has been worthy to stand there for England even if he had been a batsman whom the horse and roller followed in a knowing way to the crease. It is no secret that the England selectors, in picking their wicket-keeper, are guided largely by the opinion expressed or, transmitted to them, of cricketers playing regularly in the County Championships. It is known that this opinion has, with few exceptions, plumped for Ames in the last seven or eight years. That's good enough for the selectors; and it should be good enough for Mr Thomas Smith, scowling over the absence of his own favourite stumper.

Other wicket-keepers may have hands as sure, may even be more consistent in form; for Ames needs the great occasion to extort his full powers, and, like the late Harry Smith, of Gloucestershire, he enjoys and often asks for a run-about in the field, where he is a fine extra cover-point. But he excels as a wicket-keeper by reason of the same qualities that have brought him eight Test centuries and, in summer 1933, an aggregate of 3,058 runs – balance, speeed of foot, and thought. He is a quiet, smiling executioner; as near, I have always felt, to being sorry for his victim as his lethal profession admits. But there is an old prejudice against versatility. That Ames should do two things superbly seems to aggravate many who cannot do either of them at all.

Good slow bowlers make a wicket-keeper's records; and Kent, who had such men as Blythe, D. W. Carr, and Frank Woolley for Huish, have provided Ames with Freeman (A. P.) and C. S. Marriott. Even so, Ames's performance is wonderful. Here are the three best years – 1928, 121 wickets and 1,919 runs; 1929, 127 wickets (the highest yet recorded) and 1,795 runs; 1932, 100 wickets and 2,482 runs. You can't talk that away.

As a batsman his style is what may be called the correct-aggressive. His speed of foot makes him the equal, often the master, of the best slow bowlers he has met; his courage is unaffected by a violent attack. All his strokes are easily made, with supple wrists; but the game's best strokes are his own best, the off-drive, the forward-cut, and those which indescrib-ably partake of both.

There is an echo of W. R. Hammond about his batting,

which is not surprising, for they have been much together both on and off the field, and they share the gifts of determination, humour, and courtesy.

R. W. V. Robins — *Middlesex*

However big the crowd or serious the occasion there is something about the cricket of Walter Robins which suggests half-holidays and kicking your hat along the pavement. Perky is the word.

For business reasons he was unable to accept MCC's invitation to join D. R. Jardine's team for Australia in 1932. That was a pity. His levity, never broadening into buffoonery, would have come in handy. Before the balloon turned into a bomb he might have pricked it. Either he would have done that or else would have passed the months in a prolonged fishing expedition. He was not made for controversy, though no opponent is more likely to find the right answer in action or word.

He is one of the few first-rate all-rounders in English cricket, having escaped the bonds of specialization. In his last season at Highgate School, 1925, he was a medium-fast bowler and a forceful, if correct, batsman. This style of batting remained with him throughout his three years at Cambridge, and in 1928 brought him scores of 53 and 101 not out against Oxford. Late in his Cambridge days he learnt the leg-break, top-spinner, and googly. His spin is acute; his pace slow, even for this style; his flight high, and, at best, very worrying. Even more than most of his kind, he varies from brilliance to futility.

There was no hitch in his progress. In 1929 he took 162 wickets in first-class cricket, made 1,134 runs, and appeared in a Test against South Africa. In 1930 he played for England against Australia at Nottingham and Lord's. He struck a shrewd blow in Australia's second innings, bowling the great Bradman when he had made a century. It was a googly, mistaken for a leg-break. England won by some 90 runs. In 1935 he played three times against South Africa, including an innings of 108 at Old Trafford. In 1936–37 he went with G. O. Allen's team to Australia, and though his bowling was rarely effective he contributed an innings of 61 at Melbourne and, more still, a wise and genial support to his captain more valuable than runs. In 1937 he captained England at home in the three Tests against New Zealand.

As a fielder he is great, excelling at cover-point. Very quick in judgment and movement, he makes some wonderful saves on the backhand, so to speak, and he throws nearly as well as Bradman. With advancing years his batting has become more eccentric, and he has evolved a technique of 'advance and retire' peculiarly his own. He is a master of the unexpected and enjoys a late cut from the top of the middle stump.

Many think that he is a batsman who doesn't care; but this slap-dash method comes from an impatient and nervous temperament. As a cricketer he lives on a sharp edge, and sometimes, as a captain, his keenness would turn to anxiety. For which reason I think he is better as second-in-command than as leader.

He is a cricketer to go and see. He is entertainment in failure or success, and it is almost worth the gate-money to hear him laugh.

A. R. Gover — *Surrey*

The Oval, in normal times, is where you go to see people bat. There may be other more important, if less relevant, purposes; but since the heroic days of Lohmann, Lockwood, and that lion of bowling, Tom Richardson, batting has been the chief thing at the Oval.

Now this is a credit to that remarkable groundsman 'Bosser' Martin, recently retired, and it's very nice for the batsmen and their averages; but the tiresome fly in the beautiful ointment is that far too many mediocre batsmen have made far too many runs at the Oval. Yet they would have made goodness knows how many hundreds more if Alfred Richard Gover, fast bowler, had not been there to stop the nonsense.

He left the homely atmosphere of dear old Leyton for the not more conspicuous beauties of Kennington when he was scarcely out of his 'teens, tall and lanky, about 1928. He had been told all about the Oval, and still he came. Which was, like

Gover, brave and optimistic.

He had much, besides batsmen on the other side, to conquer. His run-up to the wicket was, and remains, a little disjointed and exciting; rather as if he were exchanging insults at extreme range with the flighty conductor of an omnibus that had the legs of him by half a mile per hour. Spectators and critics fixed on this, and ignored or couldn't see the excellence of the action at the moment of delivery, the full follow-through of the body, and the admirable timing of the propulsion. Luckily, a few people who mattered saw these things, and, more luckily still, Gover began to take wickets, and good wickets, too. But, in certain quarters and for some years, the prejudice remained, the ridiculous assumption that a bowler takes wickets with his boots.

Throughout this period of probation, as it were, Gover continued to try as hard as any fast bowler has ever tried. Sometimes he might have been a little hasty or testy, but what's the use of a fast bowler with no temperament? They are racehorses, not cows.

The Oval crowd, in their rough and friendly way, began to understand this Gover. To them he could never be Bill Hitch, as 'our Bill' was on a hot August Bank Holiday against the men of Nottingham. But they admired the persistence. The laughter and criticism began to fade.

By the middle 1930s he was established. In 1935 he took 4 wickets with 4 balls at Worcester. In 1936 he took 200 wickets at 17.73 each, and played for England against India at Manchester. Next year he took 201 wickets at 18.98 each, and played for England against New Zealand at Lord's and the Oval. I wish he could have been picked against Australia, if only once.

It is a simple history; and a threefold triumph – over himself, over the crowd, and over the best batsmen that the other counties could put against him.

W. E. Bowes — *Yorkshire*

William Bowes, of Yorkshire, the best bowler of his kind in cricket today, is a very learned looking man. I have sometimes suspected that 'Bowes' is only a term he uses for cricket, and that, like Will Hay, he conducts private research under his own name, and probably lectures to a small but discerning coterie of fellow-scientists. In the lounge of an hotel, the evening before an Australian Test of 1934, he presented, for my solution a geometrical problem over the sherry. He might as well have invited Professor Einstein to field for him at close short-leg.

In the same way that the heron gives a false idea that it is flying slowly, Bowes seldom impresses the spectator with any sense of speed or effort. His run up is somewhat shambling. His whole approach to the supreme task in cricket suggests, quite falsely, indolence, negligence, almost reluctance. But, if you watch closely, you will see the full use of great height, strong shoulder, and pliant wrist. His direction is unusually accurate; he can swing even a worn ball very late from leg, and make it leave the pitch very fast, and often with an awkward kick.

In his earlier seasons – he began regularly in 1931 – he sometimes exchanged accuracy for mere bounce, but this practice became rarer, and, having learnt to fuse restraint with hostility, he stands out as the most difficult fast-medium bowler in the country. Against Australia, at the Oval in 1938, he gave a wonderful exhibition of sustained accuracy and controlled swerve, and in the first innings took 5 for 49 in 19 overs.

For some years he was under contract to the MCC, and it was a strange, if instructive, sight to see him, fresh from some triumph for Yorkshire, attuning his art in the practice-nets at Lord's to the imperfect batsmanship of some member who doubtless went away thinking himself something of a player after all.

Bowes went to Australia with D. R. Jardine's team in 1932–33, but appeared in only one Test, when he caused Bradman to play on first ball. As a batsman he is seldom seriously extended, and not always included in the season's averages; but occasionally he silences criticism with an off-drive so regal that I wonder what might have happened if he had focused those spectacles exclusively on the study of batsmanship.

C. B. Harris — *Nottinghamshire*

Cricket should be heard as well as seen; and, as an idle dream I should like to field for an hour at slip with C. B. Harris, Nottinghamshire, batting; Major J. W. A. Stephenson, bowling; Brooks, of Surrey, keeping wicket; Sims at silly-point; and William Reeves as bowler's umpire. I doubt if Mr George Black has ever devised so rich a show.

In print Charles Harris is no more than a number one batsman of moderate pretensions, of sufficient success, and little more, to keep him in his place, which, from an earthly point of view, is mainly at Trent Bridge; but his spirit and imaginings are not to be confined within the bounds of that practical and historic arena.

For Harris is a dreamer. He is a strange addition to Walter Keeton as they walk out to open an innings; Keeton strung up, concentrated, quick-glancing; Harris serenely distrait, revolving idealistic strokes against an attack that will not occur; lagging sometimes a pace or two behind, like a boy with parent on an unwilling Sunday walk.

His methods, when he cares to apply them, are cardinally sound; his execution even has beauty; but he seems to pursue triumphs in another dimension. Sometimes, when runs are wanted quickly, he plays back-strokes of scholarly care to half-volleys, drives long-hops over mid-off, and dabs a late-cut at a full toss. I think he would like to be another George Gunn. But George Gunn occurs only in the singular. And so he has not made so many runs as some less gifted batsmen; though sometimes he appears in the big figures. He and Keeton put up 277 for the first wicket in 1933 against Middlesex, of which Harris's share was 234. In the next year he had an aggregate of 1,891. He could have kept to this standard, even improved it; but his peak is not a thing of seasons, but of hours, moods, moments. He has made the mistake of deserting art for artiness.

Among other eccentricities, he sometimes likes to act as his own commentator and critic. Having played at and missed a ball, he is heard to remark: 'At Trent Bridge yesterday Harris was below form; his footwork was slow and his strokes were not suited to the occasion.' Or, in times of unusual disappointment,

'Oh, Harris, Harris, what has come over you?'

As in batting, so in fielding; he can be brilliant in the outfield, a long thrower, fast, and a sure catcher. At other times he seems absorbed in a hat in the crowd; or a cloud formation in the sky attracts his inquiring eye.

The handbooks will say: 'Harris is a medium-paced bowler.' This is like saying: 'Mrs Sarah Gamp was a nurse.' For who could describe or understand the schemes which have gone to the making of one half-volley from his hand? In 1938 his 5 wickets cost 79.8 runs each. In 1939 he took fewer wickets at less cost – 2 at 45.5 each. A remarkable man.

C. J. Barnett — *Gloucestershire*

Of all cricketers, next to W. R. Hammond, I should like to be C. J. Barnett, also of Gloucestershire.

His batting, like his outlook on life, is strong, free, yet controlled There is a gusto about it. It is not merely hearty, which implies an absence of brain and a slap-happy ignorance of the quality of danger. It is of the stomach, in the old English sense of pride and valiance. It is the batting of a man who, having weighed the full power of an opponent, honours and yet derides him.

There are successful batsmen who remind you of hot-houses and adding-machines. Barnett suggests the leaves running before the early autumn winds. He is no ledger-bat. He is the master, not the servant, of decimal points and averages and ruled red lines. As a number one batsman, for his county and England, he is a rebel against stale custom. He is like the office boy who kicks the wastepaper-basket against the head clerk's shins, gives notice a second before he receives it, and runs out to slide on the pavement.

Being of such a sort, he makes what the book and the critic might call colossal blunders. He cuts the ball in the first over of a Test match, and the ball flies past the head of an outraged gulley, who was dreaming of stalemates and composing himself to eternity. Or it doesn't fly past, but sticks in some hand; and in a second, by the measurement of a few inches and by the miserable judgment of a pavilion, genius has turned to folly.

As an example of the futility of statistics in the judging of values, take Barnett's innings of 126 for England against Australia at Nottingham in the First Test of 1938. In that strange drawn game there were five individual scores of over 100, two of over 200: 1,496 runs were made for the loss of only 24 wickets, an average of 62.3 per man. To adapt the phrase of an old champion of billiards, a score of 50 was a blooming miscue!

But in that match two batsmen played innings that were great: S. J. McCabe for Australia (232); Barnett for England. McCabe's greatness was in rescue crowned by attack; Barnett's was in an opening attack which took the bowlers 'between wind and water', ridiculed length, and so scattered any gathering of ideas that the England batsmen who followed found them, as it were, lying about on the grass as they walked in.

It should be added that Barnett is a fast-medium bowler of no mean ability, and a strong and active fielder, especially at mid-off.

May he long retain his skill, and may selectors retain the wisdom to use it.

C. V. Grimmett — *Australia*

Clarence. A strange name for such a man; a name connected with one who got inside a butt of wine, and with many who got outside hundreds of butts. And Grimmett, even among Australians, ranks as a champion tea-drinker. He is compounded of tea, leather, patience, and subtlety.

With his small, stringy frame and his weary, surprised smile, as if the slaves of the leg-breaks shouldn't expect to hear or transmit anything funny, he might have been what is known as a pathetic figure. The constancy with which he took the best wickets in England stopped that idea. But even that success did not stop him, at the end of his over, from using Groucho Marx's walk to his place at cover-point.

You could not say that Grimmett was old or young, or in any known state of age at all. He and the calendar have never reached any proper understanding. Just as Mr Pickwick was obviously born in tights and gaiters, so Grimmett surely began with a large-peaked dark-green cap and ripe views on the status of the top-spinner. When he came here for the Tests of 1930, and stepped gravely from his cab at Lord's, an English friend met him and said: 'Well, you don't look any older'; and one of the jocular juniors of the team, Stanley McCabe, I think, said: 'He couldn't'; and walked away whistling, while Grimmett smiled paternally at this playful ambiguity.

The records, which must not omit anything, say that he was born in New Zealand on Christmas Day 1892. A Rogation Day would, perhaps, have been more proper to a man of so many lbw's, stumpings, and catches at the wicket. He played for Wellington, then, moving to Australia, for Victoria, South Australia, and Australia. He was thirty-three when he played in his first Test against England, which was the fifth of the series during A. E. R. Gilligan's tour of 1924–25. The Australians had won the rubber; Grimmett had something of his own to win. He meant to prove the virtue of round-arm spin bowling. In the first innings he took 5 for 45; in the second, 6 for 37. England, out for 167 and 146, lost heavily.

Arthur Mailey, most imaginative of modern leg-break bowlers, and a rich wit, has told how Grimmett approached him some twenty years ago with acute questions about their art, and Mailey, then the world master of this form of conjuring, told him till he could tell no more. Grimmett said 'Thanks', and went the way that led him to equal fame. Years afterwards, either forgetting himself in some unhabitual revel, or feeling that he had never quite caught up with the master, Grimmett said: 'Arthur, you told me all wrong about the googly.' Rather as if Virgil had tricked Horace on the number of feet in a hexameter.

There is no need for a hail of numbers to show that, as a Test bowler, Grimmett in Australia was only an intermittent success, in England an almost perpetual triumph. Nor can the matter be wholly explained by difference in pitches. There was something in the English air that increased his trickery, that raised his spirits and charmed his fears. One morning, when he arrived late on the ground at Oxford, he found that his side had taken 5 wickets for 15 runs. 'This,' he said, 'would never have happened if I had been here.'

He has always been mysterious. None can say whether his jerking round-arm action is a throw-back to George III or a projection to H. G. Wells. 'Do you think you ought to do this sort of thing?' I asked him once. In tired, metallic tones he said: 'Never communicate your intentions.'

He produced a book on how to take wickets, but only told us how he took them himself. Besides, you might as well have read Dan Leno on the art of making faces, or the wind on the art of blowing.

W. M. Woodfull — *Australia*

Bill Woodfull, the famous Australian batsman and captain, had the gaze of a mariner and the mind of a master who gets the whole school to and from a bank-holiday picnic without losing his reason or a boy.

Of all the protagonists in that fiercest controversy of cricket, I should say that he alone came out of it with reputation heightened and personal friendships increased. He neither concealed nor exaggerated a difficulty; and, whatever place he is to hold among Test captains, he remains the only man who has twice come here as challenger and twice carried off the victory.

As a batsman, he was noted for monumental defence and an unusually short lift of the bat. When Walter Hammond bowled him in the Fifth Test of the 1928–29 series in Australia it was the first time that his stumps had been hit for a year. The true stonewaller spares the bad balls; but Woodfull never did that; he was a heavy, strong man, and he could lean on the long-hops and half-volleys, and he scored faster than many a more graceful player.

Woodfull played for Victoria against A. E. R. Gilligan's team in 1924–25, and was close on thirty years old when he first came to England, under H. L. Collins in 1926. In those Tests he made a century at Leeds and Manchester, and headed the Australian Test averages with 57.93. Then, during A. P. F. Chapman's captaincy in Australia, he added three more centuries, and his stature was evident. He was elected captain for the 1930 visit to England.

It was the peak of his career. He had with him two of the greatest of all Australian cricketers, Bradman to make runs and Grimmett to quench them. He himself scored 155 in the first innings of the Lord's Test, topped 50 three times, and ended with a Test average of 57.55. As a speaker he was both witty and tactful.

During D. R. Jardine's tour, 1932–33, he played one of his greatest innings, carrying his bat, for the second time in Test matches, for 73 in the second innings of the Third Test. He had been injured during the first innings. Then, during his second captaincy in England, 1934, his personal skill at last began to wane; but his influence and leadership, in no easy atmosphere, were greater than ever. Further, Bradman and Ponsford were making the runs of at least four batsmen, and Grimmett had O'Reilly to help him. At the Oval Australia's triumph was complete.

In victory or defeat Woodfull remained the same quiet and, may I add, lovable character. Throughout his cricket career he won the respect and affection of both sides, and he was a man indeed.

W. A. Oldfield — *Australia*

W. A. Oldfield, of Australia, was, as near as man may be, the perfect wicket-keeper in style, demeanour, and effect. If Mr Turveydrop, that touchstone of deportment, had included wicket-keeping in his academic syllabus he would have said to his pupils: 'Yes, very elegant, my dear young man, very elegant indeed, but not quite as Mr Oldfield would have done it.'

There was a genius of apology in his work, as if he, and not you, had made the mistake; and how sociable was that meeting at the crease! He was like a dentist who seeks to obliterate the paraphernalia of action by conversation; on politics, the latest book, or the state of the family's health. He held short tryst with each batsman with an airy intimacy peculiarly his own.

Some of the nastiest bowling in the world was to be faced in a few seconds; but, first, the little talk. The response was almost universal. Of a few batsmen Oldfield says: 'They would confine themselves to "yes" or "no" or "maybe"'; but mostly they caught the idea, and it is reported that once Hendren, during the

172

taking of guard, discussed his West Indies experiences, and the Test Match just waited.

Oldfield first came to England as a member of the Australian Imperial Forces team in 1919, and with him was that great, if then wild, fast bowler, Jack Gregory. Back in Australia, he kept wicket in the first three Tests against J. W. H. T. Douglas's side and scored 50 at Adelaide. He was then displaced by the fatherly H. Carter, a wonder of unorthodoxy, who caught and stumped from four feet behind the wicket. In 1921, during W. W. Armstrong's captaincy in England, Oldfield continued to understudy till the Fifth Test, when he allowed only 1 bye in 647 runs.

During this season he made one catch that never appeared in the records but will always stay in my mind. Batting just above the extras for Oxford, I snicked a ball from Hendry that broke back and kept rather low. It hit the leg edge of the bat and also the pads, and Oldfield caught it in both hands near the ground. The appeal was turned down. At the end of the over Oldfield quietly said: 'You did hit that, didn't you? Ah, I thought so. Oh, it doesn't matter about the decision. It was the catch I was thinking about.' So am I, still.

From that season he kept wicket in every Test against England till the end of G. O. Allen's 1936–37 tour, except once, in 1932–33, when he had missed a hook at Larwood and was hit on the head. Of this ball he said: 'It was very short and pitched just outside the off stump.'

Of all wicket-keepers he most admired Herbert Strudwick, 'because of his ability in all circumstances and on all wickets'; a judgment that fits Oldfield. Without question he was the greatest wicket-keeper of this generation, and in days to come he will be talked of with Blackham.

W. J. O'Reilly — *Australia*

Bill O'Reilly was a fighter. He looked as if, under necessary circumstance, he might have founded or sacked a city. It was a face and form such as you might have seen in a picture of explorers or pioneers. At cricket he would have bowled till his boots burst, and after. If only one cricket ball was left in the world, and that one came to pieces in his hand, he would whiz down a leg-break with the largest fragment. Like Colonel J. W. H. T. Douglas, he had the inspired joy of battle; not the prone hope of the mere sticker, but the last fiery gift of the craftsman. And, with all that, he had gaiety not far latent.

He was a schoolmaster aged twenty-seven when he first played for Australia against England, having done well for New South Wales. It was D. R. Jardine's tour of 1932–33. Through the din of controversy a report, then an idea, reached us here of a new and important figure in cricket; of a bowler who on an Australian pitch could bend them from leg at nearly medium pace, and last all day. In those Tests he twice took 5 wickets in an innings and, in all, 27 wickets at about 27 each.

In 1934 O'Reilly came here under the calm, genial, and astute captaincy of W. M. Woodfull. To a stranger it was a strange bowling action. As with those more florid opponents of legendary heroes, there seemed to be more arms than Nature or the rules allow. During the run-up, a sort of fierce galumph, the right forearm worked like a piston; at delivery the head was ducked low, as if to butt the batsman on to his stumps. But it didn't take long to see the greatness; the control of leg-break, top-spinner, and googly; the change of pace and trajectory without apparent change in action; the scrupulous length; the vitality; and, informing and rounding all, the brain to diagnose what patient required what treatment.

His greatest triumph was in the First Test, at Nottingham. He took 11 wickets for 128 in 78.4 overs, and England lost that remarkable struggle against O'Reilly, Grimmett, and time. At Manchester, in the Third Test, when England's total stood at 68 for no wicket, on the cosiest of pitches, he took the wickets of Walters (52), Wyatt (0), and Hammond (4) in four balls. England went on to score 627 for 9, declared. O'Reilly took 7 for 189 in 59 overs. In that Test series he had 28 wickets at 25 runs each.

Against G. O. Allen's team in Australia, 1936–37, his skill was, perhaps, more consistent than destructive, but he topped the 20 wickets. And so, with the wonderful Grimmett now bowling as it were from memory and left behind at home,

O'Reilly came to England under Don Bradman in 1938. It was, surely, the most brittle bowling team that Australia has ever sent. It might, and it might not. On the whole, it didn't. But O'Reilly's genius, winning that glorious game at Leeds, kept the 'Ashes' in Australia and disaster at a distance, until that last resounding crash at the Oval.

Here he struggled on, frequently unaided by anything that mattered at all, sustained by his own will and his captain's example. In the total of 903 for 7 wickets he took 3 for 187 in 85 overs of which 26 were maidens. Hard pounding. Here he was outdone. But only once in those Tests did I see him over-matched, and that was when Hammond, in that wonderful 240 at Lord's, made pigmies of all rivals.

Off the course, as they say, he is a man of variety and humour. There is a story, too good to enlarge, of a goat found at midnight in an hotel bedroom, dressed austerely in a waistcoat, watch-chain and an inquiring look. O'Reilly insisted that it was the manager, but of what team or enterprise he would not say.

To end on more terrestrial matters, he was a dangerous left-handed hitter at the tail-end and a prehensile fielder. In all Anglo-Australian Tests he took, in nineteen matches, 102 wickets at 25.36 each. A great heart, and a great bowler.

G. A. Headley — *West Indies*

A writer of discernment has described how, in the late April of 1933, he met George Headley, the great Jamaican batsman, and found him 'tickled to death' at being described in the English newspapers as 'a frail sort of man'. 'Look at me,' said Headley, with the frankness of Micawber inviting inspection from young Copperfield, 'I am ten stone and six pounds.'

Whenever I have had the fortune to see this wonderful and quiet cricketer governing the bowlers, flashing into it at cover-point, musing among the less-advertised birds at deep third-man, or enjoying a moderately accurate and self-conscious little spell of bowling, I have felt that he was 'tickled to death'; not cynically, but as one who only chuckles, from cap to boots, at the responsibility of fame.

No young batsman can have come here from abroad more loaded with expectation and runs. At the age of nineteen, in 1928, he played an innings of 211 for Jamaica against a strong team from England. At twenty, still at home, against MCC, he made a century in each innings of the First Test, then packed that down with 223 in the Fourth. This innings took six hours and a half. His ripe temperament was as much noticed as his freshness of stroke.

His visit to Australia in 1930–31 with the West Indies team a little diminished his average and greatly increased his powers. He learnt the meaning of such experts in spin and length as Grimmett, Oxenham, and the left-handed Ironmonger. They, too, learnt something about Headley, for in the Brisbane Test he scored 102 not out in a total of 193, and in the last Test, at Sydney, which the West Indies won, he made another century. Home again in Jamaica, against Lord Tennyson's team, he blunted the pencils of the scorers and sharpened the hilarity of the crowd. His runs read like a bowler's dream after lobsters.

And so to England, under G. C. Grant. Much of the medium and fast-medium English bowling was pitched, defensively and dully, to a little short of a length. This suited his style, which delights in hooking, in delayed deflections to leg, and in cutting square or late. In these arts he has no living superior. His driving, when invited, was very good, but not overwhelming. In the Test at Old Trafford he made 169 not out in a total of 375. At Lord's he looked set for a century, when he was yorked by G. O. Allen, a fast bowler who has shown little interest in mere bouncing. Not long afterwards he became absorbed in Northern League cricket.

In 1939 Haslingden released him for his greatest triumph. At Lord's, in the First Test, he scored 106 out of a total of 277 and 107 out of 225. Those figures record but cannot express the scene of Headley against England on those days; the cool and equal command, the acquiescence of genius in patience and sense.

Great batting often has the beauty of the blast or the grandeur of the gale. In Headley's art there is no poise. But it answers the test of greatness. As he walks down the pavilion steps you expect, in hope or fear. Only three or four can do this for you always.

Sir Aubrey Smith — *Sussex*

If Sir Aubrey Smith could have joined the company of King Arthur he would have introduced cricket and become captain of Camelot; for none has shown better how to play both on and off the field.

Knighthood, conferred in his eighty-first year, has long been his unwritten title. It was awarded not so much for acting, in which art he has answered a need rather than reached an unusual excellence, as for showing how to employ success, that is, how to live. On the screen, and in daily life, he has been the world ambassador for the English gentleman, that character which persists in surviving clever imitations, contemptuous songs, dank intellectuals, and the cartoonist Low.

The son of a Brighton physician, C. Aubrey Smith went to Charterhouse, thence to Cambridge, and four times played against Oxford at Lord's, being three times on the winning side from 1882 to 1885. In 1883, he took 6 for 78 in the Oxford second innings, having helped to bowl them out for 55 in the first. Tall and strong, he had a high action and persistent accuracy, cutting the ball in from the off with purpose rather than subtlety. From 1887 to 1889 he captained Sussex and acquired the name of 'Round-the-corner Smith'.

An eminent player-critic has assured me that, when bowling, Smith did not arrive from round any corner at all, but approached on a logarithmic curve, and bowled as if the wind was always behind him. He was a long-reaching batsman of both vigilance and power, restrained from riotous hitting only by respect for convention. At slip he excelled, having enormous hands and the telescopic arm. In the winter, he was a noted Association outside-right for Corinthians and Old Carthusians.

In 1887 he went with Arthur Shrewsbury to Australia at the invitation of the New South Wales Cricket Association, and, in the next year, captained the first English team, sponsored by a Major Wharton, in South Africa. They did not call them Test matches in those days, but the two matches played against 'Eleven of South Africa' have since acquired Test status. Aubrey Smith played in the first of these, at Port Elizabeth, taking 5 for 19 and 2 for 42.

177

Those were the happy times before cricket had become an international bother. The game in South Africa was an infant, but their hospitality was ripe. Of the nineteen matches played, mostly against odds, four were lost: and the annalist remarks: 'All the beatings were sustained in the early part of the trip, and it is no libel to say that for a time generous hospitality had a bad effect upon the cricket.' Such is the difference between a trip and a tour. Expenses exceeded receipts.

Aubrey Smith was nearly thirty before he went on the stage, and he began on tour as Bootles in *Bootles' Baby*. In 1895 he first appeared in London, at the Garrick, as the Reverend Amos Winterfield. Soon, he passed from the Church to the peerage, where, histrionically, he has lived most of his life. In 1920 he played Professor Higgins in Shaw's *Pygmalion*. He also appeared in silent films, and several times visited the United States.

Then, when he was verging towards seventy, but still in the autumn of a virile middle-age, he took his superb nose and eyebrows to Hollywood, and to such notable films as *The House of Rothschild*, *The Garden of Allah*, and *The Prisoner of Zenda*. He took with him, also, his beloved cricket, and has found converts from San Francisco to Mexico.

Tom Hayward — *Surrey*

Tom Hayward, in his early fifties, used to bowl off-breaks in the practice nets of the Oxford Parks from about sixteen-and-a-half yards. He was preparing us, in his Thomasian manner, for the match against his native Cambridge. He used to say: 'Oh, what a shot, sir,' or 'Hit 'em hard,' or just, 'How's that?' Professionally, he said nothing else; but, in a private capacity, he sometimes turned to encroaching spectators and said : 'Cut along now, you boys'; no matter of what age they were.

To say that Tom Hayward batted at number one for Surrey and England is like announcing that Milton wrote poetry or that Disraeli often spoke in the House of Commons. Sometimes we asked him to bat in those nets because we wanted to see something of that greatness; but he only did it once, for a few minutes; he made three or four off-drives of calm splendour, deflected some off-breaks with the back-stroke that had been the despair of fast bowlers and the glory of a generation, and returned to his bowling, an art of which he remarked: 'You see, sir, I made a mistake. I let Surrey find out I could bowl as well as bat, and it was too much work; far too much.'

It brought him nearly 500 wickets at 23 each, and two hat-tricks in the season of 1899; and, two years earlier, he and Tom Richardson put Leicestershire out twice for 35 each innings. Too much work.

Tom never talked about his batting unless you dragged him on. Then he would speak as of something that had happened at least a century earlier, something that no one else could have done in the same way; not with pride exactly, but as if the whole performance were a mystery of which he alone had the key. He would stop speaking suddenly and turn aside, in that basement dressing-room, with its rough matting and smell of bat-oil, to pick up a new bat which, though he had sold you one yesterday, he would handle with a vague idea of imminent sale. 'Comes up well, Tom.' 'Yes, sir, but how does it come down?' That was his gentle and unchanging joke. It had to be said.

During our matches in the Parks you would see his florid face under the brown Surrey cap, his quasi-military moustachios, and the enormous collar of his sweater poised over the wall by the pavilion. No wickets for 30 at lunch, perhaps. 'Farther up, sir,' Tom would say; you must pitch 'em; any fool can hook; make 'em reach, make 'em reach. Now, what about a little massage?' He had a weakness for his emollient art, and for bandaging, holding no diplomas, and regarding it as a more integral part of his day than bowling off-breaks in any net. Indeed, with Tom, whim and kindness often ousted the intentions of his employers.

The books will tell you of his many triumphs; the world's fourth-wicket record, 448 against Yorkshire with Robert Abel; for forty-one years the champion aggregate, 3,518 in 1906; the 104 centuries, and how he was next after Dr Grace to do this feat. His last century, 116, was played, doubly rightly, against Yorkshire, at Lord's, where Surrey had two matches just after the start of the 1914 war.

But, as Tom would have said: 'That's enough about me, sir. . . . Cut along, now, you boys.'

E. Robson — *Somerset*

Ernest Robson, a Yorkshireman who went to Cheshire, then played as a professional for Somerset from 1895 to 1923, was the most accurate right-hand bowler of medium pace that I have ever seen; a man, also, of unequalled tranquillity in good times and bad.

Whether, in one over, he took three wickets or was hit for 20 runs, he merely curled and nursed his great moustache; and his unchanging answer to congratulation, blame, or a suggestion that he might with profit transfer second slip to short-leg, was 'Thank you, sir'.

In those many years, no one, perhaps not even his family, found out if Robson's calm concealed profundity, or what. I fancy he had early decided that batting, bowling, and especially fielding for Somerset was to be a hard job, and that he wasn't going to waste ideas, let alone words. Sometimes, between innings or the fall of wickets, I tried to coax from him views on the present or memories of the past. Little came out, though he did once remark of a famous batsman whose wicket I despaired of taking: 'What you want to do, sir, is to pitch one on his leg stump and hit the off. That'll fetch him.'

Robson fetched many a batsman by this ball, for he could make them swerve very late and wickedly from leg, and Jack Hobbs has said that he feared no bowler of this kind so much as Robson. He was forty-eight when I first played with him, and he was still doing it, with a few steps for a run and an impassive countenance. When he first saw my exaggerated use of inswing from the off, he curled his moustache and smiled, as at a child enjoying a toy soon to be thrown aside or broken.

He was also a batsman. Here, he relied much on the forward stroke. He belonged to that time when batsmen, like golfers, had pride of manner and flourish, before style had been clipped and dulled into utility. At the age of fifty he took a 50 off Middlesex at Lord's, batting at No. 10, and scored one straight six into the pavilion with no more than a full forward stroke. In the next summer he made the winning hit, a 6, against Middlesex, at Weston-super-Mare, off the second ball of the last over from J. W. Hearne. His partner, Bill Greswell, tried to nurse him away from the bowling, but Robson said: 'You leave it to me, sir.'

Twice he had days of triumph against the Australians. In 1896 he took 6 for 22; thirteen years later, at Bath, he took 8 for 35, including Trumper, Noble, S. E. Gregory, Armstrong, and Bardsley. Against Sussex, at Hove, he once bowled 50 balls without a run being scored off him. Length and Robson were inseparable companions; and I heard him dismiss all fast, bumping bowling with the comment: 'Silly, chucking 'em about like that.' He appealed in a very high voice, which, when the batsman unexpectedly got his bat there instead of a leg, changed into a strangled squeak.

In the winter he played skittles and went shooting, and was expert in both pursuits. He retired from first-class cricket at the end of 1923, and had been appointed an umpire for the Championship of 1924, but he did not live to stand in a county match.

Robson's name should be included among notable all-rounders, for he was a good batsman and, in his hour, a great bowler; and his placid brow and rolling moustache recall an age which rejected the nonsense of hurry.

A. C. MacLaren — *Lancashire*

A. C. MacLaren's name will live, not only among cricketers, but, which is the sign of greatness, with those who, only seeing or reading of him, knew him for a man.

He was a 'magnifico', and belonged, as if by some right recognized by fate, to the golden age of English batting. It was an age which, in other fields than cricket, despised uniformity, allowed for, expected, and admired the separateness of the great, and kept modernity's delight, the little man, kindly but firmly where he belongs, among the little men. And the public knew their heroes. There was no mistaking the batsmen of those days; W. G. Grace, in mellow splendour, K. S. Ranjitsinhji, C. B. Fry, F. S. Jackson, G. L. Jessop, J. T. Tyldesley, L. C. Braund. No one of these could pass for any but himself, so long as the spectator could see as far as the pitch; various in style and glory, united only in greatness.

As captain and batsman, MacLaren was a calculating attacker. His delight was to scatter the enemy by the strong stroke of bat or tactics. He was not to be tied down by a bowler or a convention. In both arts, batting and leading, he pushed daring up to but never over the verge of rashness; florid perhaps, but never theatrical; and few men can have cared less for the views of rival captains on his own side or in the Press.

Coming from Harrow, for whom, at the age of fifteen, he scored 55 and 67 against Eton at Lord's, he began for Lancashire in 1890, with a century against Sussex at Hove, early showing that which was to remain the particular glory of his batting, the full drive to the off and past the bowler. Four years later he went to Australia with A. E. Stoddart's team, and at Melbourne played an innings of 120, which went far to deciding the issue of the Rubber.

It was in Australia, which he twice again visited, on the second occasion as captain, that he showed the full MacLaren, and in Sydney he still remains the nonpareil among England batsmen. In England he did enough for fame. There was his 424 at Taunton, which stood as a record in first-class cricket for twenty-seven years; and his 88 not out at Lord's in 1899, against all that Ernest Jones could hurl or Noble and Trumble devise. But in England he was often short of practice, attacked by illness, hampered by a variety of businesses for which he was not by nature designed. His freedom of style needed freedom from that care which lay not far below the surface of courtesy and wit.

His speech, like his batting, avoided the irrelevant. Once, in the course of business, he was trying to persuade a reluctant client to buy some tyres for a new car. The hour was late; the client, anxious for bed, at last capitulated, and snapped out: 'All right, I'll buy one of your tyres.'

'Good G——,' said MacLaren, 'has your car only got one wheel?'

C. B. Fry — *Surrey, Sussex and Hampshire*

For combined excellence of mind and body Alfred Lyttelton might come up for comparison with Fry, but even he must surely retire before the Commander's overwhelming versatility.

In ancient Athens, perhaps in the Ideal Republic, Fry would have been raised by natural acclamation to eminence. In modern England he was thrice baulked at the first hurdle of the political race. He was born for the highest work with men of the highest ability; as a young man, he was rated as at least the equal of such as Lord Birkenhead and Lord Simon. But, by the very diffuseness of his genius, he became, as it were parcelled, or watered down. He had ambitions rather than ambition. He was too various for the single aim; he lacked the ruthlessness that is ever present, however deftly disguised, in the careerist.

He was a continual shock to the mere traditionalists. 'I was not,' he has said, 'popular at Lord's, being regarded in the light of a rebel.'

Lord Birkenhead, standing with him one summer day in the rose gardens of the training ship *Mercury*, said: 'This is a lovely place and a fine show, C. B. But for you it has been a backwater'; and Fry replied: 'The question remains whether it is better to be successful or happy.' Not quite as the world judges, Fry has been both.

He has admitted of himself: 'I am d – d lazy, with a huge fund of energy; and I'm no use till I am cornered.' He was 'cornered' very early in life. Money was short. In 1891, he went from Repton to Oxford with thirty shillings to spend and an eighty pounds p.a. scholarship on the books of the Bursar of Wadham. He had been meant for the Indian Civil Service, but side-stepped it, for want of mathematics. He was first on the Wadham list of scholars, one F. E. Smith being fourth, 'with a Lancashire accent that would rival Gracie Fields'.

Fry began with a Blue for association football, soon to make a famous partnership at back with W. J. Oakley. In athletics he was first string against Cambridge in the hundred yards and the long jump, but, Fryesquely, fancied himself most as a high hurdler. It was on the Iffley Road track at Oxford that he set up the world's record long jump of 23 ft 6½ in, a performance that his classical tutor had been invited to witness, but had dismissed with: 'I am afraid that would not interest me.' In cricket he played four times against Cambridge, scoring 100 not out in 1894, his year of captaincy. His fastish bowling is almost forgotten; but he took six wickets in an innings against Cambridge in 1895, and twice did the 'hat-trick' against the MCC, his victims including A. E. Stoddart and T. C. O'Brien.

After Oxford he drifted, briefly and for the only time, and the stream carried him to teaching at Charterhouse. There he decided that journalism would give him three times the income for a tenth of the time expended. In various magazines sketches of famous cricketers appeared under his name at a time when it was thought vaguely improper for an amateur to make money out of his knowledge of games. His connection with the *Manchester Evening News* ended when he telegraphed 1,200 words from the Outer Hebrides at the ordinary postal rates. He transferred his pen to Sir George Newnes's new venture, *The Captain*, and in 1904 Newnes made him, in preference to the vegetarian Eustace Miles, editor of *C. B. Fry's Magazine*.

It was in the early years of this century that his talent as a batsman blossomed into genius and he became one of the greatest, and surely the most scientific, players in the history of the game. Together, K. S. Ranjitsinhji and he became an almost insoluble problem to those who bowled against Sussex. In 1901 Fry scored six consecuitve centuries. Numerically, Don Bradman equalled this feat during the Australian season of 1938–39, but, in quality, Fry's six centuries must be held the greater, as his opponents included Yorkshire (twice), Middlesex, Surrey, and Kent, at an age very rich in bowling. In 1902 he played at back in the association football cup-final for Southampton against Sheffield United.

So far he had won fame as an athlete and a living as a writer. But he had used only a fraction of C. B. Fry. In 1908 he cast the whole of himself into the work of the training ship *Mercury* at Hamble, on the Southampton Water. He is there still, in spite of offering himself as a coal-miner at the age of seventy.

Fry denies that he was in any sense 'called'; he was simply annoyed at the sheer stupidity of allowing such a work to die with its founder, Charles Hoare, the banker. But he found both interest and funds lacking. His own and his wife's enthusiasm supplied the first need, his ingenuity and power of appealing, the second. From the start he combated the notion that a training ship was a form of reformatory and he persuaded *Punch* to publish a cartoon with a lad looking at Winston Churchill, then Home Secretary, and asking him whether he couldn't be trained for the sea without first robbing a till. Fry gave to the *Mercury* its distinctive spirit of service and self-reliance, and the *Mercury* gave to the Royal Navy and the Merchant Service those who have shown that Britain does not rule the waves merely in the words of a song.

In 1912, Fry took time off from his now established *Mercury* to captain England in the Triangular Test tournament against Australia and South Africa. At first, the Selection Committee had invited him as captain for the first match only; Fry, typically and rightly, said: 'All or none.' He led England to victory, playing a great defensive innings of 79 in the Oval Test against Australia.

Soon after the first European war, he went to Geneva as an associate with Ranjitsinhji on the Indian delegation, and worked most industriously on the Finance Committee. He was also a strong candidate for the vacant throne of Albania, whose head delegate, a bearded bishop, was looking for 'an English Country Gentleman with £10,000 a year'. But 'Ranji', perhaps unwilling to part with £10,000 and a valued friend simultaneously did not encourage the project.

Returning home, Fry was again offered, in his fiftieth year, the cricket captaincy of England against Australia. For Hampshire, he scored 59 and 37 against the formidable Australian bowling; but an injured finger settled the question. There followed years of routine work, one serious illness, and silence.

Then, one May morning of 1934, at Lord's, there stood on the steps outside the pavilion, a man with a monocle, writing; gaily and fluently writing. He appeared to be something between a retired admiral and an unusually athletic Oxford don. He wore marine gaiters and one of those waistcoats that are born to put the whole race of pull-overs to shame. No cricket had started; so I presumed to ask him whence came the facile stream. C. B. Fry said: 'My dear fellow, I am describing my idea of how the game should go, if it were going.' The *Evening Standard* was at work. He had been given an assistant to handle his 'copy'; and this worthy technician, meaning so very well, said to the master: 'Why, Commander, you might be a journalist yourself, instead of just an amateur.' And C. B. Fry said . . .

L. C. Braund — *Somerset*

A critic once wrote, with truth and traditional ceremony: 'Braund (L. C.), of Somersetshire, is undoubtedly the most accomplished all-round cricketer of the present day.'

Separating the individual from his profession, I should add that Leonard Braund is one of the characters of England.

He has an air. The tilt of his bowler-hat challenges and easily defeats Fate, who has come back at Braund often, fiercely, and laughably in vain. It is a very smart hat, renewed and therefore, as it were, plural, but of one particular era, and therefore singular; it suggests Romano's and company, and unboastful naughtiness.

He has a slow voice, with a natural and inquiring drawl. When he is inclined to speak on cricket he speaks with long wisdom and a humour that has little respect for persons, and none at all for averages, records, and clumps of figures. He tells of great cricketers, and why they were great; of little cricketers, and why they don't understand their littleness.

He illustrates a stroke with casual cane, or a spin with a snap of the fingers; then suddenly dismisses all with a bout of damnation on coupons, long-hops, of the degeneracy of beer. He may remind you, with a still half-incredulous chuckle, that he refused a second Benefit match at Taunton because he had lost money on the first.

But he will leave you to know or discover that in one series of Tests in Australia he scored a classic century and also took 8 for 81 in one innings, with leg breaks of nearly medium pace; that on his first appearance for England against South Africa, at Lord's, he made 104, that he once caught the mighty

Clem Hill at fine-leg when his official and starting place was at slip.

I count myself lucky to have stood for one August next to Braund in the slips, for the sake of his conversation, for some unlikely catches made so easy, for some easy catches floored with a 'Now, would you believe it?' In batting the style, but no longer the full effect, of greatness was upon him. He had given up bowling; but he would roll a few down between the fall of wickets; and he gave rich advice to the young. Then, they didn't always take it. Now, the advice lives in the mind; its giver in the heart.

W. Bestwick — *Derbyshire*

In the pavilion at Taunton there hung, and, if justice abounds, still hangs, a photograph showing William Bestwick, of Derbyshire, and John Cornish White, of Somerset, shaking hands on the cricket field at Derby. During the two days before, June 20 and 21, 1921, each had taken all ten wickets in an innings – White, slow left-hand, against Worcestershire at Worcester; Bestwick, fast right-hand, against Glamorgan at Cardiff.

In the ensuing match of mutual celebration, White bowled 75 overs and took 13 wickets, Bestwick bowled 58.1 overs and took 5 wickets. They were not of the sort that leans back on a laurel. They were natural men of work. White tilled the face of the earth, Bestwick dug in its bowels; together, they provided good things to eat and a good fire to cook them by.

It is twenty years to this day since Bestwick played in his last match. Among many reasons, technical and social, why he should be remembered, the strongest is that he belonged to the now less fashionable school of faster bowlers who, having been put on, are left on; or, rather, left alone; not interfered with. He arrived into cricket at that era which was golden for batting and iron for fast bowling.

The art of nursing had not yet come to relieve and insult the toilers under the sun. Bestwick, tall enough, and tremendous of shoulder and arm, didn't need a nurse. A batsman who could fight, an umpire with two out of his five senses, a quart or so of beer at mid-day and sunset, earthy laughter and cursing – these were his game.

His entry into county cricket, at the age of twenty-two, could excite little notice from any but the chroniclers, and, possibly, his own family. He played in eight matches – bowling average 53.75, batting 2.75. 'Other way round, now,' he said to an earnest inquirer, 'and what a laad I'd a'been.'

But Derbyshire, soon to be deprived of both the Davidsons, stuck to him, and in his fourth season he came out top bowler of the bottom county. Three times he had his 100 wickets, then retired, with the encouragement of the committee, to cricket in South Wales.

Here he exercised his strong arm and stronger conversation till, in 1919, Derbyshire, discovering themselves with some to bat but few to bowl, recalled Bestwick, now forty-three, but with native skill unsullied and with native accents unimpaired. He took 89 wickets for them. No one else could do better than 31. Next year, again bitten by the wander-bug, or by some unanalysed form of disgust, he removed his services to the League.

His only bowling that summer for Derbyshire yielded him 7 wickets for 97 runs in 53 overs; his batting, 1 and 5, both not out. But back he came to his own, and to that triumph of 1921; 147 wickets at 16.72 each, with 7 for 84 against Yorkshire at Hull, including Sutcliffe and Holmes for 13 between them. In 1919 he bowled for the Players at Lord's, but fared poorly. He was less than himself in the London air. But he was considered for England against Armstrong's Australians. 'So was the whole —— country,' he used to say.

Now he stayed at home. In his fiftieth year he took 7 for 20 against Leicestershire at Burton, missing victory by one wicket. Some ten days afterwards he played his last game for Derby, fittingly, at Cardiff. Cyril Walters and Dai Davies were the last two victims of one who, as a lad, had taken the wickets of Brockwell, J. T. Brown, and A. O. Jones.

His bowling being finished and nearly 1,500 wickets taken for under 20 each, Bestwick stood umpire, vastly, for a few summers in county cricket; full of rough comfort and homely counsel for the young imitator.

B. J. T. Bosanquet — *Middlesex*

'Some other experimental beggars may have fooled about with the googly, but it was I that put the thing on the market; and it sold; oh, yes, it sold a good many.' So spoke B. J. T. Bosanquet as we waited on the sixteenth tee of the Worplesdon golf course and watched an old gentleman enjoying his sandbath in a bunker guarding the green.

'Bose' was not inclined to verbosity on his invention, and he kept a stock of very versatile information for any whom he suspected, even faintly, of an improper gravity of mind. This was not unnatural in one who planted on cricket the greatest double-bluff in the game's life; for, not only did he sell to some of the most accomplished and dignified batsmen of his day a leg-break which proved, on bitter reflection, to have been an off-break, but, for a whole year, he pretended that this upstart of a ball was a misbegotten and unfortunate mistake; in short, that he was the suffering father of an undesired, and undesirable, offspring.

Arthur Shrewsbury, one of the finest batsmen of his own or any other generation, said in the year 1900 that this sort of bowling was unfair, and was little comforted when Bosanquet replied: 'No, not unfair; only immoral.'

At Eton, Bosanquet found his way into the Eleven as a medium to fast bowler and a hard-hitting batsman who, though 'having no grace of style to recommend him', scored 120 in two hours against Harrow. In the course of three matches for Oxford against Cambridge, 1898–99–1900, he took 12 wickets and scored 140 runs. So far, respectable, even interesting; not unusual.

But within the next five years, he so tempered the roughness of his batting that he twice scored a century in each innings for Middlesex at Lord's, so translated his bowling that he twice won a Test match for England against Australia, first at Sydney in 1904, then at Nottingham in 1905, and became, for thousands, the object of contemporary wonder and of subsequent imitation.

'Bose' attributed the birth of the googly in equal proportion to hot afternoons and wet mornings. 'On the former,' he said, 'I had a natural disinclination to bowl fast-medium; on the latter I felt the need for some indoor pastime that was both new and difficult.' So he invented 'Twisti-Twosti'.

His object in this parlour game was to bounce a tennis-ball on the table so that his opponent, seated at the other end, could not catch it. On this table, which now, doubtless, supports the inkstand of some unwitting Oxford scholar, the 'Bosey' was born. It was tried out at stump-cricket; then, amid hilarity, at the practice-nets in the Oxford Parks; a monstrous child, as yet without discipline or any settled name.

In July 1900 Bosanquet's googly took its first public bow, and wicket. Sam Coe, a sturdy left-hander of Leicestershire, being stumped at Lord's at 98 off one that bounced four times. In August, at Nottingham, it had the great William Gunn stumped, when ten yards from his crease, and a Mr C. E. Dench lbw. It may be added that in the former match Bosanquet scored 136 and 139; in the latter, 53. The early googly, like the early peach, was very expensive; just the ball, as its author used to say, for a mental millionaire.

In March 1903 it popped up for the first time in a first-class match in Australia. The only Victor Trumper was batting in the second innings of New South Wales against Lord Hawke's touring team. He had scored 37 in twenty minutes. Then Bosanquet, after two leg-breaks, sent down, with muttered hopes, one of 'those', and back went the middle stump. He brought it out again next winter, and won that 'Rubber' Test at Sydney.

And so to Nottingham in 1905. Australia in at one o'clock, with 402 to win in four and a half hours and only a draw to hope for; Trumper, unhappily for Australia and England, disabled by a strain. An hour after lunch, the opening pair, J. Darling and R. A. Duff, were still together; total 62. Then Bosanquet caught and bowled Duff. With nine wickets down and the light like 'darkness visible', Trumper bravely struggled as far as the pavilion gate. But he couldn't do it.

For 107 runs Bosanquet had taken the wickets of R. A. Duff, M. A. Noble, W. W. Armstrong, J. Darling, S. E. Gregory, C. E. McLeod, and F. Laver.

He never bowled the googly again like that; soon, he never bowled it at all. He passed it on, the googly, the wrong 'un, the Bosey, the ball that squints – to the great, the good, the less good, and the uncharted host of gay but innocent deceivers.

E. R. Wilson — *Yorkshire*

In combined accuracy of bowling and of memory no known cricketer has equalled E. Rockley Wilson. As no other, he could drop a ball on the needful spot and his mind on the required incident.

Yet, for a player of eminence, his appearances in first-class cricket have been few. Winchester needed him from May to August, to coach cricket and to teach French in his inimitable and metaphorical manner, and, in August, not even he could command a set place among the pick of Yorkshire. Then, in August of 1919, when he was forty, he came out to show an ignorant and negligent age the meaning of length, taking 36 wickets for Yorkshire at 16.58 each, including Jack Hobbs, when well set, at the Oval.

In 1920 he took 39 wickets at 15.48 each, and remarked, with that jigging push at the knot of his neck-tie, 'I was the discovery of the season.' Anyhow, the selectors noticed him, and he went on his first trip to Australia, under J. W. H. T. Douglas. In the Fifth Test match, at Sydney, he took the wickets of Kelleway, Mailey, and Collins for 36 runs.

As a Rugbeian freshman at Cambridge in 1899, he was also a very skilled batsman. In his first match, for A. J. Webbe's team against the University, scores of 117 and 70 suggested that he was playing on the wrong side. He got his Blue, a year too late to receive if from his brother, C. E. M. In his third year against Oxford he scored 118 and 27, and took 5 for 71 and 2 for 38. This season also marked the last of his youthful appearances for Yorkshire. They were far from unsuccessful, but too many were waiting to play. Eleven years later he played eight innings for Yorkshire, and, against Essex, at Bradford, socred 104 not out, 'driving in great form'. In 1922 he took part in a last-wicket stand against Lancashire at Old Trafford during the last over of which that calculating genius, Rhodes, with four runs needed for victory, made no attempt to score from a no-ball, and the match was drawn amid a silence as of the tomb. In this match Geoffrey Wilson fell ill, and Rockley Wilson, assuming the captaincy, led Yorkshire to victory in the Championship.

Throughout these years his art was infused into many general tions of Winchester cricketers. As a coach he can have had few equals. He not only knew the game, science and soul, and, to the finest shade, what a young player could be induced to learn, but, like Alfred Shaw, he could pitch the ball pretty well where he liked. 'And now I'll hit you on the toe,' he once said, and hit it. In the middle he was almost certain death to the firm-footed hitter and the shuffling prodder.

The full Rockley Wilson is locked away in the hearts of many friends and pupils, to be brought out, with due and affectionate exaggeration, at reunions and chance meetings. His exquisite wit and impromptu felicities should not wear the dull garb of print; but among the Rockleiana there is one comment too perfect to omit. A noble cricketing lord, whose awful majesty hid a kindly heart, was holding select court in a pavilion, and, seeing Rockley, gave him a shake of the hand. Rockley turned to a friend and whispered: 'Lucky to get a touch.'

P. R. Johnson — *Somerset*

Certain records of cricket in 1901 refer to 'Johnson, a highly erratic fast bowler'; which is rather as if, in some early Edwardian critique, mention should be found of 'Thomas Beecham, an eccentric piccolo player'; for P. R. Johnson's fame rests on batting comparable in style and fluency to that of Lionel Palairet, also of Devon and Somerset. Tall and graceful, Randall Johnson in play against fast bowling is something to remember; and once, when he was bowled in the thirties, I heard an opponent, not fond of words or losing, remark: 'Well, I *am* sorry; that's the best of day gone.'

Coming from New Zealand, Johnson went to Eton, thence to Cambridge. Another stone of weight might have gained him a Rowing Blue. Instead, he played against Oxford at Lord's, where, in the words of S. H. Day, his captain, 'he mixed up wides and wickets like a right-handed Tom Emmett'. Among the victims of this pleasing variety was that vigilant Scot, W. Findlay, then wicket-keeper of Oxford, and, later, secretary of MCC; and, had a decision over a low slip-catch by E. R. Wilson gone the way of fact, Johnson's bowling would probably have won the match.

In that same year he went to the United States with a cricket team under B. J. T. Bosanquet, and, in the following winter, accompanied Lord Hawke to New Zealand. Six years later, this number nine batsman of Cambridge made a century in each innings for Somerset against Middlesex at Taunton. The romantic bowler had become the classical batsman. But work, and the Stock Exchange, not always synonymous, made Johnson's appearances for Somerset an only occasional delight.

After war service, and severe illness, in Mesopotamia, he reappeared to captain MCC at Lord's in 1921 against Warwick Armstrong's Australians. Whatever this captaincy may have foreshadowed, Johnson, having a bone in his hand broken by a very fierce one from J. M. Gregory, dropped out of cricket for some weeks; then came back to play a glorious innings on a fiery pitch against Essex at Southend, a performance matched in splendour, though not in grace, by P. Perrin of Essex; and their combined age was eighty-six.

Young Somerset players of those years will remember some one-handed catches by Randall Johnson, made as if the ball were joined by elastic to his palm; his many words, too, of encouragement and thinly deserved praise; his liking for a game of poker on Saturday evenings and a bout of Charles Dickens in his bedroom on Sunday afternoons.

And one player, particularly, recalls at will Johnson's last century for Somerset, at the Oval. The last batsman came in to help him make 220 to win, and somehow stayed for 136 of them, and somehow dodged those whizzing drives from the other end, and then was caught at wicket off an imitation leg-break from Douglas Jardine, leaving the maestro in possession – 117 not out.

C. H. Parkin — *Lancashire*

Cecil Parkin, of Lancashire and England, could bowl every known kind of ball, except very fast, and several that were all his own invention; and, as it was often his whim to try to fit them all into one six-ball over, his time was very full.

He enjoyed fantasy, experiment, and laughter. He loved

cricket from top to toe, and he expected some fun in return; but, when a bowler's task towered, bristling and hostile, in front of him, he attacked it with a stern Northern resolution and with every resource of his consummate art.

In county and England cricket, his career was short, too short. He went to Australia in 1920 under the captaincy of J. W. H. T. Douglas, and in five losing Tests he was second in the England bowling averages, and, in the process, made comments, richly personal and fiercely descriptive, which cannot find their way into print.

In summer 1921, he continued the losing, but to him nearly always humorous, struggle against Warwick Armstrong's great Australian side in England, and his battle with H. L. Collins in the Fourth Test at Manchester was a match in itself. He again appeared in 1924 for England against South Africa at home, but soon afterwards he accepted a Northern League engagement.

To this concentrated type of cricket his genius was perfectly suited. He was a born showman, and he had much to show. Further, his great skill in bowling off-breaks, mostly from round the wicket, was just the thing for the slower turf of the North. His facial and verbal expressions, his very gestures and movements, were natural entertainment. No cricketer so easily indicated surprise, anger, or resignation, and, when life and the batsmen were dull, he would conjure the ball from or into his pocket, or flick it up from boot to hand like a Cinquevalli or a Rebla.

In the years of his fame and prime, the middle 1920s, his figure was trim and lithe, and he had a beautifully high and easy action. At his best, which was nearly always, he was the most artistic and various of bowlers. Only sometimes his temperament boiled over, and he would say, and perhaps write, things which, as intended, shook his audience with rage or merriment. His satire had pepper as much as salt.

But, in essence, Parkin was a lover of life, and of Lancashire life above all. He always seemed to have something generous to do, something good to say. In later years, when he had put on vast weight, he was an integral part of Test matches at Old Trafford, surrounded by friends and bursts of laughter. And how those friends will miss and remember him.

H. A. Gilbert — *Worcestershire*

In the years since top-hats faded from the heads and book-makers from the elbows of cricketers, H. A. Gilbert has prob-ably been the best and surely the most thoughtful, of medium-paced right-hand bowlers produced by Oxford University. His views on the bowling art, his remarks on dry-fly fishing, rare European birds, and the oddity of man, sometimes drift to the fortunate ear at Lord's. They have the dreamy authority and irregular logic of a conversation between the White Knight and Tweedledee on some Carrollian day separating Saturday from Sunday.

As a boy at Charterhouse he appeared one summer from the ruck of nowhere in the first eleven and took 38 wickets at 17 each on that iron-hearted pitch. In three seasons for Oxford, 1907–8–9, he took, in all first-class matches, 142 wickets at 16 each; against Cambridge at Lord's, 20 wickets at 14 each. In 1908, for the Gentlemen *v.* Players at the Oval he took 9 wickets, including Hobbs twice, Tom Hayward, Hardstaff, Arnold, and A. E. Trott. In 1909, for Oxford against M. A. Noble's Australian team, he took 8 for 71 in the first innings, among that eight being Noble, Ransford, S. E. Gregory, Armstrong, Trumper, and Macartney.

This feat brought him to Edgbaston as a reserve for England in the First Test. He also bowled against the Players at Lord's and the Oval. In 1910, after taking the wicket of Hirst in the second innings of Gentlemen *v.* Players at the Oval, he receded from the upper spheres of the game to pop up, three years later, comfortably at the head of the Monmouthshire bowling aver-ages and, nine years after that, still explaining and exhibiting the old art to a new generation, as the mainstay of the Wor-cestershire attack.

Gilbert wove into his bowling, which could touch greatness on wet pitches, all the garnered lore of the countryman, with refinements, sometimes over-nice, perhaps, as to wind and sun and the consistency of turf. He never just bowled. He played on the observed weakness and strength of each batsman, stock-ing many sizes of out-swerve and off-spin like a chemist's bottles, and was ever ready with scientific apology when the patient refused to die. His own, not infrequent, failures as a batsman he only regretted because they interrupted him in his assessment of the offending bowler, and he regarded fielders chiefly as devices or instruments wherewith to prove or explode some Gilbertian theory.

As in cricket and philosophy, so in ornithology, his pursuit of the truth carried him afar; and he tells how, after vain search for a rare bird in its bespoke and appropriate places high on the mountains of Switzerland, he saw it at last, as his homeward train drew out, perched unconcernedly on the edge of the platform.

J. J. Bridges — *Somerset*

It is seldom that any county is blessed with two opening bowlers who think themselves not only capable but even deserving of opening the batting as well; but such was the happy lot of Somerset and John Daniell when James Bridges and I stood between the batsmen and the extras.

Each of us privately regarded the pretensions of the other as totally absurd. Bridges could see little to praise in one who couldn't tell a leg-break from a googly, and I could hardly applaud the orthodoxy of off-drives that sent the ball at a great pace to the fine-leg boundary. But these criticisms remained unspoken. We mentioned, rather, the dozen we had put on together against Yorkshire and what fools the bowlers looked when they found the sort of thing they were up against.

Sometimes there really was a last-wicket stand. One of these Bridges incontinently ended by walking briskly back to the pavilion under the impression that an incidental, and doubtless dental, noise by the Worcestershire wicket-keeper was the old familiar rattle of wood. In the excitement of the moment, they stumped him in his absence, but, as he was walking at right-angles with the crease, the umpire gave him the benefit of topographical doubt. He resumed, and we troubled them for some fifty runs. As we finally walked away, he said: 'He won't bowl another one like that this year. Just a fluke, Glasgy, just a fluke.'

He began as a professional some years before the last war; after it, he played as an amateur. At his best, he was a very fine bowler, fast-medium, with a high action, great pace from the pitch, and a very late dip from the off; sometimes he could bring an inswinger back from the leg off the pitch and leave the batsman strokeless, and W. H. Ponsford met one of these at Taunton in 1926. Many good wickets as he took, he would have taken far more under the later lbw rule, for batsmen had brought pad-play to a distressingly fine art.

He had temperament; in success his face lighted up as if from within, and then he was ready to bowl out the world – Grace, Trumper, Ranji. Again, the slips would floor a catch, or a short-leg would seem to stray, and darkness came down. He would frown hugely, close his mouth on a medley of oaths, and signal fielders hither and thither without success. But he had endurance and would bowl from memory rather than give up.

Weston-super-Mare was his town. It was there that he made his famous 99 not out against Essex, the last man being run out trying for that desperate single. He was missed a few times, but his comment was: 'You need a little luck, even when you're in form.' It was there, too, that I met him again a few years ago, and he told me that he had been bowling. 'They didn't like *that* one,' he said, indicating an inswinger over the unconscious hat of a passer-by. I asked him about the batting. 'Batting?' he answered; 'better than ever. You know, Glasgy, we never had our rights. You and I should have opened the innings.'

A. Skelding — *Leicestershire*

I suspect that Alec Skelding's cricket luggage was essentially a bowler's bag, with a spare shirt and a pair of bootlaces, a few informal appendages of the game, and indications of other lives than bowling for Leicestershire.

For Skelding is a man of variety, and of a wit sharpened in the school which wags its head at failure and regards success with that eye which the regulars reserve for the over-dressed stranger in the village pub; a man of comic irony, like the late William Reeves, of Essex, with whom, in later years, he sometimes stood umpire in county cricket and white boots, and brought rare theatre to pitches and pavilions.

Skelding was a fervid, forceful bowler, and no mistake; fastish by habit and, in spasms, fast. He housed in a slight, if wiry, frame a spirit that mocked tiredness and unbending slip-fielders. To the batsman, he was a whizz of arms and a glint of spectacles. 'The specs,' he once remarked, 'are there for the look of the thing. I can't see without 'em, and on hot days I can't see with 'em, as I'm bowling with steam in my eyes; so I do it on hearing only, and appeal twice an over.'

Skelding appeared in the ranks of Leicestershire cricket in a year when their annual report read like something between a charity sermon and a funeral oration – 'over the doings of the eleven last season there is no temptation to linger'. His maiden season of 1912 yielded him eight wickets, including those of E. G. Hayes, Major H. S. Bush, and Bill Hitch. In December, a special meeting was called to consider the position of the Club. Skelding was retained; as if Dan Leno had poked his face round the wings during *East Lynne* and been asked to join the company.

In 1913, he took over 50 wickets; in 1914, 72, with 5 for 58 against Kent at Ashby-de-la-Zouch. Skelding seemed to be arriving, but, when cricket was resumed five years later, other and swiftlier moving avocations claimed him. He bowled only 62 overs, and took 11 wickets; seven of them fell in one innings by Yorkshire at Huddersfield, including those of Sutcliffe, D. Denton, R. Kilner, Rhodes, and Hirst; and the other four at Old Trafford, including Hallows and E. Tyldesley.

Skelding had neither the opportunity nor quite the gift of consistent excellence. 'Bowling,' he would say, 'is more often a headache than a headline. Leicester's a well-known town – for stockings and rugby football.'

He is not one who deserves to fall among mathematicians. He knew and exemplified that by which the game lives; service, hope, and laughter; and, when the Leicestershire committee rewarded him with a benefit in 1927, they were thinking of what he was as much as of what he had done; an award that suggests a lesson for a wider world.

Percy Holmes — *Yorkshire*

There is a chance that Percy Holmes, batsman, may become forgotten except in Yorkshire, and that would be wrong; for there were suggestions of greatness in his play. Only fate and the committee made him an opening batsman during the long reign of Hobbs and Sutcliffe.

In county cricket they used at first to say, 'Holmes and Sutcliffe', or 'Sutcliffe and Holmes', indifferently; but, after a few seasons, Sutcliffe, junior by seven years to the day, assumed by right the seniority in the partnership, till the firm expanded to its final shape: 'Sutcliffe, Sutcliffe, Holmes, Sutcliffe, and (possibly) Holmes.' No praise, no blame, could shake Sutcliffe from his high and earned place in cricket; but I like to wonder what Holmes might have done against Australia with equal opportunity.

In 1920 he scored 2,029 runs, average 54.83. Against Hampshire, at Southampton, he made 302 not out; against the Red Rose, at Old Trafford, 126 and 111 not out. That autumn he was not picked for J. W. H. T. Douglas's MCC team to Australia. In England, he played against Australia once, in the First Test of that crazy 1921. In the first innings, opening with D. J. Knight, he made 30, by ten runs the highest score in a total of 112, facing the whirlwind of J. M. Gregory and E. A. McDonald for an hour and a half. Holmes was also a crisp, even a brilliant, fielder anywhere. In the second match he was displaced by the worthy Dipper, and disappeared from Australian Tests for ever.

He graduated from the Yorkshire Second Eleven in 1913, appearing with irregularity but promise. In 1919 he began with 99 against MCC at Lord's and, in June, against Nottinghamshire at Trent Bridge, started the coalition with Sutcliffe. In the following years these two put up a hundred or more for the first Yorkshire wicket sixty-nine times, a record that remains. 1925 was Holmes's summer. Against Middlesex, at Lord's, he played an innings of 315 not out, beating William Ward's 278 for MCC *v.* Norfolk and three given men, a ground record which had gone strong since 1820. But Holmes's record was snatched in infancy by Hobbs, who, in 1926, made 316 not out for Surrey against Middlesex.

He battled with a sort of volatile precision entirely his own. He was like an ostler inspired to cricket; nimble, quick in glance of bat and eye, jocular and stern in rapid alternation, excelling in the cut and in the eyebrow hook from imprudent risers, strokes which the Yorkshire coaches teach pre-eminently well. After a defensive back-stroke he would switch his bat curtly downwards, as though to complete a drill-movement and to say: 'There; how's that for correctness?'

What a pair, Sutcliffe and Holmes, to bowl to or to see coming from the gate; a liner and a tug. Sutcliffe walked out as if to lay with a golden trowel the foundation-stone of some hostel for deserving cricketers; Holmes, as if he were off to Aintree or Harringay, in merely incidental white flannels. After thirteen years together they set up their record, at Leyton, 555 for the first wicket against Essex. Sutcliffe 313, Holmes 224 not out. The junior partner was in his forty-fifth year.

To Holmes decline came abruptly. He had always laughed at the years, and suddenly they won. When he failed there were few bouquets. But those who knew his batting and enjoyed his delightful ways will hand him a laurel.

A. A. Mailey —
New South Wales and Australia

In his last Test match for Australia against England, at the Oval in 1926, Arthur Mailey bowled Jack Hobbs with a full toss. In the same innings, but with more propriety, he also bowled Sutcliffe and Woolley, had A. P. F. Chapman stumped, and G. T. S. Stevens and Wilfred Rhodes caught. But Mailey liked that full toss best. He said it was as good as a Saturday afternoon.

As a bowler of slow leg-breaks and googlies, Mailey was imaginative and experimental. He would invite a batsman's contempt with a wide, lull him with long-hops, then send him witlessly pondering to the pavilion with one that struck venomously from leg-stump to the top of the off. Like P. G. H. Fender, he was never devoted to precision for its own dull sake, but to the supreme art of conquering a batsman according to arrangement. 'Sometimes,' he once remarked, 'I am attacked by waves of accuracy; and I don't trust them.'

Such a bowler needs rich support from his own batsmen and fellow bowlers, and for most of his Test career Mailey had it. Unsolicited help, too, came in his first series, 1920–21, from those of our own batsmen who, in a manner always surprising to the Australian, regarded leg-breaks as a form of voodoo, and awaited execution with hypnotized acquiescence.

In the following summer, in England, Mailey was equally great. The extent of his work was diminished, but its performance made easier, by the preceding attack of Gregory and McDonald. The batsmen who survived those masters of pace seldom retained the freshness of mind and body needed to combat Mailey's guile. In the same season Mailey took all ten Gloucestershire wickets in an innings at Cheltenham.

But many will remember him rather by the wickets that he didn't take, in those matches which rarely escape into print. In these, working on foreknowledge or a whispered suggestion, he would dispense tactful full-pitchers and self-starting boundaries, and, in the long intervals, gladden autograph-books with quaint pictures. Yet he was never just the famous fellow, relaxing.

To him all occasions were equally great, or small. He went into a Test match, as Joe Coyne used to go on to the stage, apparently because he happened to be walking that way. He gave of his wonderful best, and, if it failed, well, there was a conversation to renew with that comical gate-keeper, or an exceptional moustache to be sketched down there behind square-leg.

When he had retired from playing Test cricket he used to come over to England to report and depict it with a sort of casual exactitude entirely his own. He was exquisitely tickled by the solemnity that often overwhelms the Press, and once, while dozens of pencils were immortalizing some maiden over or no-ball, he leant over and whispered: 'Will you join me in hymn number 403?'

Mailey and Grimmett fall to be compared for excellence, and it could be a long argument; but, whatever be the answer on their performances in England, Mailey, with his severer spin, was the man in Australia. Both, in their own line and time, were better than anything of that kind in our own cricket.

H. S. Altham — *Hampshire*

Harry Altham is the best living historian of cricket, and I should place him ahead of the late Mr Ashley Cooper, who, though excelling as a student-researcher, fell short in both interest and technical appreciation once the wickets were pitched, and was held by the figures, not the fight, by the minutiae, not the moil. Altham was a very fine batsman, and still is a model of orthodoxy for the young cricketers of Winchester, and he has the happy power of communicating the love as well as the knowledge of the game.

As a boy, he was at Repton in its richest years of cricket. From its teams of 1903 to 1908 could have been picked an eleven good enough to play for Oxford or Cambridge, perhaps even for the Gentlemen of England. In those years played R. A. Young, batsman-wicket-keeper, who later captained Cambridge and went to Australia with MCC; A. F. Morcom, one of the few amateur bowlers with the sustained skill of a professional; J. L. Vidler, for three years opening bowler of Oxford; W. T. Greswell, master and pioneer of the inswinger, who once had both Hayward and Hobbs on a plumb wicket at Taunton, and who returned, years later, half-forgotten, to surprise the ignorant; Walter Franklin, wicket-keeper-batsman of Cambridge and Bucks; I. P. F. Campbell, admirable as batsman and fielder; and, greatest of all schoolboy cricketers, J. N. Crawford, who, as captain in 1905, liked to employ Altham's lob-bowling in the nets so as to hear the tiles tumbling from the distant pavilion. Altham himself was captain in 1908.

At Oxford, a then unsound defence kept him from his Blue in the first two years; but in 1911, after being one of J. F. Ireland's hat-trick in the first innings, he made a 47 which helped towards a brilliant, if unexpected, victory. In 1912, for Oxford against Hampshire, he had C. B. Fry missed at 180 off a lob, the maestro then proceeding to 203 not out by using the bat as a croquet-mallet swung from between the feet. Against Cambridge at Lord's, he was run out at the crisis, that remarkable cover-point, S. H. Saville, hitting the one visible stump. There followed some August matches for Surrey; then Altham joined the staff, and that great coach, Rockley Wilson, at Winchester.

In the war of 1914–18 he won high distinction but had time also for an occasional game on matting at Etaples, where J. W. H. T. Douglas was to be seen, worrying his batting-gloves as if Hordern were at him.

After the war Altham played sometimes for Hampshire, and an innings of 141 against Kent at Canterbury was a performance of Test match quality. But most of his cricket was with the Oxford Harlequins, where the play is as good as the fun, and he never missed an August tour from 1911 to 1939. Among many centuries, perhaps the best was one against Arthur Mailey, who had been attracted to Hythe by the air and the company.

In his writing, as in his batting and coaching, nothing but the best will do. There is a rounded thoroughness in it all. His lob-bowling I must leave to the judgment of C. B. Fry and J. N. Crawford. For the purposes of instruction at Winchester, he long ago adopted a more perpendicular manner.

A. P. Freeman — *Kent*

The performance of A. P. ('Tich') Freeman, the Kent leg-break bowler, stands unrivalled of its kind in English county cricket; yet, against Australia, in the highest Test, he was almost nothing. Such triumph set off by such failure is without parallel in modern cricket.

His career proper began in 1919. When he retired, at the end of 1936, those eighteen seasons had brought him 3,775 wickets at 18.43 each – that is an average of 209 wickets a year. Wilfred Rhodes took 413 more wickets, but his career covered twenty-nine seasons.

During the four seasons 1928–29–30–31, Freeman took in all 1,122 wickets, an average of 280 wickets a year. In 1928 he took 22 wickets in the three Tests against West Indies at 13 each, yet only twice did he play against Australia over there under A. E. R. Gilligan, and then he distinguished himself only by an innings of 50 in the First Test at Sydney, when he helped Frank Woolley to score 128 for the ninth wicket. Again he went to Australia, in 1928, under A. P. F. Chapman, but played in no Test at all; this after taking 304 wickets in an English season.

Yet there is no mystery. Against the best county batsmen Freeman was a threat; over the worst, a tyrant, even a magician. For he turned them from men to sheep . . .

> '*as one after one*
> *So docile they come to the pen-door till folding be done.*'

Docile. That was the secret. Upon so many English batsmen Freeman imposed the belief that he could not be either played or hit, and he winnowed the faint-hearted like chaff. This was his greatness, and no slow bowler within memory has cast such a spell on batsmen short of the highest class. He dictated defeatism. Only against such as Hobbs, Hendren, Duleepsinhji, and Hammond did Freeman relapse into the ordinary and ineffectual. Their quick feet beat him.

The Australians were not afraid of him. Nearly every club in Australia had its leg-breaker, who imposes no terror by wizardry. Such batsmen as Ponsford, Woodfull, Bradman, and Kippax were not going to be subjugated, and it was Freeman who retired baffled from these encounters.

Technically, he was at the top of his craft. His length was wonderfully accurate. Many leg-breakers can spin the ball away from the off-stump and from just outside it. Freeman, on his best days, spun it fiercely from leg-stump to off. His top-spinner brought him hundreds of wickets. Though small, he was tough and wiry, and, so long as things went well, he could endure for very long spells, and it should be remembered that he was thirty-nine when he took his 304 wickets. But he could be, and was, batted off the pitch by the few great, and, when once struck down, he did not re-arise. He retired to cover-point, shrugging his whole body.

Yet Freeman remains a marvel in cricket. Three times in successive years he took all ten wickets in an innings, once against Essex, twice against Lancashire. Forty times he took thirteen wickets or more in a match, and no bowler in our time, except Larwood, so excited expectation when given the ball by his captain.

C. F. Root —
Derbyshire and Worcestershire

Someone once said that no jokes about other people's names should be made before six o'clock in the evening and none after six either. But the bald line, so familiar and pleasing to readers of cricket scores twenty and thirty years ago – 'c. Beet, b. Root' – might even now titillate the flattest melancholy and melt the iciest propriety.

They were Derbyshire cricketers, these two, in times when Derbyshire did not often interfere with the plans of Yorkshire and Lancashire. Beet has been seen on many ocacsions at Lord's, standing umpire with Fowler, unforgotten jests on his tongue, intimations of victory on his face. As a wicket-keeper Beet was tough, resilient, and short.

Fred Root went over to Worcestershire in 1921. He took his hundred wickets in 1923, and again in each summer till the end of 1931, except in 1925, when he took over 200. Powerful and enduring in physique, endowed with contempt for adversity and all pettiness, he fought and toiled and joked through any-thing that batsman or climate could set against him. No other bowler could watch him without admiring him and catching something of his spirit.

His method in his famous years was the inswinger, delivered at a brisk speed, dipping in from the off unpleasantly late; toe-teasers, with the usual complement of close leg-fielders; the same method that was used by that grand Philadelphian bowler, J. B. King, by the South African, B. G. von B. Melle, of Oxford University and Hampshire, by W. T. Greswell, of Somerset, who, in artistry, was the best bowler of inswingers that I have seen.

In 1926 Root played for England in three of the five Tests against Australia. At Trent Bridge rain prevented him from bowling. Soon afterwards it was decided that Root and his bowling were secrets, to be released upon the Australians at Lord's. He even gave a radio broadcast which began: 'Evening, everybody: this is Fred Root speaking, mystery bowler,' and in good Derbyshire manner made 'bowler' rhyme with 'howler'.

In the Lord's Test he bowled well, taking the wickets of Collins, Woodfull, Andrews, and J. M. Gregory for 110 runs. Missing Leeds, he played at Manchester, and in Australia's only innings he took the wickets of Woodfull (117), Macartney (109), Ryder, and Gregory; 4 for 84 in 52 overs, 27 maidens. He was then thirty-six years old.

In 1928 he scored over a thousand runs. He loved to drive hard and high, and his defence was roughly correct. In the same season, at Taunton, when I had scored a leg-bye off him towards mid-wicket, he said: 'Hip-bones driving well today, eh?'

We shall want a few Fred Roots in post-war cricket.

A. S. Kennedy — *Hampshire*

Alec Kennedy's cricketing life began when Dr W. G. Grace's was ending – if, indeed, Grace ended at all – and stretched to the time when Hutton and Compton were making ready to be famous.

During those thirty years Kennedy took nearly 3,000 wickets, and five times brought off the 'double'. Others bowled for Hampshire; but, in attack, he and J. Newman *were* Hampshire. Yet he played for England in only one series of matches, when, in 1922–23, at the instigation of Mr Solly Joel, the Hon. L. H. Tennyson, as he then was, captained an English team in five unofficial Tests in South Africa. In these Kennedy took 21 wickets.

The variety, freshness, and intelligence of his bowling were remarkable in one who had every inducement to settle into a hack efficiency. I doubt if he has ever in his life sent down a ball just to get rid of it. He was a business letter written by a human being.

For only medium pace, his run was long, and included in its middle a sort of chassis or double-shuffle. He could swing the new ball very late either way, and knew the value of the early half-volley. He kept the inswing as a surprise; 'a stick', as he said, 'not a prop'; he bowled it from the same place, close to the wicket, as the other, and he had little use for an assembly of

206

short legs awaiting glory or death. He used both spins, but did not advertise them by obvious finger-grips, and was compact of disguise and artistry. On a sticky or broken pitch he approached S. F. Barnes in skill, for he could cut the ball sharply from leg at a pace that allowed little chance to smother it.

He was only sixteen when he began for Hampshire, in 1907, having taken that 'road with a view', as recommended to Scots by Dr Johnson. In 1909 he played regularly, took 139 wickets in 1912, and 162 in 1914. So far, he batted among the bowlers.

From 1919 onwards he was an all-rounder, that is, he was allowed to be also interested in batting. In 1922 he took 205 wickets and scored 1,129 runs, and for another ten years he remained a cricketer of high distinction. In 1927 he took 7 for 8 against Warwickshire at Portsmouth, and at the Oval took all ten wickets for the Players against the Gentlemen for only 37 runs. Strong and swarthy, he never showed weariness.

His batting varied from the studious to the violent. He appeared in every position from one to eleven, and knew all the bowlers as well as they knew themselves. As an adviser on bowling, I never found his equal, and in a swift soft flow of words he would sweep away doubt and resolve mysteries. The Ulysses of the game.

J. C. White — *Somerset*

John Cornish White, slow left-hand bowler, and the pride of Somerset, first went to play for England in Australia in 1928, at the age of thirty-seven. He perplexed and imprisoned their best batsmen by an accuracy of length, a subtlety of flight, and a pertinacity of spirit which can rarely have been combined in any other cricketer.

In the second innings of the First Test, at Brisbane, he took 4 wickets for 7 runs in 6 overs. They could not decide whether to play him or to hit him, to go forward or back in defence. In the Fourth Test, at Adelaide, in blazing heat, with an oven-breeze, he bowled 124 overs, 37 maidens, and took 13 wickets for 256. England won by 12 runs. Of this performance White remarked: 'I used a few shirts and several whisky-and-sodas.'

Jack White is the yeoman, four-square. His work on the field, either cricket or farm, is conducted with an unhurried certainty and an unsurprised understanding of natural obstacles. Whether it was cows or batsmen, he had the treatment for the trouble. In play, he was serene, but not merely placid, for the artist in him could resent too much luck in an opponent or too little attention in a fielder.

The secret of his bowling could be seen, if never quite understood, only from very close. For, besides the length and direction and the variety of flight, he made the ball 'do a little' each way on the truest pitch without any advertisement from his fingers; and he made the ball bounce high even on a wet slow surface, often hitting the splice or near it with the threat of a catch to himself following up, or to silly-point, John Daniell in early days, Arthur Wellard later. These three missed very little.

Like C. Blythe, he often started the attack with the new ball. Old or new, it was all the same to him. Occasionally he would bowl a huge and obvious off-break, and smile paternally at his enormity.

By observation and industry he rose to be a competent batsman. He tried nothing beyond his self-known limits, and I never once saw him throw away his wicket. In defence, he was a believer in pads as well as bat, remarking: 'You know, the umpire's often wrong in the right way.'

He began to play for Somerset, intermittently, when he was seventeen, in 1909; regularly in 1913. In every full season from 1919 to the end he had his 100 wickets; in 1929 and 1930, his 1,000 runs as well. He played for England fifteen times, and in all first-class matches he took 2,358 wickets at 18.56 each. He would come from a morning's haymaking to his 40 overs and 6 or 7 wickets at Taunton, then return to more work on the farm, or stay for some poker, of which game he was technically and temperamentally a master.

On sticky pitches there have been, among modern cricketers, more difficult slow left-hand bowlers than Jack White; but on all pitches, none, perhaps, so persistently great.

P. G. H. Fender — *Sussex and Surrey*

For sheer entertainment, I doubt if any modern cricketer has surpassed P. G. H. Fender, of Surrey and All England.

He hated the dull finish, the formal declaration, the expected stroke, the workaday over. He rescued treasures of cricket from dust and oblivion, snatched off the covering, and showed them to an astonished and delighted public. He would assail a famous batsman with a sequence of dropping full-pitchers. I have seen him, and him alone, cut a ball square for six. He would declare an innings closed with an abruptness which threatened committeemen with heart-failure.

Yet he was no calculating showman. His schemes were born from one of the acutest and quickest brains ever applied to cricket, and he had an unquenchable love for a gamble. His handling of a thin Surrey attack was a recurring act of mystery; he made a feast from short commons, an opera from a song in the street. One puff of victory sighted on the horizon, and he rode straight for it. Only when plans had miscarried, and the way was lost, his leadership sometimes failed. He could communicate disappointment.

As a schoolboy from St Paul's he first played for Sussex in 1910. By 1914 he was helping Hitch and Rushby in the last Surrey team which won the championship, when Hayward and Hobbs used to open the batting.

In 1920 he went with J. W. H. T. Douglas to Australia and learnt much from five consecutive Test defeats. In 1921 he succeeded C. T. A. Wilkinson as captain of Surrey, and played against Australia at Manchester and the Oval. In the next eight seasons he did the 'double' six times. Further, he was a slip-fielder in the Jack Gregory class. In 1929 he played for England against South Africa at Edgbaston. Three years later the Surrey captaincy was handed over to D. R. Jardine; but Fender continued till 1936 to play occasionally, both under Jardine and E. R. T. Holmes; advisory, loyal, and with little sign of the years.

As a bowler he seemed sometimes to lose himself in the search for variety; but, when he concentrated solely on the slow leg-break, he could be as great as any of them. At Lord's, in

1927, he took five Middlesex wickets in seven balls. Alike, he was the man to take a difficult and obstructive wicket and to confound the tailenders. In batting, he lived on risk and his wrists. He made nearly 20,000 runs at an average of 26; yet it was not figures that he went after so much as the ruining of the bowler's confidence and length.

With all this flair and adventure on the field, his habit and speech were of a conventional, even serious, turn. He liked circumlocution; he did not 'think about' things, but 'gave them his earnest consideration'. In all, he was a wonderful figure in or near the game. I wish he could have captained England; for surely he earned it.

D. J. Knight — *Surrey*

Hero-worship was an innocent wisdom, and to those of us who pursued cricket with a shameless joy and cricketers with a shocking pencil, the name D. J. Knight stood only an inch or so below Jack Hobbs, and many yards above Mr Asquith. Dorando was merely in the running.

For, in 1914, D. J. Knight was fresh from doing what we were still in the process of failing to do. At Malvern he had stepped into the First Eleven in his first summer and, for five seasons, had averaged 50. Thence he had gone to Oxford and, with an innings of 64, done much towards beating Cambridge at Lord's. Besides, what young bowler, with the weakest flame of sense, does not sometimes long to be a batsman who takes nine-tenths of the talk and can even hold, for an odd minute, the wayward interest of the ladies? And Donald Knight made his runs so easily, as if the best bowling were but the vehicle and servant of his skill.

1919 was his year, when people went to the Oval to see Hobbs and Knight open the Surrey innings. Many then did not know, or care to ask, which was which, satisfied to watch the joint approach to perfection. Against Yorkshire, Knight made a century in each innings, full of those strokes which started, for some, memories and murmurs of L. C. H. Palairet and R. H. Spooner. For Oxford, against Cambridge and a fine burst of fast bowling by Arthur Gilligan, he played a 70 in the manner of a Test batsman, which he became two years later, against Gregory, McDonald, Armstrong, and Mailey, at Trent Bridge and Lord's. It was a season of flux and failure for English cricket. In his four Test innings Knight's highest was 38 in a total of 147.

This setback would surely have been corrected, forgotten; but he went as a master to Westminster, and soon was one of those occasional names who fade easily from the purview of selectors and slide from the gossip of the game. He did play for Surrey in the August of 1923, heading their averages at 53; and in 1925, at Taunton, in some midjudgment over a snatched run, he gave up his wicket to Hobbs, who went on to equal and surpass the centuries of W. G. Grace. But, mostly, he took his wonderful batting to the Oxford Harlequins and the Old Malvernians, and the art that long remained international in quality became a familiar but local delight.

Not long before the Hitler war he came back to a regular place in the Surrey side; a welcome, but not wholly satisfying, return. Years and absence had imposed some bluntness; for now he was just a good batsman among good batsmen; a style that recalled; a hint of greatness.

F. J. Durston — *Middlesex*

At the bottom of the Middlesex bowling averages for 1919, as recorded in the most blameless of Cricket Annuals, there may be read the name Dunston. Thus, under an alias, ungarnished by any initial letter, fore or aft, unaccommodated with even a speculative Albert or a fancy Henry, and amplified only by the statement that he took five wickets at 74.20 each, did Jack Durston enter the lists of higher cricket.

Within one year from then, he had taken his full part in the August victories of Sir Pelham Warner's last Middlesex team, also 113 wickets at 22 each in the season. By 1921, he was established as the county's opening bowler. For MCC against the Australians he took 7 for 84 in one innings, and, in the Lord's Test against Australia, the wickets of T. J. E. Andrews,

H. Carter, C. G. Macartney (twice), and Warwick Armstrong (bowled for 0). He also played for Players *v.* Gentlemen at Lord's and at the Oval, but never again for England.

Those who live on memory like to tell us, what we may already suspect, that few bowlers have been fast and that, of those, only a handful have been great. The tiresome implication is that we may write off the nearly fast and the sometimes nearly great, the ambitious workmen of the game. Among these, Jack Durston, stands high, six and a half feet, no less. In action, he was high-geared, long-levered, and, if he had not the catapultine propulsion of an Ernest Jones, Cotter, or Larwood, he could make the ball whistle and kick, and the batsman spar and dance. Also, he could last, and, like all proper bowlers, he could appeal.

Five times in his earlier years he had a 100 or more wickets in the season; then, as weight and wisdom grew, he passed, by convenient stages, to the art and practice of off-spinners. It was a vast sight; the umpire was a white pigmy beside him, Jim Smith a moderate fellow; and the ball shrank to a cherry in his hand.

His batting, without violent variation in result, developed from the painstaking to the eccentric, and he once answered my inquiry on his progress with: 'Gave up style this year, and jumped to thirteenth for Middlesex.' His highest score was 92, against Northamptonshire at Lord's; but his innings that I best remember was conceived at Portsmouth, late in his career. He was aiming, vainly and regardless, to hit every ball to square-leg; Goliath swatting at flies with a pencil.

Durston never retired; he merely left the three-day toil to spread abroad skill and entertainment. None handles a charity cricket match with quite his wisdom and geniality, nor so modestly yet deftly persuades local batsmen that they have played the innings of a lifetime. His encouragement to the young and his advice to the perplexed are implied rather than given. His presence is a reassurance, a restoration; and to meet him is like leaving a political rally in Trafalgar Square for the Still Life room of the National Gallery.

J. Mercer — *Sussex and Glamorgan*

Less gifted bowlers than Jack Mercer have played for England. For fifteen seasons up to this war he opened, continued, and closed the Glamorgan attack, and welcomed with an unfailing humour the reluctance of the batsman to depart, of the umpire to agree, and of the fieldsman to bend; the Mark Tapley among cricketers.

Sussex could have had Mercer, for he was born, in 1895, at Southwick, near Brighton. He spent the summer of 1913 at the Hove Nursery. In 1914 he returned from Russia, where he was pursuing avocations unconnected with cricket, to join the Sportsmen's Battalion. Commissioned thence to the Royal Sussex Regiment, he was wounded in the fighting in France, and later held a Staff appointment in London.

In the Sussex cricket of 1919, he hardly 'got a touch'. Too many bowlers were doing the same sort of thing, among the exponents of medium and fast-medium attack being the brothers Albert and Robert Relf, Vallance Jupp, a certain Maurice Tate, and H. E. Roberts. Mercer had two innings, 8 and 1, and no bowling at all. In 1920 he took 16 wickets at 31 each, but in 1921 relapsed to 2 at 67. It was time to migrate.

His start for Glamorgan, in 1923, was, as he has remarked, almost imperceptible, his 8 wickets costing 33.50 each; but, early in September, he startled the bowlers of Hampshire and the citizens of Cardiff with 48 scored at number ten in thirty-five minutes. In 1924 he rose to the respectability of 39 wickets at 21.12 each. Next year he had his 100 wickets, a feat that he was to perform eight more times. In 1926 he and the brilliant but temperamental Ryan took 219 wickets between them, and Glamorgan rose from bottom to eighth in the Championship. That November he went with the MCC team to India, where he took 46 wickets at 21 each.

No modern bowler has surpassed, and few have equalled, Mercer in simplicity and ease of action. He used both swerves, as servants, not as toys, and he was a master of the late-swinging half-volley. But he was not reliant on the new ball for his effects, showing dexterity in off-spin and in an occasional googly of laughable dimensions.

Above all, he had that spirit without which the highest skill remains but academic, never refusing a task or admitting a conqueror. In 1936, at the age of forty-one, he took all 10 wickets for 51 runs in an innings at Worcester. In all, when the war came, he had taken 1,593 wickets at 22.84 each, a great achievement for one who, being at once the spearhead and the stay of his team, could not afford the luxury of weariness.

In batting he was economical, dividing his two important strokes equally between attack and defence. The back-stroke he called 'Cautious Caroline', and the one that sent the ball to the square-leg boundary was 'Saucy Sally'.

Akin to his bowling, he has a gift of conjuring, and, after causing a batsman to be caught at slip while playing to short-leg, he would, under persuasion, produce a comforting number of half-crowns from his victim's ear.

A year or two ago, at the end of a war-time match at Lord's, I asked him how he was bowling, and he said: 'On principle. The rest has gone.' But it will be remembered.

Maurice Tate — *Sussex*

Maurice Tate, as fast-medium bowler, has had many imitators but no equal in English cricket of the last twenty years.

Tate was also a batsman, and began as such for Sussex, with the addition of a pleasing gift of medium-paced bowling, to evoke easy if delusive comparison with his father, F. W. Tate, an admirable cricketer, to whom some erect no kinder memorial than a catch missed in 1902 off Joe Darling's bat at Manchester and deep square-leg, both difficult places. His son, Maurice, was early called 'Boundary Tate', from a habit of freedom in wrist, shoulder, and heart, but he was no fool-hitter, having also a strong and stylish back-stroke which he could apply opportunely, but not without mental strife, clothing his laughter in the hired weeds of gravity.

His custom of topping a 100 wickets in the season began in 1919; and when, in 1922, an aggregate of 1,050 runs was joined on, years of all-round competence were forecast; perhaps something more; perhaps not. Then, in 1923, Tate burst into greatness as a bowler to be spoken of, if not in the same breath, at least in the same paragraph, as S. F. Barnes and J. T. Hearne, a bowler who made the wicket-keeper's gloves crack like a pistol-shot and Jack Hobbs push back his cap and walk pensively out to prod the blameless pitch.

After a short, galumphing run, like some policeman easing his conscience by a token pursuit of the uncatchable, Tate hurled into his delivery the harmonized strength of loins, back, and fingers; a perfect engine. He has been accused of lack of variety in design; but Tate at his zenith had no need of conscious variety. To what purpose should skill be decorated with deception by a bowler who, without change of action or angle of delivery, sent stumps whistling towards long-stop with an out-swinger or break-back at nature's sweet will?

In that summer of 1923 he took 219 wickets; in 1924, 205; in 1925, 228. In each of these three seasons he had his 1,000 runs; a feat with no numerical and hardly a physical parallel in cricket. But his runs, which later included a Test century against South Africa, were to become obscured by the grandeur of his bowling, to be part-forgotten, like Swift's verse or Disraeli's novels. From all this some relief was found in bending an ever-broadening beam at short-leg and telling the umpire from behind a confidential hand that the sun was hot and the rain uncommonly wet. But he missed little that you hit into the region of his management.

Arthur Gilligan shared with Tate the opening attack for Sussex, captained him from mid-off, and received with a nod and a smile those flingings of the arms when the paint on the stumps was too thin. Some raised crusty objections to these semaphorings. But they were part of Tate, like his huge outward-turning boots, and his weird ejaculations – he once said to me as I fell to earth in catching him: 'Why, you came down that pitch like Abraham' – and a bowler who cannot curse with either mouth or hand is first cousin to an inbred slug and not worth the twopenny tram-ticket to go and see him with.

With Gilligan, in 1924, Tate shot out South Africa for 30 in forty-five minutes at Edgbaston, and under him, that winter he attacked the Australian batsmen with a sustained and solitary magnificence. He took 38 wickets for 23 each, a record for all Test series between England and Australia. Of those 38, 28 were the wickets of acknowledged and principal batsmen. That was Tate's way. He fired away his powder on the big game. The rabbits could die on their own. He went again to Australia under A. P. F. Chapman. Tate, at thirty-three, was not quite the bowler of four years earlier; besides, he was now part of a scheme, not the corner-stone of the building. But he was never collared, sometimes deadly, always reliable. His last visit to Australia, under D. R. Jardine, was a mistake; not his own. But he enjoyed the fishing.

Even in his decline, during the middle 1930s, Tate was feared for his fame. He never bowled loosely; he couldn't; and, for three overs or so at the start, the batsman would pride himself on surviving a brave imitation of the Tate who could once silence a crowd by expectation alone. Perhaps the boys, whom in heart he most resembles, enjoyed him most; and they took their autograph-books to him not merely for the sake of their collection but to be near a man and to share in the bulky wonder of his greatness.

C. S. Marriott — *Lancashire and Kent*

When C. S. Marriott had bowled out a batsman, he used to stand with his hands clasped behind his back, leaning inquiringly forward, like a doctor watching a patient from the end of the bed. Very potent was the medicine.

He had a short, prancing run, like a development of 'marking time at the double', which his long legs began from the environs of mid-off; just before delivery he whipped his right hand behind his back, and the batsmen had no sight of the intended spin, leg or off, till the ball was in the air. His pace was above slow, his length teasingly accurate, and the spin, imparted by unusually long fingers, sufficient without exaggeration. A batsman, beaten by this spin, would often be perturbed to see what appeared, falsely, to be a smile on the face of the bowler. But the expression was not attributable to amusement; it was a natural, if mysterious, spasm.

In games, bowling at cricket was the one thing that Marriott did supremely well; and this art he rarely presented to the public view except in the month of August, when he would emerge from his Dulwich schoolmastering and coaching to join Freeman of Kent in a spin-ensemble such as no other county could remotely rival. In that month he seldom failed to take some 50 wickets at low cost.

Marriott was educated at St Columba's, Dublin, and first played for Lancashire, the county of his birth, in 1919, taking 26 wickets at 26 each. Going up to Cambridge at the age of twenty-four, he soon showed himself to be one of the best slow bowlers ever seen at Fenner's. In his first summer term he took 50 wickets at 13.58 each, and he had 7 for 69 against Oxford. In 1921 he took 57 wickets for Cambridge at 18 each, and his bowling, 5 for 44 and 2 for 67, contributed to the heavy defeat of Oxford. 'I shall catch you at wicket off a leg-break from Father Marriott,' said M. D. Lyon, as I took guard, and then missed me off him from my very first ball. Soon afterwards Marriott bowled with success at Lord's for Gentlemen against Players. In the same summer, he was one of those picked for the Manchester Test against Australia, but was left out.

In 1924 he began to play for Kent, and in that August he took 43 wickets at 14 each. In the following winter he went to South Africa under Lord Tennyson. But not till he was in his thirty-eighth year did he play in a full Test for England. Then at the Oval in August of 1933 he baffled the best batsmen of the West Indies, taking 5 for 37 and 6 for 59. It was artistry of the highest order.

In batting he was a natural number eleven, but he once helped Ames to save Kent against Surrey at the Oval, and once when overweening, I said to him down the pitch, 'Father, I am going to bowl down your stumps,' he hit the next ball clean out of the ground.

G. Duckworth — *Lancashire*

George Duckworth, wicket-keeper to Lancashire and England, lived a noisy life on the field and enjoyed it. One over, he was falling sideways with a crash to hold a wide and fiery one from Ted McDonald; the next he and Richard Tyldesley were hunting an lbw together, the stumper's falsetto baying discordant assent to the bowler's declamatory tenor; and when they brought their turn to a Yorkshire ground, the Saturday crowd, uplifted by refreshment and party, liked to join in the concert; and Emmott Robinson, perhaps, would be batting, and he, too, would have his say, and brandish his bat, till nearly everyone was at it, and the umpire 'signified disagreement', and the crowd roared, and the match battled on.

Duckworth's art was like that of the old music-hall players who scorned suavity and suggestion and sang their lines as fast and as loud as they could, who took their jokes and threw them slap against the spectators' faces and would have starved rather than crooned. But Duckworth *was* an artist, for he made the sternest batsman feel uncomfortable. As a batsman, square and correct, nearly all pads and obstinacy, he was no easy target, and once he played on three days of a Test in Australia for 39 runs.

His first appearance for England was at Old Trafford in a match without cricket, against South Africa in 1924; and, as the rain poured, Duckworth, in that huge-collared sweater, was able to explain Manchester to his companions. Four years passed before his second chance came, at the Oval against the West Indies, and he took it. In that season he shared in the fall of 107 wickets, 77 caught, 30 stumped, and was picked to go to Australia under A. P. F. Chapman. He played in all five Tests, as he did again in England during the Australian visit of 1930. To Duckworth there has been no captain like Chapman, 'the skipper' then and ever since.

Under Chapman again, he went to South Africa in 1931, but fell ill after three Tests, his place being taken by the able Farrimond, the man who would not desert Lancashire. In 1932, he and Ames went together under D. R. Jardine to Australia. The wicket-keeping in the Tests fell to the younger man, and Duckworth, who knows no envy, used to help Ames buckle on his pads and give freely of his rich and humorous advice. In life as in wicket-keeping he has missed very little.

In all that he does and says there is a rough kindliness and a gusto that seem to grow best together in Lancashire.

K. S. Duleepsinhji — *Sussex*

K. S. Duleepsinhji's cricketing career was short and great. In 1925 he was given his Blue at Cambridge; by August 1932 he had played his last match for Sussex and England, and at the age of only twenty-seven had begun the life of an invalid. He had just been invited to go to Australia with D. R. Jardine's team, but Australia never received, in a full Test match, this prince of style and master of footwork.

In these eight seasons – hardly eight, for besides his early retirement in 1932 he was cut short in May of 1927 – he made 50 centuries. On his first appearance against Australia, at Lord's, in 1930, he scored 173, followed by 48 in the second innings, Even for him this was a wonderful year. Playing for Sussex against Middlesex, at Lord's, he scored 116 and 102 not out; for Gentlemen *v.* Players, at Lord's, 125 and 103 not out; for Sussex *v.* Northamptonshire, at Hove, 333 in one day, the highest innings ever recorded for his county. In the last three Tests, respectively at Leeds, Manchester, and the Oval, he made 38, 10, 54, 50, 46.

For Cambridge against Oxford he made no century; but his 75 as a Freshman in 1925 was a fulfilment of something more than promise at Cheltenham. Two years later he began the Cambridge season with 101 against Yorkshire; then came that 254 not out against Middlesex. Soon after, he fell ill and went abroad for the winter. In 1928 eleven matches for Sussex brought him 1,082 runs, with six centuries. In 1929 he made seven centuries, including 115 and 246 in one match against Kent, on the Hastings ground with that free pavilion on the distant hills. So to his 1930 season, after a visit with A. H. H. Gilligan's MCC team to Australia and New Zealand, in which his Test average against New Zealand was 89.

In 1931 he became captain of Sussex and headed their averages. In that season he made nine centuries, four of them in succession. He played in the three Tests against New Zealand and scored a century (107) in the Oval match. In 1932 he had an innings of 132 for Gentlemen *v.* Players at Lord's, and he was leading Sussex in a close struggle with Yorkshire for the championship when his health broke. In Test trials he had scored 92 not out at Cardiff and 128 for South *v.* North at Manchester.

Among great cricketers he was at once the most retiring and the most candid that I have met. I have heard him, after making a century for Sussex, say: 'No, it was not good; the bowling was nothing.' Again, after a score of some 20 or 30: 'That was my best innings this month; there was something to do.' Quiet, discerning, and witty in conversation, he seemed gently to transfer to the admiring spectator most of the responsibility for some fine performance of his own; yet he knew, without belittlement or exaggeration, the exact scope of his own powers, and he compared them without vain modesty or silly envy to those of the few great batsmen of his day. But with his uncle, 'Ranji', he encouraged no comparison, either of himself or of others, 'Ranji' was the oracle, the incomparable, 'Uncle said . . .' That was enough.

In 'Duleep's' batting, beauty and orthodoxy were perfectly wedded. Lithe, strong of wrist, quick in eye and foot, he had neither cause nor inclination to fear any bowler. In the killing of slow bowling he had no superior, perhaps no equal, in England. From duels with 'Duleep', only Clarence Grimmett, among leg-breakers, emerged with something near to equal honours. Besides his batting he was a great field at short-slip, standing closer than is usual.

It is a tale of concentrated glory, sad but triumphant. In success or failure, health or illness, he has never varied. As friend or casual acquaintance, companion or opponent, he is courteous and courageous, interested and interesting; 'a very perfect gentle knight'.

C. F. Walters —
Glamorgan and Worcestershire

Cyril Walters hardly gave himself time for fame, but, for sheer grace of batting, he was not surpassed by any cricketer of the inter-war years.

In the summer of 1934 he burst, like the welcome sun, upon a half-ignorant public, once as captain and nine times as opening batsman of England against Australia. In the year before, he had played in the three Tests against the West Indies, then accompanied D. R. Jardine's MCC team to India, where he played an innings of 102 in the Test at Madras.

Even so, he was not yet earmarked for England. His style was admired, but his solidity was questioned by the commercial school of criticism, whose eleventh commandment was 'Thou shalt not adventure'. In the shadow of this drab academy even the great Hammond was stifling his genius. And here was a young man who opened an innings against Australia as if he were enjoying a practice-net.

Walters was a reflection, a recapture, of the Palairet and Spooner manner. He walked to the wicket like a free man, one going out to a hard, but agreeable task. Medium of height, trimly knit, he had the dancer's balance. He used the whole crease, as the saying goes, and held orthodoxy as servant, not master. He answered the bowler on merit, not on reputation, and he suffered from no clogging respect for the occasion. He was never 'set', a state which implies a growth of confidence. He jumped to his high noon.

Thus, he was as likely to fail at 70 as at 7. He had all the strokes that need a full swing and a free wrist, excelling at those played to the off side off the back foot. Only he lacked the metallic certainty of a Bradman, the intensity of a Sutcliffe; a choice of temperament rather than a want in technique.

His figures in that series against Australia are worth recalling: 17 and 46 (out of a total of 141) at Trent Bridge; 82 at Lord's; 52 and 50 not out at Old Trafford (twice putting on 100 with Sutcliffe); 44 and 45 at Leeds; 64 and 1 at the Oval. An average of 51 was fine going for so debonair an artist.

Welsh born, Walters for three or four years played for Glamorgan; then he qualified for Worcestershire, for whom he was first secretary, then captain. He had a habit of making a century against Warwickshire and Northamptonshire. Then, in 1933, he first topped the 2,000, scoring 226 against Kent at Gravesend. In Walters, the Nawab of Pataudi, Nichol, and Gibbons, Worcestershire had four opening batsmen to compare with any in England.

For England against the West Indies he played an innings

of 51 at Lord's. In 1934 he again exceeded 2,000 runs, and, beside his Test performances, he shared with R. E. S. Wyatt in an opening stand of 160 in eighty minutes in the second innings of the Gentlemen against the Players at Lord's; the basis of victory. Then, midway through the season of 1935, he left first-class cricket for domestic reasons. He was only twenty-nine; and his twenty-third and twenty-fourth years had been lost in the tiresome process of qualification.

Cyril Walters was of those who –

> 'play their music,
> Play, and are gone on the windy highway.'

But the tune will be remembered.

E. F. Longrigg — *Somerset*

E. F. Longrigg has told me how, at the end of his first match for Somerset, a fellow-player, only five years his senior, said to him: 'You know nothing at all about cricket, but don't let that worry you.' It was unlikely to do so in a county that remembered Sam Wood's words to a new cricketer in his team on his first day at Bradford against Yorkshire: 'Hullo, my dear, I don't remember seeing *you* on the train. What's your weakness? Batting? or bowling?'

'Bunty' Longrigg – for nobody calls him by his name of Edmund – has been the most consistent amateur batsman in the Somerset team since the prime of J. C. W. MacBryan and M. D. Lyon; and, being left-handed, he was little troubled by the leg-breakers who were so baneful to the airy notions of his right-handed companions. My strongest memory of him is his playing the subtle and gyratory 'Tich' Freeman firmly in the middle of the bat, while others groped vainly for the truth. Against the fastest bowlers he was less sure, being apt to spar at the rising ball; but the infrequency with which he gave a catch to wicket-keeper or slips made me almost believe his assertion that he was 'just leading them on'.

Longrigg was in the Rugby School eleven for four years; in his third, he averaged 40; in his fourth, when he was captain,

53, with a highest score of 159; and his right-handed slow-medium bowling gave him 11 wickets at 9.27 each. 'I used to keep the batsmen wondering,' he said, 'wondering when the ball was going to break.' In that same summer, 1925, he played for the Lord's Schools against the Rest, and scored 57 for the Public Schools against the Army.

John Daniell summoned him from Bath to Taunton, where, from the first, he found Harry Fernie's pitches well suited to his style. After being one of those who were privileged to field out to Jack Hobbs's two centuries that equalled and overtook the record of Dr W. G. Grace, he began on his own account with a chanceless 60 not out against Kent. This he followed with 44 not out against Middlesex, and 47 against the champions, Yorkshire.

Going up to Cambridge, he did not find a place against Oxford in 1926, but again showed a liking for the Yorkshire and Kent bowlers at Taunton. Next year, he won his Blue, and in the second innings against Oxford, helped A. K. Judd to put on 108 for the second wicket. In 1929, he topped 1,000 runs; in 1930, he did so again, and scored four centuries, including 205 against Leicestershire at his favourite Taunton. In 1931, he achieved the desire of all batsmen with 100 against Yorkshire, again at Taunton.

In the years that followed, torts and conveyancing often kept him from the field, but, having a natural gift of eye and wrist, he could strike form with the minimum of practice. In 1938, he succeeded R. A. Ingle as captain, and, at Bristol, elated the right-thinking half of the bank holiday crowd with 187 not out. In leadership he showed keenness, judgment, and a nice satirical humour. To which of these he owed his 2 overs for 13 runs and 0 wickets it is hard to say. In the last year before the war he was again captain. The first year after it found him ready to write his name not too low in the batting order at Taunton.

A. H. Bakewell — *Northamptonshire*

A. H. Bakewell, of Northamptonshire, sometimes showed an ability shared by only some half-dozen batsmen in this generation; fate also willed that the show should be given during just a few seasons and, mostly, to a half-empty house.

He began in 1928, aged twenty, first topped the 1,000 in 1930, touched the heights in 1933, and was stopped from batting by a car accident in August 1936 on his way home from an innings of supreme skill.

Between 1931 – when he and J. Arnold, with an aggregate age of forty-five, opened the innings for England against New Zealand – and 1936 he played six times for England; but never against Australia; and how Sydney would have enjoyed him; for his batting was nature without veneer; he feared neither tradition nor bowlers, and he hated convention as a boy hates tight collars and polite talk.

Therein lay his strength, and his weakness. He did not bother to hide his love of freedom and company, and he remained the boy who just wouldn't touch his cap to the important visitor. He was Huckleberry Finn with no Mississippi. He needed a leader-manager, not merely a captain, and it was not all his own fault that he never found one.

He would have caught the eye as a fielder alone, for he seemed to be three short-legs at once, hovering for the kill. In his first season he made eight catches in one match against Essex at Leyton. In batting he had a stance to make the purists mutter, wide-straddling, rather crouched, and very open; but this idea straightened itself in time for a sufficiency of defence, and in attack his design was bold, his footwork very nimble, his execution crisp.

The artistry was always there, waiting to be uncovered, but among the bright colours there lurked a dull thread of negligence, even apathy. Neither his own temperament nor external comment could always make him care; but, when his mind and his fortunes were warm, he could have batted with Bradman on not uneven terms. For most of 1933 he held this mood. He made 257 against Glamorgan at Swansea, the highest innings recorded for Northamptonshire.

After being twelfth man at Manchester, he took Sutcliffe's place against the West Indies in the Oval Test, and scored a century of power and ease. But the best of all was his innings of 246 against Nottinghamshire at Northampton, when Sam Staples set the leg field for his accurate off-breaks and Bakewell again and again drove him from the leg stump crack against the rails through vacant extra-cover.

Though he later played once for England against India and twice against South Africa, that season of 1933 was the climax of the story. It is well to think of men at their best. Many like to talk of what a player Bakewell might have been. It is better to remember how great he often was.

The Nawab of Pataudi —
Worcestershire, England and India

The Nawab of Pataudi was one of the great batsmen of his short day, and fortunate were the few who saw him and Cyril Walters matching each other's artistry on the Worcestershire pitch by the banks of the Severn.

In style, Pataudi was a quietist, a deflector rather than a driver, supple of wrist; he had long patience, the quickness of foot to counter spin, and the heart to sustain pace. Above all, he loved a match that mattered, a fight, one in which fast bowlers and strong talkers could be heard prophesying what sort of things were going to happen to the other side. He needed stimulus, such as was given him by Cambridge at Lord's in 1931, when Ratcliffe set him the figure of 201 to aim at and lesser batsmen bowed to the fury of Farnes.

In 1926, at the age of sixteen, Pataudi came to England from the Chief's College, Lahore, where he had been coached by M. G. Salter, the former Oxford University and Gloucestershire cricketer. Living in the Tonbridge district, he was further instructed by Frank Woolley. The pupil moved his master to unusual expressions of praise. Going up to Oxford in 1928, he missed his Blue that summer, but in 1929 he saved Oxford from defeat at Lord's by innings of 106 and 84.

It was natural that he should be compared with K. S. Duleepsinhji, his senior by five years. In power of attack, Pataudi was not the equal of 'Duleep', who could make a bowler, especially the slow leg-breaker, doubt if the whole thing was worth while. In grace of movement there was nothing between them; and both were beautiful fielders.

In 1930, Pataudi failed against Cambridge, but next summer he broke records right and left, scoring 1,307 runs for Oxford at an average of 93.35. At one time he made five centuries in six consecutive innings, including two at the Oval, in the match against Surrey, and his captain withdrew him from the final match against MCC, in case, as he said, Pataudi should 'waste the runs that he was going to make against Cambridge'. There followed his memorable innings of 238 not out, which may stand for many years as an Oxford *v.* Cambridge record. Only F. R. Brown sometimes troubled him, but he gave no actual chance. Such was the nervous and physical strain of this performance that he collapsed on returning to the pavilion. His average against Cambridge in three years was 113.

In 1932, he first played for Worcestershire. For the county in that season he did nothing out of the way, but at Lord's, for Gentlemen against Players, he rectified his failure of 1931 by an innings of 165, adding 161 for the third wicket with Duleepsinhji and 160 for the fourth with D. R. Jardine. This performance won him a place in Jardine's team for Australia.

There, he began with a century against Western Australia and another against the Combined Australian Eleven. Then, in his first Test, he scored 102. It took him over five hours. In the Second Test he failed, and was dropped for the remaining three. Once more he played against Australia, at Nottingham in 1934, scoring 12 and 10.

In 1933, he scored three double-centuries for Worcestershire, but soon afterwards his health broke down. He recovered enough to play intermittently for the county, and his last century for them, against Hampshire in 1938, was one of the most brilliant that he ever made.

When first-class competitive cricket was resumed in 1946, he came to England as captain of the All-India touring team. Pataudi, considered at his best, will always rank among the masters of batting.

Facts and Fancies

The Stylist

I came upon him while looking through some old photographs
and groups of our first school, standing trim, bland, gorgeously
flannelled, in the back row of the Second Eleven. We called
him 'The Stylist'. As to technique, he knew it all – left foot,
balance, and eye well over the ball for the off-drive; left elbow
out and hands in front of blade for forward defensive stroke.
He imitated admirably the maestros of the day, and understood
the value of the Hobbs twirl of the bat-handle and the Philip
Mead habit of gardening on the pitch.

A casual spectator, passing by for one over, might approve
his promise and grace, but his intimates knew better. For he
made no runs; or nearly none. Of course he was always going
to make some. It was strange how little this unfortunate flaw
affected his reputation, and other boys continued to ask his
advice, and he continued to give it. For he had a smooth and
pleasing manner in transferring knowledge. He was oracular
without obscurity; didactic, but never dictatorial. He was
the triumph of pure reason.

Then, for some years, I lost him. It was understood that at
his public school he fell among those of ruder technique, who
preferred practice to theory. But he did not cease, so it was
rumoured, to dress perfectly for the game. He lingered for a
time in the Second House team, but was no longer consulted
on matters of style. He became assistant telegraphist on the
First Eleven score-board, from which position he rose by
diligence to be head scorer.

At the University his services on the field entirely ceased
to be required. He became just an opinion. But he joined
several of the less celebrated London and District Clubs to
whose members his powerful car was useful and his manner
pleasing. His equipment remained unexceptionable; a cricket-
bag, large enough to suggest county form, contained two bats
in oilskin cases, innocent of all marks except a few on the outer
edge, and two pairs of boots kept in bags bearing his initials
in blue; one pair, it was said, was reserved – perpetually – for
bowling. In the field he preferred mid-on.

He passed, as if by right, into the Diplomatic Service. He

does not aim to be an ambassador, as he hates publicity. So I hope that his eye does not fall on this light biography.

The Fathers' Match

I look forward to the revival of the Fathers' Match, pleasantest of cricket's civil wars. For some of us, some time ago, it used to be a day when you rushed to the window first thing in the morning. School matches could be postponed for rain; but, even in the golden days of Edward, fathers could come but once for cricket, and so the sun must shine. The match was near the end of the term, when the calendars were almost pencilled off, and examinations were near, and the last penny of private income had been blued on a veteran tennis ball.

For those who had fathers coming to play there was the pleasure of seeing them, mixed sometimes with the fear of seeing them make asses of themselves; a pleasure and a fear probably not confined to the sons. It is an ever-present anxiety to the schoolboy, as it is a sort of fearful hope to his companions, that a close relative should commit some public indiscretion. Mothers and aunts, certainly, are allowed a wider scope of eccentricity. They are expected to transcend convention; and I remember a Ladies' Match in which a boy in imminent danger of being torpedoed, piped out: 'I say, pitch 'em up, auntie, and Pax on grubs.' But fathers are given no points. Though with strict regard for politeness, their deportment is closely watched and, at times, discussed.

An eminent county cricketer has told me how he went down to his son's school and happened to play an innings of some distinction. He is a short man. His son's best enemy, fixing on this point and disregarding the innings, remarked to a friend: 'I say, hasn't —— got a putrid little pater?' The deadly insult reached the ears of the little pater's son, who, when there were no parents about, challenged, and, after a stiff fight, annihilated the slanderer!

And then, what blazers were to be seen on that day! I recall one of such complicated design and startling colours that it cancelled all impoliteness of staring. There was azure in it, and yellow and green; the sort of thing that Mr Pecksniff might have worn if, in his capacity of non-playing chairman, he had been offering some bland comments on the village cricket season, and giving away bats to which he had made no personal subscription. On one head, too, there was a funny little cap, like the Panjandrum's; as if the owner had invented a club of his own, of which he was sole member and perpetual president. There was, too, a very slow bowler with a deceptive double-wiggle in his action, who generally took wickets, partly because boys cannot play slow bowling, but chiefly, I think, because he distracted attention by what were surely the tightest trousers on record.

Afterwards there was the supper, at which hilarity was 'tempered with a modicum of decorum'; except once, when a meringue was, quite anonymously, thrown. Speeches were made, and the best school cricketers were praised, and blushed. Songs were then sung: 'The four-horse charabanc', 'Put a plaster on my chest', and 'The choir boy', whose voice was so beautiful and a little higher than the rest.

The Catch That Never Came Down

'What you tell me is very interesting,' said Drayson; 'but did I ever tell you the story of the catch that never came down?'

I stirred uneasily. Distant rumours of this – well – story had reached me some years before. There was a ruminative wildness in Drayson's eye. He helped himself to a cigarette, settled into his chair, and said: 'You don't believe it, of course. No one wants to believe it. It doesn't suit them. It cracks science from top to bottom. It wrecks Newton and Einstein; Jeans and Horstfloobler and that bunch would have to think again. But I know. You see, I was the bowler.'

'What and where was the match?'

'I'll leave you to guess, and just tell you what happened.'

'Ah.'

'We were sworn to secrecy. You see, it would have been awkward for the Club, if it had got around. Either everyone would have wanted to come and play there, to see if it would happen again, or else no one would have consented to play on a ground where a ball might disappear upwards for good. Nervous cricketers could never have stood the suspense. Any moment it might have come. A casual jerk from third-man; gone for good. A promising leg-break; switched away into eternity. Cummings, the treasurer, foresaw the implications; and already he had to answer to the committee for the unaccountable absence of a new ball. But it never happened again; and now the ground is built over.'

There was a short silence.

'It was in the second over that it happened, on the first ball. Curlew, our fast man, had opened in a very erratic manner. His first two balls went full-pitch to Wilkinson, the wicket-keeper, nearly vertical wides. The next two were long-hops, which the batsman hooked for four each; then two more full-pitchers. The second of these was immensely, almost inhumanly, fast; and it nearly decapitated Wilkinson. I remember it bounced back an unusual distance from the screen. I asked Curlew at the end of the over what he was up to. He was puzzled, and said the ball was very slippery; dangerously slippery, he thought, and it didn't feel quite like an ordinary ball. It was warm, he said, to the touch. He was right. There was an unearthly warmth about that ball.'

Drayson sat up straight in his chair. He spoke more slowly, and in a lower tone. 'I recall the start of my over,' he went on, 'as if it was yesterday. Two women had begun to settle in front of the screen with a picnic-basket and a small dog. It took some time to move them, also to shift Gandars, a minor poet, who was lost to the world at square-leg when he should have been at mid-on. I was itching to bowl; for the ball was getting warmer. It had reached the temperature of an unsatisfactory hot-bath. You know my style; slow tempters, with a bogus twirl of the hand to indicate leg-break. I tossed it up. The batsman mistook it for a half-volley, as so many have done to their cost. The upward sweep of his bat caught the ball on the rise, and it soared into the air.

'A slight breeze seemed to be wafting it towards Wilkinson at the wicket. I called his name, and he began to revolve, in his clumsy manner, underneath it. Gandars, for no apparent reason, shouted "Mine!" and teetered in on his toes from mid-on. Cover-point began to interest himself; and I stood half-way down the pitch, in an alert posture. Then I noticed something. The ball was not coming down. It went on up; slowly, slowly, getting smaller and smaller. Ganders, who is short-sighted, was the first to give up. He shouted "It's gone. Holy mushrooms. That's done it!" and put his hands in his pockets. The batsmen, after running three, stopped, and both stared into the sky. The ball was now only just visible, about the size of a moderate spider, some 150 feet up. There, for a space, it stopped, hovering in miraculous indecision. If it came down, it was going to be the catch of a lifetime. If it didn't, well . . . It didn't.

'One spectator thought we were being funny, shouted something about "horse-play", and left the ground. Cartwright, the groundsman, walked out to the pitch, looked steadily up at the ball, then at me. "Who done that?" he asked, unanswerably; then felt he was a fool; which he is; and began to laugh stupidly. Then the batting side came out, mostly running. Wilkinson wanted to send for a gun. "Extreme range," he explained, "but it's worth trying." Suddenly the ball shot up again, and in a second was lost to view. It just went, I tell you, slap into the void – empyrean, if you like.'

'Did you get another?' I asked.

'Oh, yes,' said Drayson, 'we got another; and we finished the game, though I can remember next to nothing of it. It fell pretty flat, you see. At tea we arranged to keep the affair a secret, and the spectators, just a handful, agreed. But now, of course, it doesn't matter who knows.'

'I wonder if it ever came down anywhere, Drayson.'

'I should doubt it. In fact, I hope not. I prefer to think that for one instant in the world's history the laws of gravity were suspended.'

The Best Company

I have sometimes wondered in which reign, as the schoolboys say, and with what men, I should most like to have gone cricketing. Our own age is the best, no doubt; but we need not incur the charge of escapism, levelled by the angular-minded at those who play nine holes of golf or read Trollope, if we choose to imagine, for a few minutes, that we were present to hear the talk of the spectators when Edward VII, then Prince of Wales, was bowled for nought by an over-excited man in East Anglia; or that we were near at hand when, between the battles of Trafalgar and Waterloo, William Lambert, the Surrey professional, bowled a 'stick' of wides to the Reverend Lord Frederick Beauclerk, on purpose 'to put him out of temper'.

In those days there was no penalty for bowling wides, a pleasant and expansive state of affairs. Beauclerk did become very angry, and was soon out. The match was a two-a-sider. On the morning of it, Lambert's partner, Mr. G. Osbaldeston, was ill, and wanted to postpone it. But Beauclerk said 'No; play or pay.' So, 'Osbaldeston tottered to the wicket, made one run, and then retired, thus securing a substitute to field'. Lambert, a sort of Ajax of a man, scored 56 and 24, bowled 3 wickets, and caught and bowled the other. He won by 15 runs. Thus his lordship lost his temper, his wicket, the match, and the money.

His partner was one T. C. Howard; a mere name; the phantom of an else forgotten accomplice; pale satellite of tyranny. What, I wonder, did Mr Howard say? Was he allowed even to think? He was not consulted, I fancy, on any point of strategy. He was caught up in the clerical storm, roundly cursed, forced to lend his favourite bat, then blamed for defeat.

It always seems a little strange to me that most of those who con antiquity should fret so much about the erstwhile nature, shape, and position of buildings, and so little about the conversation of those who once laughed, worked, wept, or idled within them. These devoted students will argue for many months about the probable construction of a Forum. Many of us wouldn't give a sausage for all that, if we could only know whether that windswept gap in the corner was once full of shoppers on the verge of conflict about vegetables, while outside there stood a Roman tout passing betting-tablets and the subtlest information on the afternoon's chariot-racing. So it is, in a minor way, with cricket. Nyren and Pycroft have done their best; their pen-pictures of the old players are exquisitely drawn.

But both they, and to a greater degree those who followed them, have sometimes allowed themselves to be drowned in a flood of mathematics about the size of wickets, and bails and bats, to be parched by annalistic dust, and confounded in a maze of geography. I would like to know what Mr Osbaldeston said when that two-a-side match was over; and whether there ever passed through Lord Frederick's mind the shadow of a conviction that the ethics in his sermons were not wholly consummated by his own conduct on the field. Perhaps he didn't care.

These were the men, when history had not long staggered out of legend, with whom any one might have been happy to play. Character may sometimes have been questionable, but personality was richly varied. The cold hand of progress had not yet slapped the world into dull obediences and mass-conduct.

Others, perhaps, will praise the mid-Victorian times, when Dr Grace was beginning that career. For me, the earliest tours abroad read very invitingly, when the hospitable Americans played 'Rule, Britannia', as the opening English pair went out to bat. And the long trip to Australia, in spite of the waves, must have promoted, and strained, social harmony; when there was some pushing to sit next to the captain, and the first mate argued the room empty with a dissertation on the decline of back-stopping.

The Lost Average

Tellson, who is quite an important man these days, and has recently won a sharp bout of official correspondence, ought to be happy. But when I met him the other day, expecting to see a glow of bureaucratic-well-being on his somewhat ovine features, I found him, instead, a little petulant and almost difficult. He was, as the poet succinctly says, 'in pale contented of discontent'. He looked unconcentrated, like a sufferer from the grasshopper-mind; far other from him at whose arrival the clerks push funny postcards hastily under the ledger.

It seemed, after a short silence, followed by semi-courteous rumblings, that he was annoyed about his bowling average, or, rather, the lack of it. Circumstances had allowed him to appear in but one match of cricket this season. It had been a scratch affair; and his captain, a sort of vague tea-planter on leave, had mistaken him for a batsman of the same name. Couldn't be convinced to the contrary. In the reluctant guise of that other Tellson he had gone in, dazed, if flattered, first wicket down, and had been bowled second ball by a full-pitcher, that may have swerved, on the bottom of the off-stump. He hadn't liked that; but he had sunk the failure in the expectation of a spell of first-change bowling.

'Do you mean to tell me,' I said, 'that you were not put on at all? "First-change Tellson" not put on?'

'I had two overs, right at the end, after they'd won the game.'

'Well, that's not so bad, you know. Why, one day last June, when I was supposed to be opening the bowling, heavy rain came on just before the start. So I went off and had a nap. When I came back the other side had lost 7 wickets for 112——'

'But——'

'A fine example of the dispensability of the individual. I was given one over. It was a formal maiden. Then we declared. But tell me about your two overs, Tellson.'

He rescued his memories from engulfing wrath.

'They cost me twenty-seven runs, eternally curse it. You know how I like my field placed.'

'Yes, Tellson; scattered about. Fellows who are handy at catching the return throw from the spectators.'

'No, you fool; you know what I mean. One out, one in; a double ring; look after the singles and the fours. Well; this wallowing dolt of a captain – I should like to report him to a proper authority – shouted "Come on, Tellson, old man, see if you can make it. There's only ten minutes left!" '

'What's the matter with that? Very genial, I call it. Is that all?'

'No, it's not. He also said: "What about a trundle before the cows come home?" A trundle, indeed! Phssht! Then he told the fielders to go where they liked. They did. Long-leg sat down in a deck-chair, lit a cigarette, and engaged himself in talk with some footling woman. The wicket-keeper stood twenty yards back and pretended to knock at the knees. An undiluted travesty. If there's one thing I cannot stand at cricket it's——'

'What about your umpire?' I asked. 'I suppose he wasn't there. You know the one I mean. The fellow who has a nervous click in the nose, and whose moustache is longer on one side than the other. The one to whom you used to give tickets for Wembley each year.'

'He was not there, if you mean Lushington. The umpire I had was mad. He stood in my way. You know how I corkscrew out and come in again. He wouldn't budge. Insolent, too; said it didn't matter if I ran up backwards and bowled out of a mirror. I was hopelessly put off.'

'But did no one know that you were not the other Tellson, the batsman, I mean?'

'I cannot be sure. If they did, they pretended they didn't. I was subjected to continual badinage.'

'In what way?'

'It appears that this other man was a heavy drinker. At the start of the innings, when the field was being placed, our captain turned to me and said: "Well, where will it be today, Tellson?" And that wicket-keeper said: "Don't put him in the slips. He'll take them on the knee-cap. Try deep third-man, where he can predict them by sound and put his foot behind the middle one of the three." I tell you——'

'Too bad, my dear chap, and now your favourite beach is closed, where you might have made up your lost average in a sandy seashore game. Too bad, altogether. Come, Tellson, whichever Tellson you be; I'll give you lunch, and we'll forget your tea-planting captain in the restricted pleasures of the table.'

The Bottom of the Bag

My heart sticks to old things, which, in their turn, often stick to each other in affectionate adhesion at the bottom of the cricket-bag.

Strange inhabitants sojourn down there, and the other day I disturbed their slumber. There is a left-handed batting-glove, of neat design, but underdeveloped at birth. It had one short innings, but was so small that the finger-nails creaked for tightness. Its right-handed brother is not present, but must somewhere be incommoding the knuckles of a nameless batsman.

Next to the glove, oddly enough, is a pedometer. Whether it was bought, borrowed, or stolen, or just descended like manna, who could say? Perhaps it was once used by a disgruntled but scientific fielder, who wished to be able to tell his captain just how far he had travelled, walking once every two and a half minutes from long-leg to long-leg, and, in an unguarded moment, he lent it to me and went in to bat. Then, tucked away in a corner are two cricket balls, dishonourably acquired long ago, and now fallen into a disreputable old age; one, smooth and bald, and tolerably rhomboid, the other bearded at the seams; a disgraceful pair. The rhombus will be consigned to the nets, where it will flatter the bowler and alarm the batsman by making spontaneous breaks. The beard I shall give to the dog.

There is, too, an old score-book, full of junior games and resounding inaccuracies; telling, almost aloud, of scorers pressed into service, whose pencils were a mockery and whose hearts were far away; with signs of impatient, even fraudulent, umpiring, the letters 'lbw' being followed often by question marks, and, in one instance, the word 'rot'. Once someone, with frantic conscience, has tried to annotate the analysis; but soon resigned the task, with the absolving comment, 'and soe on and soe on'. On another page a batsman, who made nothing, is said to have been 'cort and boled' – it sounds like some obscure but comprehensive Saxon punishment – but there is nothing to tell us who was the 'boler'. Some primal wit here and there creeps in. A match played in July some years ago is stated to have been between 'the Rumtifoozlers' and 'The Duke of Pumblechook's Team'. The ducal retainers won by seven wickets, in a feudal sort of way, possibly because the captain did not bat.

There are also two old score-cards from Lord's; tales of a match which, though recent in years, seems now as forgotten as the most distant generations. These sheets ought, I know, to be reminders of happiness. I cannot now find them so; they are too melancholy, as if in the papers of one long gone we should find a sprightly invitation to dine.

Last, there is a bat, almost new; but one which, as the young say, never worked. It still flatters in aspect, balance, and grain. But I know it to be a hoax. It was born too beautiful, and it took me in like those triumphs of the waxwork craft, it has no soul. It is a

Fatal and perfidious bark,
Built in th' eclipse and rigg'd with curses dark.

I shall therefore offer it to some player who could mow a six with a coffin-lid.

Small Fry

'That's a very dangerous young lady,' remarked the third victim of a hat-trick in a match between boys under ten and girls under thirteen, when he retired with grim solemnity to the pavilion and, as captain of the sinking ship, went into conference upon means of salvation. The policy was soon determined. 'Take risks!' shouted the captain, whose caution had availed him nothing; 'take risks', as number six blocked a full-pitcher with every resource of instrument and eye. As if the whole game were not one gigantic risk, a jousting adventure with fate and the ladies who, when their turn came to bat, sat nine in a row, somewhat on the front edge of a bench, as if confronting something half-way between a cinematograph show and a lesson on the principal capes of Britain, dressed all in grave brown, some with pigtails, some without; nicely balanced, when one of their team hit a boundary, between the exuberance of triumph and the delicacy of reticence, the latter on the whole prevailing.

They had but two bats between them, no pads, resilient shins, and one dominant idea, which was to run for every hit; and that was generally safe enough, as the majority of the fielders, in the manner of the St Andrews caddies judging the probable range and direction of the new captain's inaugural drive, had picked on square-leg and close mid-wicket, where they would pounce on the ball and worry it like the Westminster pancake. Once only in the ladies' innings was the ball catapulted from the moil on to the stumps, with the runner far out – so extraordinarily far that none appealed and the innings continued. The wicket-keeper knew what he meant to do, but as, in caricature of photographs of the famous, he had adopted the posture of one weeding the lawn or awaiting the cane, he took many balls inaccurately, and byes were run while he was adjusting his features.

So the ladies just won, and it was the byes that did it. Indeed, as in the days of Mr Marcon, the Oxford fast bowler of 1844, two long-stops were needed, one to stun the ball and the other to kill it. A second innings began, but it soon dwindled to nullity when it was found that the number three batsman had, with opportune chivalry, taken his opposite number away to tea; not unlike yet another Oxford University cricketer who, when his team wanted but nine to win and had one wicket to fall, could nowhere be discovered, and became the immortal and shocking subject of the sentence. 'Close as this finish was, it might have been still closer had not Lord Ward, on the Oxford side, been absent at the crisis.'

On the same evening as this defeat by the girls the vice-captain was heard to remark to one with no official capacity, 'I see Copson's got his hundred wickets. I've only got nineteen so far.' 'Counting nets?' inquired the junior. 'Oh, yes.' 'Ah, I don't count nets.' 'No; and it wouldn't make any difference if you did, for you hardly ever bowl into the right one.' There followed the silence that confesses the unpalatable truth.

The teaching of bowling is an art so difficult that pages of weighty instruction and learned diagrams have gone almost for nothing. The variety of method in the young is startling, ranging from the boy who runs twenty-two yards, tripping up twice on the way, to the artist who, after holding the ball to the eye with an illusory air of taking aim, propels it with a petulant abruptness as if ordering the batsman to miss it. This difficulty is nothing new, for I find that 'Ranji' himself can get no farther in his famous book than: 'Bowling is an art; or rather it is an art to bowl well; and in a true sense, as all writers on the subject have agreed, it is an art that cannot be taught.' This is dispiriting, and, surely, a little severe, for it implies the dreary truth for most cricketers that 'Bowling is bowling, so it's of no use your trying to bowl!' But even this view is rank optimism compared to that of Mr Kempson, formerly of Cambridge University, who remarked: 'Bowling is an incommunicable natural gift, which can be perfected to almost any degree by practice.' Now this, if logically pursued, would lead to the closing down of all schools of cricket and the survival of a few scattered nets in which a few bowlers, like gods together, divinely conscious of their incommunicable natural gift, gave lordly practice to a few selected batsmen.

I once had under my tuition a boy who thought that he was Bowes, the famous Yorkshire and England bowler; that is, in a cricket, not a pathological sense. The delusion grew upon him. In vain I tried to coax him back into his rightful identity or ego. I even led him into the library and pointed out to him the passage: 'Sometimes the bowler takes upon himself to demonstrate the peculiarities in the styles of various great bowlers in a manner which does infinite credit to his imagination, but none at all to his power of imitation. Such useless mimicry is worse than profitless.' He read this stern rebuke in silence, then smiled – a bland and tolerant smile, such as might have momentarily illuminated the features of Charles Darwin when shown the theory of a rival scientist.

His admiration of Bowes was inexpressible in words, except that he once was heard to remark: 'Bowes is a wonderful man; he's got a very bass voice.' Ah, if all of us could but achieve excellence by so easy a process of Nature! Irrevocable laws had given him a squeaky voice, 4 ft 8 in of height, and no weight worthy of record; but he had acquired by observation something of his hero; the slow and meditative gait before turning to deliver the ball. When he felt in form he would even borrow a pair of spectacles for the occasion. He grew in time to resemble the insane gentleman in Horace who sat in an empty theatre and 'believed he was witnessing marvellous tragedies'. At length he became, in his own idea, Bowes himself. Alas, that I should have to write that the impersonation was a failure. His works dropped groundward, or else never touched ground at all, and many an afternoon 'Bowes' spent fuming at point or meditating incredible slaughters from long-stop. Finally, he became a Wet Bob. Ichabod!

The Ladies in Play

'*Ron, ron*, or you will *nevaire* egg-sell at the athletics' – thus was I exhorted, some years ago now, with more zeal than precision, by a Swiss governess who tried to initiate herself and me into the complexities of single-wicket cricket, with croquet hoops as stumps and rooks for spectators. It was my first experience of the Cricketing Lady.

There is evidence that the ladies interested themselves, at least verbally, in the game in the earlier years of George the Third, when Mrs 'Lumpy' Stevens would scream advice not unmingled with abuse at her famous husband of Hambledon CC. There are many instances, ancient and modern, of wives and daughters, and, in the greatest of all cricketing families of a grandmother, too, who have at the proper moment ceased to 'mind the distaff' and plunged into disputations on the failure of a relative. Indeed, it is on record that a certain great professional batsman was discovered by a companion wandering in a town at night with a wild mien, because, as he said in low and anguished tone: 'I daren't go home. I daren't. The old woman'll tell me exactly why I missed that ball.'

There hangs in the pavilion of the Kent Cricket Club on the St Lawrence ground, Canterbury, an old print, in the Hogarthian manner, of a ladies' cricket match; Married *v.* Single, I believe. It is not a delicate or aesthetic scene. A burlesque and corpulent figure lies sprawling after a fielding failure. Mid-wicket, too, is an object of fun, having, like the mariner's wife of Mr Jacobs, 'lost her good looks and found others'. The gentlemen spectators, scattered in small marquees, are regaling themselves with culpable abandon.

Far otherwise are ladies' cricket matches conducted in these days. Any who saw the Tests and other matches played a few summers ago between England and the visitors from Australia will recall not only the trimness of these athletes and their skill, especially with the bat, which made tough and crochety old male spectators scratch their heads in surprise, but, more than anything, the exactitude of the organization (making even the LGU seem haphazard)! and the defiance of the weather. The Oval groundsman and his staff must have regarded the next fixture between men as a rest cure!

I was once present, at all material times, at a ladies' county match, to which I must give with a sort of military anonymity the title of Wessex *v.* Loamshire, and to the players themselves, in the manner of Edgar Wallace's heroines and villainesses, spurious names that do not, nevertheless, 'have no reference to any living person'. For this is an unofficial and fragmentary account of the proceedings, and of some of the cricketers I can truthfully say that I did but see her passing by.

First, remembering the inhuman ability at catching and stopping shown by 'Twelve Ladies of the District' in school-days – the much too prehensile fingers and the skirt-protected shins – I remark with fidelity that the fielding of the ladies of Wessex and Loamshire, especially the latter, was faulty in the extreme. Cricketing ladies have often told me, with an admonishing frown, that it is not their wish to be compared with the men. Quite so; but they must admit comparison with each other, and on this occasion, had I been the Loamshire captain, I would have gathered my team at the close of play and said: 'No, Simpson; certainly not; and you, too, Jackson, and you, Micklethwaite; you may not go off to your sherry party; an hour's fielding practice for all of you; the catching was deplorable, and the throwing-in the limit.'

Perhaps it was the heat; yet this alone does not explain the garrulity of the slips, outdoing any post-prandial discussions among men. Nor am I convinced that the conversation turned solely on the artistry or eccentricities, of the opposing batsmen, but rather, I fear, on hats and cookery, or other matters of personal adornment and refection.

Wessex scored some 165 for 8 wickets, and left Loamshire two and three-quarter hours to win, which would appear a little generous were it not that the tea interval bisected the Loamshire innings for three-quarters of an hour! Ah, that's the sort of match I have dreamed of playing in!

A lady to whom I award the prosaic name of Johnson scored 90 odd for Wessex, but let the Loamshire fellows bitterly reflect on the five chances that bumped to earth. In the words of a literary colleague, 'Johnson opened very shakily indeed, and cocked up several that were put on the floor before she became at all menacing'. But she made some lovely strokes, with that full sweeping rhythm which seems to desert man in adolescence, and it took a terrific catch at mid-off to dismiss her, expiation nearly enough for the other fumblings. Sixty-eight of her runs came from boundaries, and the next highest score was a desperate 17 by number nine.

For Loamshire, Sanderson, who must have suffered inward agonies from the inequalities of the fielding, bowled 30 overs in a row, except for negligible respite when changing ends. Three for 53 was inadequate reward.

Loamshire began as if their task, even including the tea, were easy; but they were soon forced to change daring for obstinacy, two players being out for very few runs. The second was bowled by one that seemed to go sharply with the arm, but refinements in definition fall flat before another of my friend's diagnoses. 'She was bowled by a perfect length ball that obviously she knew nothing about.' That's the way that men's Test matches should be described. A simple brutality. The team was saved, as it turned out, by their number four, who was undismissed, though not entirely unbeaten, for 16, made in an hour and forty minutes. 'There was no moving her.' But there was movement around her in plenty; bowlers came and went and came again in bewildering permutation. Then one of the opening batsmen suddenly lost control, and, calling for a run for a stroke straight to close square-leg, was amply run out. The lady who had caught that great catch at mid-off, then arrived to make a hurricane 31 in thirty-five minutes. Still number four remained, majestic amid ruin, four more wickets falling with a crash. But number eleven not only averted the hat-trick but stayed for the last over and a half, with fielders perched nearly on her bat, and the stumper twice whipping away the bails more in prophecy than in hope.

A great day; but oh! those slip-fielders! If one should chance to cast her eye on these words, may she blush and amend!

West Country Idyll

Occasions had taken me to the West Country for a match of cricket in a hamlet which is set firmly, happily, defiantly on the side of the downs.

It was the day of a football cup-final, and elsewhere, it seems, the winds blew and directors and other such important folk held on their tile-hats with some diminution of dignity; but with us it was intermittently soft and sunny, by benefit borrowed, I fancy, from those Isles of Hesperus which, it is reasonably supposed, lie not many leagues away to the west.

The little place shook and hummed with the reboations of many radios telling of the doings at Wembley. We, too, had our football, most of it being transacted at close fine-leg or, if you wish, deepish mid-off, where there disported themselves in antic contest some budding but by no means mute Guthrie, some future, if temporarily inglorious Barlow, and an even smaller, footballer, gum-booted to the armpits, to whom his brother, our good captain and wicket-keeper turned, while almost in the act of taking the ball, with the remark, 'You'll be killed in a moment, and your mother will want to know why.'

Our match was not one of the 'League' fixtures – those stern and sometimes argumentative scenes – but a meeting with some pleasantly disposed military gentlemen stationed in the neighbourhood. The field needs but little description. At one end a straight hit of some seventy yards sends the ball into the churchyard; at the other (after the goalposts) stand hills of that sort to which King Lear once hurled the rebuke 'You, too, are old'. Around the prepared surface is barbed wire, for to the untechnical mind of the cow one patch of grass is as useful as another.

So, this fencing being removed, the toss won by us, and a gaggle of small boys swept away from the entry to the pavilion, a start was made; a little abrupt, perhaps, for in the first over the opposing wicket-keeper took a smart blow on the head, but, after an interval in which he reproved man, earth, and providence, he resumed his office.

Events ran against the home team. If a ball shot along the ground it hit one of the stumps instead of first slip's toes. If it rose, by way of ferocious variety, it struck the shoulder of the bat instead of passing harmlessly overhead. So five good men were out for 18 runs, and there assailed our captain and committee the horrid truth, seldom apparent in higher cricket, that there was a paucity of players. We were short by three batsmen; some of the more regular members were out a-milking, others playing football in the next village. But the situation gave our captain neither pause nor debate. Three spectators, whose interest had hitherto been purely civilian and verbal, were rapidly persuaded to put their theories to the test. One of them, a gardener of repute, long past what is called middle age, was asked if he would care to have a runner. Having removed his briar to refuse the offer, he dug himself in, as it were, with trowel, mattock, and hoe.

He fell, after three overs, to a ball for which there was no answer in horticulture. It then appeared that the same batsman came in again, imperfectly disguised. I cannot be sure. But we were out for 30 – neither good nor bad.

In spite of our second-best bowler retiring to deliver the afternoon post – a thing that he does only less gracefully than appealing for improbable decisions, five soldiers were soon out for eight runs. The rumour flew around that the men of Wolverhampton had fallen with a crash. Two of the opposing team were noticed to be fielding for us; whether by accident or request it was not known. The church clock struck five, and tea was taken in the skittle-alley. At six o'clock it was noticed that the president of the club threatened a speech, and the match was hastily resumed; so hastily that our eldest player, trying to resume his place in the field with an alacrity unworthy of him, slipped where village greens are apt to be most slippery – where the long grass joins the short – and measured his circularity on the good earth.

The shock of this event seemed to disturb the tenor of our captain's policy, for he removed a capable man who was intending to bowl, and replaced him by a youth who had hitherto shown no art except an ability to throw small stones on the pitch during the process of cricket. It soon became evident that this playful habit was, indeed, his sole visible accomplishment, and their score rose abruptly from 8 to 26, the margin of error thus becoming merely four. However, three more men were dispatched before the winning hit was made, one being run out through sheer absence of mind, one bowled because he had no spike in the end of his bat, one easily caught at cover-point when playing a glide to leg.

The winning hit was a drive that struck the bowler's boots, recoiled to the centre of the pitch, and was seemingly trodden into the ground. A diverting, if eccentric, finish. I think that the better, at any rate the less mutable, team won.

And some fools say that cricket is dull.

Manchester

Unlike the apocryphal gentleman who took the railway ticket, I am fond of going to Manchester for cricket. Others may laugh or weep, according to their philosophy, knock Manchester about with slapstick and threadbare facetiousness – I know one who always takes two umbrellas to Old Trafford – but I like it, because it's ugly. Like the poetaster of A. A. Milne who gave an incomprehensible recital, Manchester, I feel, is ugly on purpose; as if it could be quite good-looking if it wanted to be, but was above all that sort of thing; knowing that it is the respectable thing to be plain.

It is silly to hurry on your way to the Test at Old Trafford; you should wander down its more solemn streets; wide, serious, and easy to be lost in; where the constables, when questioned, point out the way to more streets, obviously relations, even twins, of the first street; whose faces hide large, old-fashioned offices where business is done by some of the kindred if not of the house of Chuzzlewit, and a Mr Chuffey still shuffles about with tight little secrets and difficult papers, and there are partners whom nothing would shock except the news that a Lancashire batsman had gone mad, hit three consecutive sixes against Yorkshire, then been stumped by four yards and several seconds.

So, by decent stages, to Old Trafford, whose beautiful turf gains glory from its saturnine surroundings: at one end is the railway, where the engine-drivers seem perpetually to be shunting themselves into position to discern between the googly and the genuine off-break; at the other, at a quaint angle, the Press Box, which suggests that it might have been designed by Einstein immediately after a reunion dinner of mathematicians: eccentric perch of the critics. It is a ground which seems to have decided, none daring to contradict, that the beauties of the cricketing art are self-sufficient, and have no need of meretricious appurtenances; it is abrupt, like a rude and true remark from Carlyle or Sam Johnson; proclaiming disdain of the soft meadows and orchard lawns of the South, of 'bowery hollows crowned with summer sea'. If you want that sort of thing you can go and eat the Lotus in Kent, elbow through the trippers for a plate of whelks at Southend, or take a cheap ticket to the wonders of Blackpool.

I have not heard that John Bright or W. E. Gladstone ever played cricket, but, if they did, they should never have played away from Old Trafford, which, on a rainy day, is the nearest thing I know to an academic speech on Free Trade. It must have taught many a cricketer its own philosophy, batsmanship such as that of Harry Makepeace or, in his stubborn days, Charles Hallows, which seldom deviated into brilliance, but flowed on with a staid majesty like the lines of Milton or a leader of the great C. P. Scott, with scarcely the easement of a paragraph, without ever the hope of an anacoluthon! Indeed, I always consider that it was almost a rebuff to Nature that Lancashire permitted, I will not say encouraged, such batsmen as A. C. MacLaren, who refused to unlearn what Harrow and youth had taught him; R. H. Spooner, whose grace was of no one county or time; such masters of bowling and clowning as Johnny Briggs and Cecil Parkin. In more modern years Old Trafford has seen the 'mutiny' of Ernest Tyldesley, whose wickets were visible when you bowled, and who might use the pull-drive in the first over; of Eddie Paynter, who sometimes plays a stroke with neither foot on the ground; great heretics all.

If you talk to the older spectators at Old Trafford you will find that they most remember the Australian victory by three wickets in 1896 with the tremendous bowling of Ernest Jones and Tom Richardson, and the 154 not out by 'Ranji' in England's second innings, when others failed and kept flicking Jones off his face to the leg boundary. One ball nicked his ear, and he remarked afterwards: 'It was very important to get the head well behind the ball to get a good sight of it!' The Australians needed only 125 to win, but it took them three hours and seven wickets, and Richardson bowled through those three hours for six of the wickets, having bowled 68 overs in the first innings. Talk of Alexander and Hercules!

Here in 1934 O'Reilly took three English wickets in one over, as it were in one flush – Walters and Hammond and Wyatt, and I can still revive the tremors of that shock. In the same match Pat Hendren made a century, flowering from the early and habitual stiffness of defence into the full warmth of extra-cover driving. Here, six years ago, Constantine and Martindale assailed D. R. Jardine with bounce and speed, and he quelled them and was caught in the end low at gully for 127, and the ground rose to him.

Manchester is a tough old nut, but when you crack it the kernel is sweet enough. Warm, even wild, are the hospitalities underneath the harsh exterior of reception; dinner parties such as only Test matches beget, and conversations that tire out the night before the talkers. But some, perhaps, have never learnt the way.

James Pycroft

'Long-stop is wholly at fault if he requires the wicket-keeper to stand aside; this would spoil the stumping.' This magnificent advice, propounded by the Rev James Pycroft in 1873, and still true today, floated into my mind the other afternoon as I watched a particularly inept wicket-keeper. There was no long-stop, alas, to 'require' him 'to stand aside'. It would have been better for his team if there had been. Instead he stood upright and very still, an angry look on his face, as if rebuking the bowler for bowling, while many a ball hurtled past him into the nettles.

I make no apology for thus bringing to light the great Pycroft. Widely though the game has altered since his day, the force of his wit, instruction, and philosophy remains unweakened. 'If you miss a ball,' he remarks to all fielders, and long-stops in particular, 'rattle away after it; do not stand, as many do, to apologize by dumb show.' He was a scholar as well as a fine cricketer, and had a boldness of phrase and full-blooded humanity not always to be found in the clerical. Writing on the character of cricket, he says that it 'affords to a race of professionals a merry and abundant, though rather a laborious, livelihood from the time the first May-fly is up to the time the first pheasant is down'.

Only occasionally does floridness overcome his style, as when he remarks of cricket in the Navy: 'Her Majesty's ships have bats and balls to astonish the cockroaches at sea, and the crabs and turtles ashore. Hence it has come to pass that, wherever Her Majesty's servants have "carried their victorious arms" and legs – wind and weather permitting – cricket has been played.' The facetious insertion of 'and legs' would, I feel, have been deplored by his bishop, however nicely it may have titillated the historian's whim!

Pycroft, stressing the Anglo-Saxon character of cricket, assets that it has never been 'naturalized in Ireland. It follows the course rather of ale than whisky.' Then he pops, as it were, into the pulpit, to condemn the use of either stimulant to give the cricketer Dutch courage. 'Feed the body,' he adjures the phantom flock, 'but do not cloud the mind. You, sir, with that hectic flush, the fire of your eyes burnt low in their sockets, with beak as sharp as a woodcock's from living upon suction, with pallid face and shaky hand – our game disdains such ghostlike votaries.' Still with the mantle of Savonarola he smites 'the pest of the cricket-field . . . who bores you about his average . . . and looks blue even at the success of his own party'.

His technical instruction is at times over-rigid, and he feels qualms, it is evident, in forbidding the use of a cross-bat to a toss, or, as we less romantically call it, a full-pitcher. This question, he finds, 'tries my rule very hard'; but after something near a spiritual and invisible struggle, he decides that 'to play tosses, and ground-balls, and hops, and every variety of loose bowling, by the rigid rules of straight and upright play, is a principle the neglect of which has often given the old hands a laugh at the young ones. . . . Often have I been amused (sardonic old bird!) to see the wonder and disappointment occasioned when some noted member of a University eleven, or the Marylebone Club – from whom all expected, of course, the most temendous hitting "off mere underhand bowling" – has been easily disposed of by a toss or a ground ball, yclept a "sneak".' I believe that the triumph most highly esteemed by the great Don Bradman was when he dismissed W. R. Hammond in a Test match with a 'toss'!

Though the author must have often afterwards seen Grace break his maxim, he teaches us 'never hit across wicket'. Which may be 'very gratifying and very effective; and perhaps you may hit over the tent or, as I once saw, into a neighbour's carriage; but while the natives were marvel-striken, a good judge will shake his head and inwardly grieve at folly so triumphant'.

Then, as now, the game met with severe disparagement. It was considered to encourage gambling and idleness. The former charge is no longer valid; the latter is true enough, though we now use the more dignified term 'leisure'. Anyhow, the distant thunder of the superfluously upright can still amuse: 'Would it not be extremely odd,' wrote a correspondent in *The British Champion*, 'to see lords and gentlemen, clergymen and lawyers, associating themselves with butchers and cobblers in pursuit of their diversions?' The writer also complains of the game being 'the subject of public advertisement, to draw together great crowds of people who ought all of them to be somewhere else'. An unpardonable intrusion on privacy of judgment! Again, at a later month, this round-headed killjoy returns to the attack: 'Noblemen, gentlemen, and clergymen may divert themselves as they think fit. We cannot dispute their privilege to make butchers, cobblers, or tinkers their companions,' but it is to be doubted, avers the correspondent, 'whether they have any right to invite *thousands of people* to be spectators of their agility. It draws numbers of people from their employment, to the ruin of their families.'

But, in the matter of gambling at cricket, undoubtedly the game at one time incurred much discredit. Old Nyren complained of 'the legs of Marylebone', sleek knaves who used to try 'to corrupt primitive specimens of Hambledon innocence'. Bookies used to attend Lord's as regularly as Epsom and

Ascot, a custom that they no longer pursue in their professional capacity. They would sit ready under the pavilion, and at least were good payers if they lost. Among other playful habits they used sometimes 'to keep a player out of the way by a false report that his wife was dead'. As a set-off to this device I have heard of a famous professional who used to make a century when he learnt that his wife was on the ground. He preferred the company of his bat! In time their very roguery beat its own ends, and, as that pioneer of forward play, Fennex, remarked to the author: 'They overdid it; they spoilt their own trade; and, as I said to one of them, "A knave and a fool make a bad partnership; so you and yourself will never prosper".'

W. G. Grace was entering on his first fame when Pycroft wrote his *Cricket Field*, and the author praises his manly and upright stance at the wicket: but 'look at the others,' he writes; 'nineteen out of twenty at least; there they stand with bended knees, half a foot shorter than Nature made them . . . some men stand at guard with a long, flat horizontal back, like cows; some seem to be holding the bat most desperately into the blockhole; some stick out behind so indecently we wonder they are not ashamed that any should see them . . . in a word, if you want to see a man looking at a deplorable disadvantage to any non-cricketing observer, only see him *in* at cricket.'

Hail to you, James Pycroft! Wise of instruction and witty of phrase! Happy were your parishioners if you preached but half as well as you wrote!

The Art of Waiting

A lady of my acquaintance whom, with that misplaced kindness that sometimes steals over us, I had invited to watch a match of cricket, answered 'No, thanks; nothing ever happens at cricket; it's just all waiting'. I overlooked the first part of this gracious reply which, at one heretical stroke, annuls myriads of runs and wickets and leg-byes, and denies what has been to many the glory of their vigorous prime and the consolation of their conversational age; but the second part made me think – 'It's just all waiting'.

Some of us have perhaps forgotten how many hours of past summers we have spent in standing outside the walls and enclosures of cricket grounds, having in one hand the unsatisfactory sandwich, in the other the insatiate son or nephew, and across our shoulders the spy-glass or other optical device that perpetually falls short of its advertised performance; while, on the greater occasions, the ever-hopeful among mankind play musical instruments for our delectation or, maybe, are strangely inspired to expect profit by reversing their waistcoat without removing their jacket.

But this sort of 'just waiting', fit subject though it be for an essay from Freud or Francis Bacon, is not quite what is meant by those ladies whom we rashly invite to use the hardly-acquired Rover Ticket. They sweep past this sort of thing into the ground, where they anticipate, it seems, the immediate presentation of a scene of animation and adventure reminiscent of the afternoons when, in imperial Rome, a Christian would sidestep a lion with an unexpected virtuosity of footwork. What the ladies mean is the waiting for a short, ugly batsman to get out and a tall, good-looking one to come in; for the deep-fielder to move aside and give a view of that graceful mid-off or that cover-point with the exquisite trousers and the fetching cap.

Perhaps I wrong some of them, but only a few. Do they ever think of what waiting means to the players? No; or, almost no. They have neither the heart nor the wish to imagine the sensations of an opening batsman who, after being out first ball, sits through rain for a day and a half while 'o – 1 – o', with hideous magnetism, keeps reminding him of the state of the game. Their careless and social minds cannot know that long-leg is waiting to be asked to bowl, that the bowler is waiting for first slip to stand where he was put, that the wicket-keeper is waiting for the unlikely moment when he will take a ball in the centre of his gloves, that the captain is waiting for some providential inspiration which will for ever stamp him as one of the captains who know, that the correspondent of the *Daily Message* in the corner of the Press Box is waiting for an epigram and the time when his colleague will desert funny stories for an interest in the cricket.

I think all cricketers may be divided into good waiters and bad waiters. Among batsmen there are those who pace the dressing-room as if it were a cage, ever and anon popping their head out of window or on to balcony to inquire the state of matters and to ask questions about bowling with which they have long been familiar. Then there are those of iron equanimity, like Maurice Leyland, whose tranquillity seems to deepen in proportion to the importance of his innings, and who bats in a Test match with a sort of stern gaiety peculiarly his own. Some possess a detachment of mind which nothing can disturb. Such was Mr C. E. Hatfield, of Oxford University, who, when he went out to bat against Cambridge at a solemn hour of doubt, stopped for a few seconds at the foot of the pavilion steps to aim his bat at the Lord's pigeons. He made 35 not out and won the match.

In boys' cricket matches the batting side is apt to wait in a row on a bench and in full panoply. Whether this habit comes from keenness or mistrust I have never quite known.

Old Clarke

Old Clarke. The adjective, so often used in contemporary conversation, so rarely retained into posterity, indicates an admixture of affection and awe; as in boys' schools, where once, in a Latin grammar, I found the memorable, if uncorroborated, statement – 'Old Buffy's ears wiggle when he is angry'. As, too, with 'Old Odell', to whom the epithet was given, not only because no brother clubman could remember him not being old, but because, like Clarke, he was, in character, something of an 'old devil'.

Old Clarke, of Nottingham, was in most respects extraordinary. Born in 1798, he made his first appearance in the Gentlemen v. Players match at Lord's in 1845, at an age when he had every right to exchange the hope of selection for the pleasures of criticism. He practised, with commanding success, a method of bowling, the ball being delivered from about waist high, which was considered obsolete, effete, and even laughable. He transferred, for his own profit, cricket from the Forest to Trent Bridge, charging 6d a head, a sum which many citizens were ready to pay for the chance of booing the financier all the way to the crease in his inaugural innings. Old Clarke, flattered rather than piqued, pretended to walk out after his first ball, and the deluded crowd redoubled their derision. This primitive trick was typical of his humour.

In 1847 he began to tour the towns and villages with his All-England team, the cream of professional cricketers. It was a vast success. Inter-county matches were almost deserted when there was a chance of seeing the All-England team in action. Nearly all the matches were against odds. W. Caffyn, the Surrey and England all-rounder, played for Clarke, and found the enjoyment somewhat marred at times by the strenuous travelling, the cricketers often bumping about country lanes all night, then nearly falling asleep in the noon-day heat of some secluded green. Nor was the pay, £4 a match, wholly satisfying to the players, and on one occasion *Wisden* 'spoke straightly', but to no effect, to the captain on this topic.

Yet, so strong was his character, that Clarke kept his team almost intact, if not entirely pleased, for seven years, when he handed over the leadership to that great leg-hitter, George Parr. During this period Clarke took 2,385 wickets, an average of 340 a season. In 1853 his bag was 467! A wonderful achievement, even though the opposition was often rather paltry, and though the captain was accustomed to keep himself on almost without intermission!

Not often did an opposing batsman in these matches reach 50; but there is report of an innings of 68 by Mr W. Ridding, who was playing for Major Willies's XXII. Ridding wore a cap that was no cap, the peak only, affixed by elastic, being retained. Happy were those who on that day both saw this sartorial phenomenon and heard Clarke's comments as, for once ineffectually, he trundled up his lobs! His bowling must have much resembled the method of Dr Grace; 'a short run, a curving flight, and a very abrupt rise from the pitch . . . a consistent spin from leg, and a positive genius for detecting the weak points in an opponent's armour'. With a view to this detection it was his custom to prowl round the nets before a match and sum up the opposition. After careful scrutiny he would retire, murmuring ominously: 'We shall have an accident with these men very soon.'

His career was full of argument with fate and man. In 1854 he quarrelled with the MCC, and withdrew Caesar, Parr, and Caffyn from Gentlemen v. Players and from England v. MCC at Lord's. He once cursed a brass band, at Bingham, for over two hours, while he was bowling. Even the mild and modest Caffyn at length parted from him, and at the time referred to him as 'poor Old Clarke'.

He was as little inclined to receive as to confer a favour; but he was one of the truly great men of cricket, which he loved in his own jealous, tyrannical, and grimly humorous manner.

H. J. Henley

He was a critic, and a ripe good one; straight of judgment, mind, and word. There was much of Falstaff about him in look and habit and love of what fell out curiously through the prank of chance and the folly of man. He did common things in an uncommon way. In ordinary company – and he never seemed to be out of company – he would suddenly crown some other's tattered and feeble remark with a golden line of his own or of some poet; he would throw out a paradox like Chesterton, or even roll a boulder from Milton, then push his hat to the back of his head and murmur, as if for the select benefit of himself and the person with whom he would have preferred to be talking: 'Never mind, old chap, let it pass, let it pass.'

In cricket pavilions he would suffer in silence a fairly silent fool; but an argumentative fool he would flay alive. His stick would go crack on the floor; he would shake theories till their wig and false teeth rattled, smack analogies in the face, unmask the fiction of facts, and, with a final shove, send the whole jerry-built theme crashing in dust and smoke. Then, as the air cleared, he would ask his husk of an opponent what he'd take to refurbish his tenantless frame and fit him once more to walk, almost erect, before his fellow-man.

Like many generous men, he enjoyed peculiar economies. He would festoon a score-card with notes of a current match –

abstruse as Hittite runes to the layman – and when these irregular spaces were filled he might feel in his pocket for the notebook that he and we knew could not be there; and I have fancied that I saw him, when hard pressed, cock a speculative eye at a stiff collar in front of him, then sigh, and reach for another score-card. He was never observed, like other travellers by train, to arrive in the compartment with an unwieldy bundle or an air of responsible haste. He did not trouble the luggage-rack with anything heavier than a tight little bag of antique design and professional aspect. Such weight as he brought was that of his own mind and body. And his conversation made the longest journey seem just a jaunt to the suburbs.

I don't think that he greatly cared for any games but cricket and rugby. We persuaded him once into a game of clock-golf on a hilly and contrary course. He was, in a sense, an unsatisfactory partner, for, after he had played each putt under doubtless faulty instruction, he kept starting to walk away from the scene, and had to be recalled. For the game was beneath the dignity of argument, and was not resolvable into a few premises and a conclusion. It was deficient in point. Also, it was abominably hot.

Surrey was his county, and Ernest Hayes his cricket hero. He was always happy talking at the one and about the other. And would that he could come back again, and bang his stick, and say: 'I don't agree.'

The Land of Might-have-been

'Well, incubus', once remarked an old friend, as we walked away at the end of a match in which he had led us to narrow defeat, 'I suppose there were seven million ways I could have won that game, and eight million I could have lost it. So what?' Whereat, with practised sidestep, he dodged a platitudinous old toucan, who was threatening to reveal one of the seven million.

Both then and later I pondered and admired that captain's philosophy, not to mention his social footwork. It was seldom indeed that he allowed himself to be cut off from all exits except a skylight, and to be confronted with the old, inexorable inquisition: 'and why?' Ah; the thoughts of some recently unsuccessful captain, cornered by the critic for the prosecution, 'were never said in rhyme', and, by their nature, do not lend themselves to published prose. He can be silent in seven different languages, all bad. It is not for him to explain the infinite permutations of chance, only to suffer the boundless idiocy of man.

Yet, in all the moans of the poets, few mental pleasures exceed the contemplation of the might-have-been. I confess that after a long and barren day of bowling I have, at a convenient moment, gone through that team like a guillotine through a Dutch cheese. In the folly or vanity or solace of imagination – call it what you will – I have begun with a wide that was also a long-hop; but, before the silence of derision has died down, I have sent Hobbs's bails whistling past the wicket-keeper, 0 – 1 – 0. That just for a start. Then, 'flown with insolence', I am not content with Surrey alone, but convoke the stars from all the counties of England to prepare for extinction. Hammond leans on one lazy four past cover, then is lbw, not under any new rule either. Next, Woolley is caught and bowled, low with the left hand; while, as the reports sometimes say, 'all eyes were on the boundary'.

In a few overs, to cut the matter short, the last man comes in 'to an anticipatory buzz of excitement'. To play this game properly, for by now the barriers of time and place are shattered, you should here introduce some visiting cricketer, say, Constantine or Macartney, or, if you like, Don Bradman, who has arrived late on the ground and for once 'betrays evident signs of nervousness'. And well he may, for he is at once bowled by an inswinger that nips from leg and knocks out the off-stump. But you must be resigned to interruption before you have taken your 10 wickets. Morning tea, someone borrowing a stud, a friend who mistakes your reverie for serious illness – any of these may smash the picture. Moreover, if you are wise, you will rectify the illusion by a glance at yesterday's score, recover humility, and so resume your place upon the earth.

And there are the real might-have-beens. I speak with the sympathy of experience to each batsman who 'rides in on the roller', whose mere appearance is a signal for the groundsman to rattle his brooms, for the spectator to edge nearer to the refreshments, for his own acquaintances to nudge each other and discuss his eccentric and imminent end. See the nearer fieldsmen gather round him like cheerful vultures. They borrow and examine his bat, hollow emblem of ephemeral office, and they run their hands along its edges as a farmer feels a goose that is ripe for the table. Perhaps he was never any good; just an untutored swatter at the neighbourhood of the ball, a crude approximator. Perhaps he was once the pride and promise of his instructor. But circumstance, length of time and shortness of breath, habit and mockery, have reduced him to this impotent husk of a batsman, this arrival and departure, this futile flail! You don't believe it? Question yourself, next time you go in, and out, last.

Some few there are who escape this awful fate; number elevens of stern will and unsmiling resolution. Such an one bats with the dignity of a number one and with a brave parody of his skill. He even refuses the peremptory and selfish call of the hero at the other end, whose century is near. He scorns short runs and silly scamperings. And when the hero, mistrustful and impatient, hits all round the half-volley, soon to be absorbed in cheers and back-smackings, he, the number eleven, the fool who *would* keep the bowling, says nothing in his corner, but wonders when, if ever, he'll find someone to stay with him. For hope, like love, never grows old.

September Fancies

There is something about early September that seems to make both people and things a little odd; more so than the better accredited period of mid-summer.

I have always fancied, without relying on safe evidence, that it was in September that Kubla Khan gave his extravagant orders to the stone-masons of Xanadu. About then, too, in times of peace, the English holiday-maker, having relegated his wife and children to the use of deck-chairs, sand, and buckets, would, perhaps, poise a periwinkle; then, strolling to a favourite house of refreshment, would push down the after brim of his straw-boater with a care-free knock, and confide to the young lady in charge of the bottles that he did not see how his boss, a man of few brains, could prosper much longer without him.

It is the time when cricket, festival cricket, merges into partridge-shooting for those whose stubble-fields happen to be graced by that elusive bird. To this combination, added to war, I must attribute a strange dream. I dreamt that I came upon a small shooting-party awaiting driven birds with their guns pushed through the loopholes of a fortified hedge. Suddenly there stood before me a figure, familiar, venerable, and tall; he wore, appropriately enough, a black silk top-hat and a mauve frock-coat. But his made-up-tie, of knitted wool, bore the colours of Marylebone. He joined the party in the hedge and all was over.

In September festival cricket, too, strange things have happened. At Scarborough, once, I bowled down the wicket of an opening batsman who afterwards declared that he was discussing the sea mist with the square-leg umpire. There, too, early in this century, it happened that there was a very high wind blowing across the ground during the Gentlemen v. Players match. It also chanced that an important lady, crowned with what an Oxford chimney-sweep once called 'my 'irsute adornment', was watching the play. The wind, in frolic, whisked off the wig, which went bowling along to the feet of a young cricketer. He fielded it, and there was a pause. Then, from the marquee a butler emerged with a silver tray, on which, with solemn care, he received and carried away the wig. Its ownership became known to the cricketers. At lunch the success-ful fielder was introduced to his hostess, who said graciously: 'Ah, Mr ——, I think we have met before.' To which came the answer: 'Well, madam, *some* of us have.'

Autumn is the time, too, when we should say a few words about spectators, especially those who haunt and, be it remem-bered, support pavilions. They have had little enough to see in recent summers, but, all praise to them, they have come to see it; with a flower, perhaps, in the button-hole, and with a more cheerful countenance than ever before. There has been heard, thank goodness, much the same sort of talk:

'He's the prettiest bat of the lot.'

'Oh, I can't see him without my glasses. I thought Johnson was played for his bowling.'

'It's not Johnson. It's Jackson.'

'Oh, old James Jackson's son, the wicket-keeper?'

'No. He never married.'

'Must be his nephew, then.'

'Ah, well, whoever it is, he's out. Stupidest shot I've ever seen. They teach these boys all wrong at school nowadays.'

Going Batting

Perhaps you remember a *Punch* drawing in the last war, by Mr Frank Reynolds, in which a small black-clothed city clerk sits in the Underground train holding a small bat – painted splice, I fear – a birthday present for his son; and a female, all hairpins and hate, says to him: 'Aren't you ashamed to go batting these days?' Well, blow me if it isn't about the best thing a man could do today in his spare moments, to go batting, if he is lucky enough to find a green, some bowlers, and 'several players stationed to "look out" in different parts of the field'.

I confess, unashamed, to an urge in this direction. The other day I had a fine view from a railway compartment of one over of a country game. Usually we flash past these parti-garbed cricketers while the captain is motioning the fielders about, or the batsman is taking guard from a paralytic umpire, or, most often, when the bowler is walking back, meditating some enormity. But this time we had stopped. Engines, like donkeys, halt unaccountably. A fat batsman was facing up to a lean bowler, who took a long run, then bowled slow. It took the batsman five balls to adjust his technique to this stratagem. Then, with the air of a man who has exploded a mystery, he swept the sixth ball from his stumps to the square-leg boundary. The bowler seemed to be cursing; the fielders, unmoved, crossed over; two boys worried the hedge and quarrelled about returning the ball. Then the train moved on, and I longed to jump down and have a go at that fat batsman who had carved the boundary, and to hit him a most prodigious slam in the waistband, then appeal for lbw – and apologize!

I should like to play again in a village 'Derby', where feeling ran high and nearly everyone appealed for nearly everything, and even the umpires scowled at each other. There must be something to it, some cup or shield or enduring emblem. Your ordinary village games, with nothing on the result, can be very dull affairs; fit enough for a little essay in a belles-lettres sort of way, touching upon the tree-tops, the sloping sun, cows, and English endeavour; but, as cricket, they're often a flop. And the same I find true of the greatest players when it doesn't matter who wins. Skill alone is not enough. I could not watch even Bradman for long in a practice-net, and I would rather see Frank Woolley making 25 for Kent than 100 for no particular side or reason.

I would, then, choose the match between G—— and S——, on the borders of Surrey; on their ground, where once we were barracked as we walked out to field, and our opening bowler, a retired constable, on having an appeal refused, was asked why he had left his truncheon at home, and our captain answered all critics by breaking a cucumber-frame with one of the highest sixes I've ever seen.

Also I wish there could be some cricket to report at Southend. I miss the 'profane multitude', the saunter from hotel to ground, punctuated by the vinegared whelk and relieved by the esculent cockle; and the comic postcard which something in the Southend air advises to send for a confusion to the breakfast-table of a rather respectable friend. There were ducks at the cricket-ground, which would quack the batsman with insolent prophecy to the wicket; and over there stood the marquee of the local yachting club, where a member might scrutinize the pitch through a marine telescope, then retire within for light refreshment.

It was on the long pier there that some of us took an England selector for a ride in 1934, soon before a Test match. We knew that he carried the English team in his skull. And we missed our chance. We should have shown him the view from the extreme end and said: 'Sir, here is the pier; there is the sea; where is your team?'

Cricket with Taste

'Through the kindness of Major A, a very enjoyable game of cricket was played on the XY Sports Club ground between P and Q. Lunch was served in the dining-hall of Z. The various items of food had been provided by the players, and these were tastefully served up by a band of willing lady helpers. After lunch the Toast to The King was given. This was followed by a speech of thanks by Mr N to Major M for his unfailing kindness on such occasions, and also a vote of thanks to the ladies who had arranged the lunch so well. After a very enjoyable game, P won by a margin of over ninety runs.'

Thus, with a mild rearrangement of punctuation and a discreet use of censorship, runs the account of a cricket match between two teams of a British colony in foreign parts. It may strike the casual reader that the section devoted to the play is meagre, that the reference to the luncheon is 'bland almost to sickliness', and that, in one instance at least, the band of willing lady helpers had arranged the less solid part of the luncheon rather too well. Someone, not, I fancy, the Lucullan reporter, has remembered to append the score. It is one deserving of a fuller explanation than it has received. For here, too, there are signs of refreshment. Of the twelve batsmen, number two does not appear to have had any innings at all, for against his name there is a mysterious blank space. Nine wickets fell for about 60 runs; but the last wicket pair contributed 92. There follows the ghostly observation '27', suspended in air and anonymity. Extras 6, and total 196. Q replied with only 104.

Be this as it may, it can be regarded as an extreme example of the laudatory method in reporting. 'Pick one thing that interests you above all others, and it is almost sure to interest your readers,' once remarked a very famous critic. In this case, the refreshments and their service have been picked on; but they excite, rather than sustain, interest. There is lacking a gracious somewhat.

Reflecting on these peculiar matters, I began to wonder whether most reporters do not habitually tend to excessive praise. In spite of what cricketers, who are scarcely less touchy than actors, may state to the contrary, we spend many hours in the search for the good and the beautiful, if not always for the true. To me, at least, the strain has often been severe. I have known an ill-suppressed longing to write some such words as:

'On the —— Ground, which, for sheer ugliness, can have few rivals, while the chimneys belched foul smoke, and a bitter wind whistled through the ramshackle Grand Stand which, by the way, is set at a ridiculous angle to the play; before a small, shrivelled, and unintelligent herd of soi-disant spectators, the match between A and B was reluctantly resumed. It had reached a condition which, except to a mind irrevocably sunk in an insane optimism, could lead only to a futile draw. Perhaps it was the continued and ungenerous absence of a sight-screen at the City End that induced C, who has seldom been seen to less advantage, to strike a paralytic attitude confidently supposed to be a posture of defence, and to remain at the crease for thirty minutes before he scored a run between first and second slip, while apparently attempting a leg-glide.' Doubtless, after this, I should not be asked to write again; but I should be able to say with G. K. C.: 'I have laid an egg; I feel better, thank you.'

Perhaps, therefore, it would always be safer merely to remark, whenever consistent with truth, that the lunch was tastefully served up by a band of willing lady, or gentlemen, helpers, and that 'a very enjoyable game of cricket was played'. After that, the score.

Old Friends

When tempers and commodities grow a little short, I take half an hour off with invisible friends. I like to start at Taunton, hoping to find the railway porter who never knew how the trains to London ran. He had heard that the time-table was being 'mucked about with'; but why, to what point, in logic or the clock's perimeter, he confessed himself to be in total darkness, and rolled the milk-cans on into the dawn of butter.

There, in the main street, outside the tobacconist, talk Sam Woods, of Somerset and the world, and Mr Lock, of the George Inn. Nothing ever stood between them except some loose pieces of an argument on whether Tyler didn't overdo the flighted off-side half-volley when Gilbert Jessop was batting and Sam was at mid-off.

About twenty minutes' talk away, on the county ground, head groundsman Fernie with one eye is daring the turf to show a weed; with the other he arrests a bounding rubber ball, and connects it darkly with a boy who generates an insane interest in the huge empty scoreboard.

I arrange for a very private aeroplane, the sort of thing that would have made Blériot laugh. It has something in common with a helicopter. In it I move, with uncertain state, over the Quantocks, and direct my telescope down on to a village where the leading tradesman, an old wicket-keeper of ideas, is deciding without pain that some advice at the pub might solve the problems of the larder. Thence, over Bishop's Lydeard, where I was once put to sing against a local basso who, in some huff, had withdrawn his sound from choir to congregation.

So to Combe Florey, where a sort of landing is made by the farm of Jack White, who imprisoned many a famous batsman with left-hand cunning and keeps cider beyond compare. From there the flight is towards the Bristol Channel and Watchet, where Harold Gimblett first showed his skill, and a Somerset Eleven used to play against a number from the district in early September; cricket which had little effect on lunch, tea, speeches: 'Mr ——, whom you all know so well as the local secretary of the . . . in whose capable hands . . . and Mrs ——, who, at considerable inconvenience has provided the . . . and the collection box will be at . . . who's got a cigarette?'

But evening is near. On the links at Weston-super-Mare an elderly golfer is rebuking a seashore bandit for halloo-ing on the stroke. There is a haze over Bath, where good Tom Young hit the Hampshire bowlers that day like flaming fire, and where, in Milsom Street, a warlike lady used to sell admonitory newspapers of limited circulation.

Soon, they say, there will be no bats or balls, no petrol for mowing. No matter. We'll snatch a game of cricket with hockey-sticks in a meadow, as they did in England before anyone thought of Prussia.

Mid-On and Third-Man

If you were taking a young lady, free from the slightest acquaintance with cricket, to watch her affianced, a non-bowler, in the field, you would probably hope to find, and so be able to describe, him as shining at cover-point. A cynic might add, that, if it were her husband, mid-on would be good enough.

Poor, humble, maligned mid-on. I have never understood the prejudice, almost amounting to a conspiracy, against that place among those whose fancy it is that they can field. I have heard an otherwise worthy man, respected in the City and kind to his wife, when he was asked by his captain to occupy mid-on, abruptly say 'No'; like Mr T. Handley denying that the day is nice. Certainly it was a Sunday afternoon. But the dissenter was not only breaking 'Ranji's' famous injunction, delivered in the Jubilee year of 1897: 'Obey your captain cheerfully and promptly,' but he was revealing a brute ignorance of the philosophy of mid-on.

I could have told him, had I not been showing an umpire the unsatisfactory shape of the ball, the many beautiful and unlikely thoughts that have solaced my mind while standing in that position as I watched short-leg chasing in youth and hope to the boundary, and waited, without care, for the captain to say, 'Well, Glasgow, what about a try at the top end? The other doesn't seem to suit you.' I could have told him about Copley's catch at mid-on which dismissed McCabe and turned that Nottingham Test. But the man was lost, as I afterwards learnt, in some misty yearnings for third-man; a silly scheme in one whose longest throw was a galvanic under-arm jerk such as testy golfers use to give their caddies a frisk from green to tee.

Besides, third-man was unsuited to his temperament, which, if this lapse be overlooked, is sociable and gustily talkative; and you are the deuce of a long way from the news at third-man, except that which you pick up, free from the crowd or from a passing newspaper deftly trapped under the boot.

The text-books tend to say that the places at cricket, though they exact from the fielder a variety of method and approach, yet demand equally the fundamental virtues of vigilance and speed. But these arid truths cannot explain the secret, which is that each place in the field has a character, almost an identity, of its own.

For cover-point is a vain fellow, who loves applause and the spotlight, who prefers speculation to a solid investment. Wicket-keeper is tough, and speaks to convince, not to amuse. Short-leg is an acrobat or pantaloon. Slip is a man of the world, glib and sharp. Long-stop is an occasional waiter, once a young and ambrosial butler. Third-man is a hermit.

But mid-on is best. He is a genial club gentleman, seasoned with the right stuff; and he knows that the ball which the hand misses will yet bounce off the boots.

The Bore

The true bore, virtuous man, nearly always speaks the truth. He chases it, like a runaway straw-hat, pins it, and holds it up for admiration. If he is a golfer, he must fix for you the number of the tree, judged from left to right, level with which his ball finished. It was the third tree; no, sorry, the fifth; a lime; or is it a Chinese chestnut? Smithers would know, if he were here. It was a number two iron. No; that had been left with the professional for binding; it was a driving-mashie; you don't often see them now; it was bought on an Easter holiday at Turnberry. As the last of his audience slinks, still thirsty, from the club, he has nailed that stroke for ever; in his own memory.

The flour of experience should be leavened with the yeast of romance. Supposing this golfer, having fixed the tree (from left to right) had suddenly gone, by his own standards, clean mad, and had said, in his laundry-mangle voice: 'And on the topmost branch of that tree I saw an African cockatoo,' or 'Between the second and third tree I saw Nottleworthy, the caddie-master, dancing the conga in a bathing-costume.' Undoubtedly there would be a rush for doctors.

But the romancer would only have been making the mistake of jumping two steps instead of one. For the right order of honours is – bore; boaster; romancer. The boaster is merely the reformed bore; the romancer is but he who has learnt that he has nothing to boast about. Speaking entirely for myself, I could not happily dispense with any of them.

There are further refinements, not easily found in common field games, but needing the ampler aether of gun and rod. 'I had just shot my fifth tiger that morning, when the Duke said: "Look here, Jack, we must leave a few for the Rajah." ' There is a magnitude about this sort of thing, not granted to cricket or football or golf. It is Big Game and, as Huck Finn would say, it lays back everything else you'll ever hear on. We bless such ballad-mongers, weaving, as it were, circles round them thrice and closing our eyes in holy dread.

In cricket boasting on a generous scale is neither easy nor frequent; for the most bald-faced narrator knows how *Wisden's* and facts can be pounced on. Avoid figures, therefore, except of speech, and adhere to such plesaing generalities as: 'So the Old Man said to me: "Thompson, you can bat last." ' No harm came, or will come, from that.

I heard recently from a Middlesex cricketer of a good bout of exaggeration. The Home Guard had been playing the Fire Service, and had won in the last over by an arguable run-out. 'After the talk in the pavilion,' he wrote, 'we repaired to the local, and the boasting began. I held my own easily. I am pleased to think I can still do it.' So am I.

All Square

How often, in cricket, sentiment dopes the conscience and makes a liar of judgment.

For instance, the season, such as it may be, has been born; in potting-sheds, outhouses, and other more scrofulous shacks practice-nets are being disentangled from mowing-machines, from shin-paring pails, from those anonymous implements that are a curse even to the gardeners, who store them against eternity. These nets are found to be more porous than ever before. They have shrunk, and their attendant guy-ropes burst like rotten suspenders.

During the popping and bending, my cross-examiner, Mr Blathers, whose livelihood is evidently earned at night, approaches with his inexorable gaiety and, overlooking a request to fetch that hammer please, remarks that we are at the good work early, aha! and implies, by a homely metaphor or two, that we and the nets are twin souls, never long, or happy, apart.

Politeness demands a grunt, which he interprets as agreement, and waxing suddenly fervid, as he can, waves a hamhand with circular gesture round trees, grass, and a passing aeroplane, and says noisily: 'This is the thing; village and country cricket; worth all the rest put together.' And, whether it is the fanatical glint in his eye, or the remembered note of last evening's nightingale, or the expectation of tomorrow's sausages, blow me if he doesn't for the moment carry me with him, so that I say, reverently if tersely, 'Yes'. And it isn't true; not for me, it isn't. One down to conscience; one up to sentiment.

Not long afterwards, without Blathers, I was able to put this right, or nearly. I went to a neighbourhood where I used to play in school and village cricket; to the school field, and leant over the gate. A sea of vegetables rolled in front of me. How useful, I thought, how very sensible. Sentiment died at birth. I had been ready to remember gentle scenes, such as the boy, now, I believe, an eminent headmaster, who, after bowling four successive wides, said 'Damn', and was sent to cool in the pavilion; or the afternoon when the choirboys had us out for 10 (3 extras) and then snatched all the cherries at tea.

Those allotments, thank goodness, dammed that gush, and, instead, I recalled one May match when it snowed, and another when I was bowled with a three-bouncer, and the ball died away at the bottom of the middle stump. Besides, how miserably small the place looked! I felt like the man who exclaimed: 'Is this the mighty ocean? Is this all!' or something of the kind.

I bicycled sternly away, noting the looseness of the front wheel, and the threat of rain. Conscience and sentiment all square.

A Cricketer

He was a promising batsman once; and once he overheard his instructor, who bowled eternal off-breaks, saying: 'Yes; with that style he might do anything.' But, ah! how nigh was night to that fair morning!

It was the style that brought him low; down only a little at first, to numbers five and six, where men are still batsmen, and are pointed out by the more knowing spectators, and have their own bats and pads and standards of dignity; then to that questionable limbo of numbers seven to nine, that bourne, let me tell you, whence few cricketers return, that doubtful habitation where, in a spasm of visionary glory, a man may remember the light and whence, for him, it once flowed; that sinking degree where, at best, you hope to be mistaken for a number three who has missed the proper train; at worst, you are asked whether it is to bowling, wicket-keeping, or favouritism that you owe your appearance in the team.

And lastly, down to that inferno, too frightful to be mentioned by Dante, where you are not a batsman but a person with a bat, which you wield as any instrument of vanity or laughter. To such a pit, to such darkness visible did style hurl that cricketer.

And so he took to bowling. In this, I believe, he was early fortified by two autographs, one of the immortal cricketer, S. F. Barnes, which he called 'Method', another of the unquenchable billiard-player, Melbourne Inman, referred to as 'Stamina'. In youth he had no other heroes except an operatic tenor who lived abroad.

He bowls right on, with a moderately high and not unpleasing action, and sets no value on spin, which is beyond his art, or on subtly arranged fields, which he leaves to fuss and his captain. He keeps a tolerable length, towards the middle stump, and, if the ball chooses to swerve, so much the better fun. His philosophy is simple. He will say: 'If I don't know what I'm doing, then how the devil can the batsman?' He never angles for catches, but aims to bowl his man clean; next best, to hit him on the fat part of the leg and appeal for lbw. He talks much; nearly all the time; especially to umpires and batsmen who require silence. He is never angry except when taken off. Then he does some muttering, and scowls at his incompetent successor.

In fielding, he most fancies the slips; for there, he says, you are in the talk, and should be able, without effort, to make all catches seem difficult. 'If you miss a sitter,' he once told me, 'fall down at once; roll on the grass, if it's dry; and don't get up too soon.' Sometimes, being a very fair thrower and catcher, he is sent into the deep; but not by captains who know him, for he is too interested in casual dogs, spectators, deck-chairs, and passing clouds.

He means to take to batting again when peace returns. I have found him reading C. B. Fry on back-play.

Who ever hoped like a cricketer?

The Questioner

His letter came from near a scene of action, and he wanted to know.

He asked what a certain corner of our West Country looked like just now, and said that he wouldn't mind 'having a smack at H——'s bowling again, especially the googlies; you know'. I do know. They are always going to do the trick. They feed on hope, die by murder, and are born again. Reasons, evasions, and open lies live around these googlies. It is the wrong end, the wrong slope, or too cold. Some day all will be warm and right. But I don't think so. Never the time and the place and the googly all together.

He inquired whether our club accounts had shown the customary half-crown credit, and, if they hadn't, what did the auditor think he was there for? As to the committee, he suggested an electoral truce, but wondered whether the three vice-presidents were still quite up to their job, and whether James, the scorer, had come safely through the annual dinner, if any.

He supposed that certain hilarious juniors would have to be promoted to the middle from uncharted cricket around the pavilion, would briefly occupy the batting space above the extras, would be given an over or two under discouraging circumstances, would be told they had much to learn and be sent, muttering, to the less spectacular places in the field. He also supposed that by now the sight-screen at the south end had fallen into two pieces, and that a certain parishioner, tethered and painted white, would form a reasonable wartime substitute.

He turned aside for a space to the land and the fighters around them; but not for long. And in the end he was speaking, obliquely, as lovers often do, of our green fields, and the elms, and the stream with the trout, and the mill with the long-silent wheel, and the dispersing laughter from the evening inn.

The Captain

He will rise no higher than his present office, and, as he is soon to go to a school where he will desert cricket for rowing, he is on the verge of retirement; but he must not go without a short tribute, not to his cricket, which is negligible, but to his control of other non-cricketers, which is unique. For he is a captain in the second game, resort of the mellow and sanctuary of incompetence.

He has no instinct for the game, being by habit a practising natural historian; besides, even Doctor Grace's love of cricket might have cooled if his first boundary had come off the knuckles in the fifth week of the season, and if his most consistent batsman had been the wides bowled by his opponents. But he knows what should and what should not be done; chiefly the latter. He knows that long-stop should not be in a position to trap the ball on the half-volley under the sole of his shoe, or, having trapped it, to throw it backwards over his head into the scoring-hut. If square-leg hides himself behind the umpire, he winkles him out and changes him with point. He allows no signs of pain in his fielders, and the other day, when his wicket-keeper was dancing about and rubbing his ankle, he told him that the game was waiting 'till you've finished having a fit'.

He will try any bowler once, for one over, except himself, whom he retains continually at the copse end, partly from the same sense of duty that keeps a sea-captain on the bridge to the last, partly because he hopes to repeat a now legendary leg-break which bowled the opposing captain round his legs and which caused the bowler to exclaim: 'I didn't know I could do that.' In the effort to recapture this miraculous delivery, he sometimes overdoes some grip or twiddle, once to the extent of hitting his own mid-on a sharp clack on the left side of the head, to whom he merely remarked: 'I did that on purpose, to see if you were awake.'

Autocracy and failure have increased his weakness for irony, and he will say to a batsman who has scythed him to the boundary: 'Were you quite ready just then?' But, in the warmer weather, when he has one eye on the cabbage whites, he reverts to open swearing, using such expressions as 'fluke', or 'bother, I mean blast'.

Common labour on the river will be a drab change from this high estate. For a few more weeks he will be a king; and then, for untold years, a galley-slave.

The Gatekeeper

Among those whom the war relieved of a regular profession was the pavilion gatekeeper; I mean the man who lets you out to bat.

He who stops you coming in was still there, probably because there is nothing else in the world that he can do. He has grown old in the business of prevention. He knows to a nicety what sort of deception will be practised at the members' entrance, discerning afar between those smaller invaders who will seek to ooze in under the shadow of a corpulent member and those who put one foot on the mat inside and remark, in easy tones: 'Oh, Mr Culpepper said he would sign me in,' and who may be overheard at intervals for the rest of the day discussing Mr Culpepper's incomprehensible absence or his still more perplexing non-existence.

This janitor of exclusion remained at his post. In war his work was more intricate, because wider and more democratic was the passage to the mysteries within. All the same, he stuck to certain standards, and he told me one day: 'Chaps without a collar or tie I do not let in.'

But the man who let you out vanished, and will only return with bananas, benedictine, and rubber handles for bats. I know, because I wrote to one who has let me out to many a snick and swat, and he said that he, and, he was quite sure, his fellow-artists, were not going to be 'brought out for an odd Saturday for any old bunch of hit-and-missers who wouldn't care what you told them about the bowling'.

I understood. He had attended for the first summer of war in a straw-hat and his old chair by the wicket-gate; but his pride had been hit. His professional advice had been questioned, perhaps derided, by some flailing sergeant who batted by numbers, bowled a mechanized medium, and, opening the gate on his own, shattered the ceremony of fifty summers and passed, unforgivable, on his ignorant road.

For there were, and will be again, subtly various ways of opening that wicket-gate. In deference to the first pair of batsmen he laid it open as soon as he saw them coming from the dressing-room, and he smiled on them as one who smiles on prosperous travellers who go on a long journey. If one of them returned unexpectedly early, he still kept a silence, at once surprised and tactful. But, if Nos. three and four also came back somewhat empty, he put two and two together; ratiocination, it is sometimes called; and he began to offer advice which, in its brief simplicity, embraced the whole art of batting. If spin was the source of trouble, he said: 'What you want to do is to stop 'em breaking. Play 'im on the dap.' If speed prevailed, he said: 'Hit 'im back past his whiskers. No bowler never likes that.'

For the last two batsmen he kept an entirely different line. I think he knew that, in their case, all technical suggestions were superfluous. They had no batting to discuss. So he stuck to merely secular affairs, observing in offhand tones: 'There's a good picture at the Regal tonight,' and, on one occasion, 'Mrs —— is expecting again.'

But he would soon return to business; for, if you looked round on your way to the crease, you would see that he had not only opened the gate, but also left it open.

The White Chicken

In a match played between Barbados and Trinidad, a Barbados spectator, carried away by the brilliance of one of the home batsmen, rushed out on to the field and presented him with a white chicken. The recipient, F. M. Worrell, a young man of nineteen, had just passed the score of 210, made in the same match by J. B. Stollmeyer, of Trinidad, and he and his partner, the left-handed J. D. Goddard, went on to set up a new world's fourth wicket record of 502, Worrell 308, Goddard 218, both not out.

But the feat of the anonymous donor is, of its kind, equally remarkable. It is not everyone that would have had a bird handy for such an occasion, or the hopefulness to convey it to the ground on so slender a chance of bringing it into play. It makes me quite hot to imagine his excitement when the scoreboard told him that he would not be required to carry his gift, a year tougher, to the corresponding fixture in Trinidad, and that he was about to make a public presentation which, though doubtless he knew it not, scarcely conceivable among those cricketing nations who have lost the dear light of simplicity and, temporarily, the majority of their hens.

In Australia, we have heard, the unsuccessful outfielder has sometimes been comforted with hot-house fruit on the back of the neck, while those beyond the range of solids receive the more abstract oblation of advice; but in English cricket the spontaneous gift is almost unknown. The generous Barbadian gave to a young man, on the nail, something intended to appeal to the appetite of youth. In England we offer, to the elderly, after a long wrangle, something designed to accelerate his retirement and obstruct his sideboard.

In higher cricket, we have never given much of a trial to the punitive or admonitory award, of that sort which has prompted the back benches of a village club to sing, 'The Dead March in Saul' during a lecture on the Significance of Art, and which once induced a friend of mine to hand the wine list to an inebriated stranger at a public dance. What a vista stretches here: – A gargle carried on to the field for the square-leg who *will* appeal for lbw; a *Bradshaw* handed silently by the umpire to the dreary batsman; a counterfeit fiver handed back by the dreary batsman to the venal umpire.

But the hen is better than these; though there is something to be said for a turkey.

April

This is the time of year when the sentimental cricketer withdraws his bat tenderly from its winter bed and croons over it, as if it were a Stradivarius or a shoulder of mutton.

If he is doing the thing properly, he allows the immaculate blade to wave him back on the zephyrs of memory, and of exaggeration, to that 50 which he would have scored, had not his partner fallen to a slow full-pitcher. He may even lock the door, put on his favourite club-cap, and go through those strokes with which, but for his partner's futility, he would have won a famous victory. If he be a bowler, and nothing but, he will pass his fingers contentedly down the bat's edge and say: 'This one bisected the slips and flew, like a scalded cat, to the boundary; that one was the off-drive which found fine-leg so fast asleep.'

Such delights are not for me; for I have no bat. The best bats that I ever had have been other people's, returnable after use. It was always so. In earliest days at school I had a bat that was lovely to look upon; the grain was straight, nor rudely broad nor miserably close; the blade was knotless, and I never oiled the splice. But it didn't work at all. It remained, like the sea-sirens, a beautiful and deadly ornament.

Years passed. I still bought a bat once in a while. I even lifted it, in response to the vendor's request that I should feel 'how well it comes up'; then I wrote my name on the back. I was using one such purchase in a match of some importance at Lord's when Tom Lowry, at short-leg, inquired: 'Tell me, do you buy your bats at Hamley's, or leave them in water overnight?'

Thenceforward I settled to borrowing. I studied the art inside-out. I came to know that batsmen who have made 0, especially by lbw, do not lend with simplicity. I learnt that bats in oilskin are untouchable; that those in cloth cases may be won by judicious wooing; that those left standing in dim corners of the dressing-room are legal prey.

Then, one day in August, having brought off a successful touch of an expansive major of Artillery, I made what was, for me, a long score. The same thing happened in the second innings; and the owner offered me the bat; a generosity the more remarkable as he had just made two with his second-best. I am glad to remember that I kept my head. 'No, no,' I said, with profuse but fearful thanks; 'keep your bat. For, once it is my own, it will turn to an alloy of teak and tin.' He kept it.

276

So I shall not be withdrawing my bat tenderly from its winter bed. But, already, I am looking around for a cheerful lender.

The Look of the Thing

A friend of mine, who sometimes cocks an eye at cricket, told me that, to his possibly cock-eyed view, everyone on the cricket field looks like everyone else.

'I do not,' he said, 'refer to their batting, which may be too slow to please the crowd or too fast to amuse the bowler. I mean their aspect; the tout ensemble; there's a dangerous uniformity.' He gazed meditatively at the Lord's Tavern, past which a citizen in once grey flannel trousers and what might have started as a dinner-jacket walked with his chic wife and two well-dressed children.

'Of course,' he went on, 'at any moment this uniformity may cease. There are, ranging about, fanatical cricketers who, owing to the parsimony of the Board of Trade and the alarming growth of their children, hurry headlong towards nakedness. Only this' – here he swept his hand towards the Members' Pavilion and the window of the Committee Room – 'only this, and the cowardice of custom, prevent these desperate men from going out to bat in a siren-suit with bowler hat, or going on to bowl in plus-fours and Home Guard boots.'

An innings ending at this moment and the fielders turning with a decent show of reluctance towards the pavilion, this critic went off to refresh his mind with the newly restored pictures in the Long Room and his body with a possible some-what in the equally important *salon* behind.

At first I let his remarks slide away as the idle passes of one who has always opposed, and beaten, the world with the rapier of levity. It was he, I recalled, who, when put on to bowl in a Club match, asked that first-slip be removed in order to provide an uninterrupted view of a lady by the sight-screen, and, when his captain wanted to know what should be done with first-slip, answered: 'That is a matter between you and your conscience.'

But, as the fielders returned in their various attitudes of

hostility and resignation, I sensed the error of his phrase, 'dangerous uniformity'; and I felt, as never before, that cricket, except to those irrevocably lost on the escalators of restlessness or in the deserts of cynicism, is one of the answers by free individualism to collective servility; and I thought of those, beyond counting, who had passed in from the noise outside not just to see the scoring of so many runs in so many hours, but to enjoy the players of their heart, the men, without the arithmetic; the monument of Dr Grace at point; Spofforth fixing the incoming victim with fierce mesmeric eye; 'Tich' Freeman shrugging his way to cover-point after an over to Bradman; Philip Mead settling into his crease like a dog into its basket; or Lord Tennyson quelling a hot one at mid-off.

Rain Stopped Play

A Family Test

It started on the home meadow, soon after the departure of Father Christmas and the arrival of the blue-nosed brothers Frost and Snow. At about the same time, the Third Test was being played at Melbourne. That match had an end, merciful, unexpected, agonizing, according to opinion's choice; but inevitable. Our own Test had no end; there is a local prejudice against stopping anything, once it has started, whether it is cricket, dancing, or a go-cart touched off at the top of the hill. But it had a sort of middle, and it was around then that I joined it.

It was a single-wicket match between England and Australia, but you could be run out at either end; or at both, one after the other. The countries were represented by both sexes. Ages ranged from 4 to 14; from deep square-leg-cum-extra-cover, who sometimes made snowballs or was taken away for an hour's siesta, to roving long-stop, who made nothing but a few unheeded appeals and took his sleep standing up. There were also two dogs; a Gentleman and a Player; and lest, in these captious times, it should be thought that I cast some slur on their social status, it may be explained that the Gentleman just watched but the Player joined in.

This Test had reached its third or fourth afternoon. No one was caring which. It was Timeless, like love, and London clocks, and the Garden of the Hesperides. One day they would grow up and discover bunions, and overdrafts, and Boards of Control. By a purely personal arrangement the England captain was batting for Australia; a guest-artist. He was accepted, like Monday morning. He said he had made 74.

At 80 he retired, because he wanted to bowl at his young sister, whose desire for success had been sharpened by insults and a prolonged absence from the crease. The wicket-keeper, obsessed by the Victorian notion that ladies need help, took guard for her. But she kicked him out of the way and was still acting the suffragette when she was bowled by a full-pitcher on the middle stump. She said she wasn't ready. What woman ever was? And so she went on batting.

After a week the players knew no score but their own. The

Australian captain claimed 694 in 23 innings, and said that, as he had never really been out, his average was infinity. At times I was asked to umpire, at others, to field 'just over there'. On the last afternoon of the holidays I was asked to bowl; not on merit, but because the two best England bowlers had been whipped away to the dentist.

Darkness was falling when I bowled a ball that pitched on a block of ice and started to return, in disgust, to its originator. The batsman, like Warren Bardsley on a famous occasion, came out to hit it. Twice he missed; the first time, because he fell over; the second, because point had meanwhile removed the ball and thrown it at the batsman's wicket, which it struck, then passed on to the back of the wicket-keeper's neck, who was arguing with long-stop. So ended that day's play, in chaos, darkness, and vulgar abuse. The dogs barked, deep square-leg was taken off to bed, and three times round the house the gong was sounded for tea.

Primrose Path

The mind, if such it be, surely works by opposites, for, as soon as I saw, from the train window, the first primroses, as usual pretending not to be there, I thought of some of the slap-up rows in cricket at which I had rejoiced to be present.

This was very wrong of me, as I had not long since been listening, apparently, to some of those speeches in which cricket is extolled as an unrivalled stimulant to rectitude of character. Of course, it may be that burglars would give up stealing if they took more interest in top-spinners and leg-glides, and Attila himself would have become more of a social success if he had diverted his energies to fast bowling; but there is something tedious, even depressing, in the thought of Sir Galahad at play. So, as the train toiled upwards through sylvan beauty, I found myself reflecting on a certain irascible Lieutenant-Colonel who, on a ground not far behind the trees to the left had been run out, by silly-point, while patting down inequalities in the pitch.

This, too, was the country of Tom Walker, whose silent invincibility at the crease provoked Frederick Beauclerk to language that was secular even for his Reverend Lordship; the country, too, of our own village cricket some twenty years ago. As I remembered it, it was not chiefly notable for its rectitude or improving moral tone. I recalled, rather, the afternoon when our team retired from the field as a protest against the opposing umpire's interpretations and left the batsmen without the means of exhibiting their skill. I thought of the ground where our slow bowler, a policeman, on being refused a decision for lbw, was asked by the spectators whether he had brought his truncheon, and where our number ten batsman, himself a glazier, had ended the match with a hit that descended from almost invisible height through the cucumber-frame belonging to the opposing captain.

But most of all I thought of our opening bowler, who operated from round the wicket fast round-arm, and appealed for every hit registered on the enemy, from top to toe. Many an undeserved favour did he scowl out of hesitant umpires, and once, in answer to some rudeness from an opponent, he pushed his face close to the offender's and muttered, 'only look, now, if you get passing them com-ments, I'll smash you'. Our wicket-keeper, too, had an artificial leg which drove like a bat, and sometimes returned the ball the whole way to the bowler. And the umpire would sometimes offend the more serious takers of guard by saying, 'That's your middle-de-diddle'.

These were the men who won us our matches, and, when they lost them, cursed and went their way to see how the other side would stand up to it in the local. And, as the primrose comes round again, it is of them that I think, with laughter and delight. Nothing flowery about them; except that they too, were the work of Nature.

A. N. Other

There was a time, which may never recur, when there was room in the newspapers to publish the names of those who were to represent their team on the field of play. It was pleasant for those who were going to perform, because everyone likes to see his name in print, except, perhaps, in the police news; and it was helpful for the performers' friends, who were thus reassured that A. E. Smith had recovered from his sprained ankle and that J. L. Jones had safely returned from a holiday in foreign parts.

Equally, it was agreeable reading for those who find innocent pleasure in deducing from a name the physical appearance of its owner. I enjoy it myself. My Johnsons are all rather short and fat and pale; my Hendersons are tall with a raking stride; my O'Briens have wild, black hair and are rude to referees.

But there was one player who excited especial conjecture, and that was A. N. Other. I first saw his name a good many summers ago at the bottom of our school cricket Second Eleven, and I thought, in common with several of my friends, that the sports master, after several promising but false starts, had at last gone off his chump. That match was cancelled owing to rain or measles, and the mysterious athlete never took the field. But many times since he has popped up, and no one has enjoyed so long a playing career.

He does not appear for the best Clubs, whose secretaries would doubtless resign rather than publish his name. But I would like to see more of him. It would be nice if he could be picked for England against Australia, at Lord's. It would be a great moment for him and very annoying for the critics. Nor should a political career be beyond him. He would look well in the Prime Minister's list of Ministers. Chancellor of the Exchequer – A. N. Other. He would be useful, too, in fictional romance – 'Why are you so cold today, Madeleine?' he asked her, straightening his cravat; 'have I done anything to offend you?' Tears welled into her ultramarine eyes. 'Lancelot,' she replied, 'I have a confession to make. I love A. N. Other.'

I have great hopes of him. He may yet win for Great Britain the hop-step-and-jump at the Olympic Games; or prove to be the answer to Bradman.

Missing Catches

The easiest catch I ever saw was one missed by a Member of Parliament at mid-on. The ball, feebly struck, seemed scarcely equal, even with a gentle following breeze, to its brief journey;

but the culprit, lost in the profundity of political cogitations, and further handicapped by tight trousers, lifted his head just in time to keep it lifted, and the ball, untouched by delaying finger, fell to the grass with an almost imperceptible and half-apologetic sound. Silence followed. The crime was beyond expiation. We could only stand helpless, as when a parishioner is seized by stomach-rumbles in the sermon or a host uses a bad word at a children's party.

There is usually a reason for a missed catch. For instance, when G. O. Allen, the England captain in the West Indies, floored a sitter at short-leg, he was doubtless exercised by anxiety as to what malady, and where, would lay low which of his fellow-fielders, and whether, to fill the widening breaches, any more cricketers could be persuaded to leave the shores of England. And, where there is no reason, there is apt to be a pretext; especially among the slips who, in moments of failure, excuse themselves by saying that the bowler bowled before they were ready; a condition that prevailed in a well-remembered match in a London suburb when my second slip, while watching his wife trying to park a car, took a snick on the back of the neck.

But the truly experienced misser is, paradoxically, the most alert. His rapidity of judgment is such that he can make any catch appear impossible. If in the slips, he hurls himself sideways or forwards. clawing the air with all the desperation of a drowning man, and so invests a bald miss with the romance of a near-miracle. If situated in the deeper positions, he realizes, as soon as the catch goes up, that if he stands quite still the ball cannot miss him. He must therefore decide which course will win him most sympathy among the dupes, to run forwards and let the ball pass high over his head, or to totter backwards and watch it drop in front of him, or, easier yet, to take a few graceful steps to the side and shield his eyes from the sun.

But perhaps the simplest method of all is to fall down. To those who favour this idea my advice is, once down, stay down. The effect is blunted by any attempt to rise; and I recall, with pleasure, the ironical applause which greeted a Somerset deep-fielder who fell while midjusging a towering hit by Percy Chapman, then half-rose into an attitude of Oriental devotion.

The lot of the bowler is indeed unenviable. Besides the

perfection of pitches and the indifference of umpires he must suffer day in and out from fielders who conjoin to natural incompetence every art of hypocrisy.

After Tea

Now should all slaves of the desk bless the name of William Willett, who wrenched for us a whole hour of daylight from inexorable Time and gave new meaning to the words After Tea.

What better time for cricket than After Tea, when the sun turns from cruelty to generosity and the umpires begin to be mellow? Dissolved are the stiffness of the morning and the heaviness of the post-luncheon hours. The spectators have discovered each other and confirmed the wisdom of being where they are. For batsmen, it is the perfect time to increase advantage gained or to defy disaster's threat. For the bowler, it is the just and natural hour. The pitch shrinks to the span of a few strides; he could almost lean over the batsman and flick away his bails. It was now that Maurice Tate was at his mightiest. The new ball came up and he made it whizz from the pitch like a thunder-flash; and the Sussex boys shouted as the stumps flew, wrote down their hero's latest triumph with unlikely pencil, then crammed another ice-cream into the invincible stomach of youth.

After Tea at lawn tennis. Gone is the constriction of politeness and introductions; unused is the apology for double-fault or drive poached from the lady's back-hand. The party waxes in warmth and thins in number. The guests invited for social or testamentary, reasons linger over a tea-cup or take departure from mere duty performed. The wilder experiments are made; balls fly uninhibited to the back-netting or startle some pensive botanist in the neighbouring garden.

After Tea at golf. It was now that Hoylake's Jack Graham, the champion who never won the Championship, burnt up his great links with a flame of threes. It was now that we played those nine holes with familiar friends, and joked over whims of style on the tee and eccentric attitudes on the green, while the westering sun shone on the coming beauty of the trees. Now, too, was it often happiness enough to play alone. There, by the third green, stooped the same gardener in the same posture. He knew nothing of golf and I knew less of gardening, and we would stare at each other in reciprocal ignorance and wonder. 'How goes the putting?' he would say. 'How go the japonicas?' I would answer.

Ah, yes; thrice blessed is the name of William Willett, sun-giver.

Seats

A friend recently requested from me suggestions for an inscription to be carved on a special seat, which he is giving to a country cricket ground 'for the use of the older and wiser spectators'. They are Yorkshiremen, and they will enjoy a place to sit and doubt if there will ever be another Stanley Jackson, Hirst, or Rhodes, or if Hedley Verity will ever be repeated. To find a suitable inscription, something between the romantic and the obvious, would tax William Shakespeare. 'Sit tight' at first commended itself for brevity and wisdom; but it was too suggestive of the scenic railway; and I seemed to hear Colonel Chinstrap say, 'I always do, sir'. In the end, I sent him some crude and unsatisfying couplet.

All over England the seats on cricket grounds are being adjusted to the necessary angle, and their prospective occupants are refurbishing their critical faculties. The other afternoon, on a village green, I saw the earliest arrival. He had beaten the cuckoo to it. He was sitting on a bench watching the groundsman, who was also the umpire and the scorer's uncle; and the groundsman was watching the pitch. Both were evidently sunk in wonder. The spectator was wondering if the groundsman was going to do anything worth criticizing, and the groundsman was wondering whether a scythe wouldn't be necessary before the mower. Neither acknowledged the presence of the other. Neither cared what Mr Molotov thought. They might have been there since William the Conqueror. The only voice was from a wood-pigeon.

There is much to be said for deck-chairs at cricket. It is

agreeable to adjust them to an angle whence only the heads of the players can be seen, and to judge the game solely on facial expression. The fast bowler doesn't laugh. He scowls with effort and the desire to terrify. The slow spin bowler smiles smugly, with conscious art, and at the batsman's incompetence in discerning the googly. The medium-paced stock bowler has no expression at all. He has conquered hope and disappointment. The years have sapped him of all emotion. He just goes on with his job, like the ticket-server at the booking-office, or a donkey pulling a tinker's cart.

But a seat at cricket should not be too comfortable. The luxury of being present at all should be nearly enough. The larger and softer the seat, the greater is the spectator's belief in the value of his criticism, and he begins to think himself more important than the cricketer he watches. There is much to be said for a bare bench; with a few rusty nails, to provoke an occasional saunter towards the refreshments.

The Start

This year my first wicket, a junior relative caught and bowled, fell to me on the last day of March. The catch was taken low and one-handed. Any spectator, however ignorant, would have recognized in this feat the delusive brilliance of immobility. One step, and it was a sitter. That was my start, and, I expect, my zenith.

And now the Universities join in. While the rest of us are wondering where to go and watch Bradman and his men, already, at Oxford and Cambridge, inveterate critics have nearly decided on the teams for Lord's.

The wise always walked to their cricket in the Oxford Parks; already flannelled; for thus you could enjoy a wholly legal triumph over those who hurried earnestly or trickled compulsively to annotate the erudition of lectures. Halting at Wadham, you could look up, not without wonder, at those windows whence, so it was said, the greatest of all Oxford's games-players had fired a shot, nearly 300 yards, on to the ceiling of the Dean of Trinity. The accused, then, as sixty years later, disproved the charge, adducing mathematical evidence miraculous in so classical a scholar. And so to the match, through the avenue of trees.

There is something unnatural, even horrifying, in a Trial game of cricket. The batsman, bowled early by a trimmer, watches, with what pleasure he can pretend, his rivals banging celestial long-hops and mellow half-volleys to every corner of the field. The bowler, having had the star opponent missed twice, at the wicket, stands at mid-on ruefully enjoying the fall of batsmen to every form of ineptitude, and, while meditating on the cruelty of chance, lets an easy one glide through his fingers. A Trial is the only match in which you play twenty-one cricketers, and two umpires, all at once.

But at last the match was over, not altogether for the worse; and, with some assurance of hope, we passed into the kindly, if casual, attention of Tom Hayward. He and J. T. Hearne looked after us in the nets. Tom said little, except 'hit 'em hard' or 'Oh, what a shot', and he bowled off-breaks from about eighteen yards. Jack Hearne dwelt more intimately on the science of the game, and never wearied of depicting the value of number eleven batsmen who avoided the insaner manifestations of violence.

But it wasn't what they said or showed or bowled that mattered so much. To be with them was enough learning. And when, on a biting morning of early May, Tom lent me his huge-collared sweater for the match against Warwickshire, I fancied that I was Hayward (T.), opening the innings for England and sending the fast bowlers about their business.

Fine Feathers

I knew a man who used to wear his club cricket cap when he listened in to wireless reports of Test matches in Australia. It was as near as he would ever come to playing for England. Capless, he would have been just one of the dumb and incompetent millions, but, crowned with his colours, he felt that, in an honorary and approximate sort of way, he was taking wickets and making runs, and he would even criticize the pitch and, on his best days, the umpiring.

Alas, for our decline from romance to utility. When eighty-five years ago, H. H. Stephenson took the first England cricket team to Australia, the band at Melbourne played their guests into the field to the strains of 'God Save the Queen'. Imagine a band at a modern Test match. I suppose it is conceivable, if they played 'Rock of Ages' and the 'Dead March in Saul'. With what finery, too, that first team cheered and enlightened the spectators. Each English player wore a very light helmet-shaped hat, with a sash and hat-ribbon of a distinctive hue, corresponding to colours set down in the score-card against each man's name. This gay conception died far too young. I like to fancy Hendren in heliotrope and Sutcliffe in sea-green. Douglas Jardine did his best with his Harlequin cap, but by then most of the Australian spectators were beyond the emollient influence of bright colours.

England and most of the counties have settled to the uniformity of the darker blues, though Surrey struggles on with chocolate brown, Worcestershire with green. It is left to the schools and clubs to illuminate the darkness. Rugby still take the field against Marlborough in light-blue shirts, and the I Zingari cap shines like a beacon in the mist. But it must be admitted that, in modern cricket, versicolority is apt to be rated as a signal of incompetence, until the contrary is proved; and it was not on merely political reasoning that a famous professional bowler used to say at the fall of a wicket, 'Here comes a ruddy college cap; give me the ball'.

But the finest feathers are still sported by those who have no claim to them but fancy. Errand boys are said to have a leaning towards the Old Harrovian tie, and many a tramp, if by some convulsion of nature he were to be stripped of his outer crusts, would be found to be holding up his trousers with Band of Brothers braces.

Only the other day, too, a millionaire, travelling on the *Queen Elizabeth* in bright blue trousers and golden socks, admitted that his red beret was that which is more officially reserved for Airborne Troops. But he couldn't resist it. This, indeed, is the right attitude to colours. Love at first sight.

Panache

Otherwise, the plume on the knight's helmet, and so, by metaphor, dignity and bravado, display and heroism, vainglory and pride; everything, in short, that tends to shock the narrow code, especially on the fields of play. We were not ever thus; not when Coeur de Lion left the throne cold and rode off in panoply and glee for an up-and-downer with Saladin, nor when Archie MacLaren dumped his cares at Tilbury and sailed out to show his batting to the citizens of Sydney.

Panache. Alan Breck had it, and, as he wiped the miscreant blood from his sword, told the old world and young David Balfour to be sure and note that he had it. Don Quixote had it, and, which was his greatness, kept it, even when he was bowled, so to speak, for 0, as he was, every day and nearly every hour of his chivalry. Herbert Sutcliffe had it, albeit of the northern and cooler sort. When his bails flew, he did not leave like one accepting the expected or expecting the inevitable, but he looked round, half-contemptuously, as if some clumsy oaf had broken a Ming vase, which would soon be replaced, with unfelt expense. Walter Hammond had it, above all cricketers of his time; from the moment that you saw him at the pavilion gate; strike or miss, to the end.

Twickenham had it, when, in the March sun, the thousands stood to King George the Fifth before England against Scotland, and Scotland brought its own panache, the crying pipes and the swirl of the kilt. Yet it does not depend merely on panoply, accoutrements, and the appurtenances of its possessor. I have seen it in a golfer with tattered coat and rusty string-flapping irons.

Sir Nigel Loring had it, though he was weak of eye and, by comparison with his Company, slight of strength. Achilles had it, shouting in the trenches; and well, you say, he might, seeing that he could return to a warm tent and a more than warm meal, and had beauty to share the one and prepare the other.

Panache fears no enemy but fear; fear of what may result from failure; from loss of face and place; fear of convention; fear of being different and free; fear of bravery itself.

Australian cricketers, especially the young and the new, have it; less easy to be recognized, perhaps, in the sombre hues and pragmatic guise of modernity, but the same panache that greets the Test with level eye and side-tilted cap.

And England has it, somewhere, everywhere. By the cuff-links of Lord Palmerston and by the Beard of Grace she needs it. For it is better than a million political speeches and ten thousand lessons on how to play leg-breaks.

The Bowling Question

Whenever, and that is daily, someone laments the state of bowling in English cricket, I think of gardeners who expect their flowers to win prizes at the show of their own accord and curse them when they don't.

For consider how we treat the bowler. We do everything possible to make him understand that it is not he but the bats-man who matters in cricket. 'How many did you make?' we inquire of the cricketer; almost never 'How many wickets did you take?' When he is young we put him to bowl in the prac-tice nets, but it is the batsman who takes the eye and the atten-tion. Then, when flushed with hope and opportunity, he reaches the first-class game we give him a heart-break pitch, and the batsman the benefit of the doubt. So the bowler fails; and, to crown all, we tell him that he can't bowl at all.

In youth it is not easy to find an instructor in the arts of bowling. The swing at golf, the right stroke at lawn tennis or swimming, these are widely taught; any cricket coach will tell a boy how to position himself for the off-drive; but how few will tell him where his shoulder and foot should be when bowling? Walter Brearley used to show what he meant in the nets at Lord's, and, when he felt that way, in the long room of the pavilion. There is a common idea that bowling, like being funny, is nature's gift, unteachable. In coaches this excuses a lifetime of silence or laziness. Yet it *can* be taught, not, indeed, implanted, but encouraged and brought out. George Geary teaches it, if I may be allowed a personal touch, at Charter-house. So do a few others – a few.

Picking his own path, the modern bowler too often arrives at in-swing. School, club and county cricket is overstocked with those who set a hopeful huddle of close leg-fielders, fiercely rub the new ball on their patient trousers, then -- wait for the next new ball. There is nothing wrong with in-swing as such. It is a good stick but a poor prop. As a sudden variant to out-swing, as practised by such artists as Emmott Robinson, Alec Kennedy, George Macaulay, and Tom Rushby, it can be a winner. But it is a vain idol, a noxious cult.

The bowler, then, needs help, encouragement. Certainly he can help himself by observation, by avoiding the automatic. But he cannot do it all on his own. He needs a stimulus to hope and confidence. In boyhood he must be given the idea of equality with the batsman; in manhood he must be given its fact. There must be a wise instructor and a wise groundsman.

Old Boys' Match

If I were allowed to relive one day from the moderately distant past, it would be a close thing between the journey by train from London to Aberdeen, which took in the Forth Bridge and the Tay Bridge at one whack, and the Old Boys' cricket match at school, which ended, so far as the public programme knew, with a supper. In the final decision, the cricket would have it. The school cook, a temperamental lady, teed herself up, as the golfers say, for that supper. Her artistry gloried in the refinements of lucent syrups and creamy curds, and her only fear was that the rope of the lift from the top-floor kitchen might snap and plunge the whole feast into the cellar.

The match was on the last day of the term. 'Last day but one, top button undone; last day of all, no buttons at all.' This school doggerel, referring solely to the supernal or upper garment, can have but little meaning for students of today, who are encouraged by the Board of Trade to dispense with jackets; a state of affairs which also casts an almost intolerable strain on the trouser pockets.

But now we are at the cricket. Each summer we were helped against the formidable foe by a sporting parson who was a proper bowler. He was reckoned to have the gift of bowling shooters at will, and there were few umpires whom he could not surprise into a favourable decision. And, by the foot of Pharaoh, we needed him. Three or four of our opponents would be very young old boys; heroic of their kind, but vulnerable; dangerous, but familiar; and, though they might pretend to manhood by smoking a cigarette or two behind the Fives Courts, we knew that it was not long since they had been among us, incurring rebuke, or even detention for neglect of irregular verbs.

As to the others. Rumour had her way. This one had played for Kent; the tall and, did we but know it, apprehensive mid-off had bowled for England; when, and with what exact result, was immaterial. The wicket-keeper whipped off the bails in an obviously international manner, and it seemed incredible that the umpire could dare to resist his appeals. But he did. And we were standing up to them and making runs. And, when it came to our turn to field, the sporting parson produced his shooter for the man of Kent, and our cricket master, I. S., standing down near the swimming-bath, caught an almost invisible ballooner as cool and clean as may be, and, at the last, it was left to the school captain of three years ago to hit a six with a great thwack on to the thatch of the pavilion and, as was only right, to save the match for his side.

And so to that supper, with speeches of neat praise and blunt humour; and the sing-song, and the short light-sleeping night before the summer holidays.

Twelfth Man

An oarsman, far advanced in fame and years, told me that if all the spare men he had met from the Oxford and Cambridge crews of the last fifty years were laid end to end, as he thought they should be, they would stretch from Barnes Bridge to Mortlake Brewery.

He seemed, as he side-stepped an ice-cream vendor and cast a contemptuous glance at the wrist-work of a citizen in a skiff, to take this matter of spare men pretty hardly. So I suggested to him that the years justify some elasticity of truth. I reminded him of the Prince Regent's celebrated appearance at the Battle of Waterloo and of Calverley's single lady who lived on

'the thought, the dream, that she had offers.'

Then, as he still wallowed in the luxury of his rectitude, I added that, in power of imagination, cricketers left oarsmen far down the course. 'I myself,' I said, 'can claim to have told a credulous questioner that I once survived an over from Larwood without seeing a single ball, and that was very odd, because, when I looked up the match in *Wisden*, I found that Larwood wasn't even playing.'

This confession halted my truth-ridden companion on the towing-path, but, before rebuke could pass his teeth, I launched another dart. 'Beware,' I warned him, 'of smugness. Why, you yourself have probably told some innocent visitor, while your wife was out of the room fetching hot water for the tea, that you might have won the Diamond Sculls but for hitting a boom in the first round. Remember, too, that you and I have no excuse for romance. Fortune, no less than skill, included you in this eight, me in that eleven. But the spare man and the twelfth man must live for years on a near miss. Small wonder that they sometimes promote fancy to fact, the might-have-been to the was.'

Besides, as any cricketer should know, the twelfth man is chosen for his discretion rather than his ethics. Uninformed opinion regards him as no more than a purveyor of unnecessary drinks and second-best bats. But he is no mere porter. He may have to start the morning by persuading the doorkeeper, and perhaps the secretary himself, of his credentials. Usurpers are not unknown, armed with every semblance of reality. He must have a cool head, the capacity both to absorb the hospitality of general supporters and to discern such patrons from those representatives of the Press who conceal under the guise of casual topics an unquenchable desire for exclusive information.

He must also be able to distinguish between the relatives of those who have been preferred to him in the team and so avoid offering warm sympathy to the mother of a batsman who has just reached his 50 or excessive praise to the aunt of a bowler who has just been struck for 20 in an over. Above all, he must look the part. If he has not been invited to take his blazer off at least he must have one that is worth keeping on.

Such is the profession of twelfth man. And, if he can't tell a few lies when he's an old man, then cricket is just a waste of time.

Waiting For It

As Gay's beggars sang, the hour of attack approaches. Nearer to Brisbane, where, eighteen years ago, Percy Chapman sent back the dread obstacular Woodfull for 0 with the catch of a lifetime, then watched his bowlers overturn Australia for 122 and 61; where the great-hearted Jack Gregory bowled his last, and Edward Paynter took leave from hospital to make that famous 83. Now they will be putting on the last touches; flattening a trouser-threatening nail or so on the 'bleachers'; testing wires for the myriad words of commentary; unloading bottles against equatorial thirst; and the groundsman will be explaining, to any who can still listen, how that wicket should surely last for a year.

Fourteen years ago I swore I would never do it again, that switching on of the radio at seven o'clock in the morning. I trained myself towards the belief that cricket doesn't matter. I practised indifference. Mr Coué would have approved of me. I was qualifying for a degree in Auto-suggestion. But at the first temptation I fell, and, before you could say Don Bradman, I found myself explaining to a deaf old gentleman who loathes cricket anyhow why some insolent conduct by the Western Australian batsmen meant nothing at all. I told him to wait, just wait.

Soon I was worse than ever before. I could tell this by the photograph that stands by the radio. When Denis Compton made a century, the photograph showed a handsome fellow, of obviously generous disposition, a credit to the family. When Hutton made some early blunder, I saw instead a semi-moron who had inherited all that was unenviable from the ancestral faces, even a slight squint. Then I joined the contemptible band of cowards and sceptics, and picked up my radio news second-

hand, with spuriously casual air. I asked the latest about
Molotov, then added, by way of conventional conversation:
'And the MCC? Don't tell me Bradman's out!'

But you get what you deserve by asking news of others.
Everyone tells you something different. The same batsmen,
you will find, has made 0, 53, and isn't playing at all. He has
been run out and lbw concurrently. I remember a lady in the
Tests of 1930, who told me that Ranji had made a century and
that 'Tate was in it'.

So I am back again, listening for myself. For, after a brisk
pick-me-up from the Ministry of Food or Fuel, what are a few
Test matches more or less?

Nottingham Characters

It was William Clarke, that man of many arguments, who first
took good cricket to Trent Bridge, in 1838. He bowled slow,
between, under, and round arm, and went on taking wickets at
an age when others are merely talking about them. He was a
close and contemptuous student of the opposition, and his
enemies said he had the instincts of a vulture.

'I have summed them up,' he would say, 'and they are worth
so many an innings. I have noted three or four pretty hitters
among them, when they understand the bowling, but they are as
good as ready money to me. We shall have an accident with
these men very soon.' This diagnosis of the day's task he would
utter sufficiently audibly for the victims; for he liked a match
with some feeling in it. He wrote a brochure of practical cricket
hints and gave it to Mrs Grace, the champion's mother. He
didn't make many gifts, and his parsimony over wages led to
some disruption in his touring All-England Eleven. Only
Fuller Pilch played Clarke's bowling well, after careful study.

From Nottingham came the greatest length-bowler the game
has known, Alfred Shaw, who began professional life at the age
of ten as a crow-scarer. In first-class cricket he bowled nearly
17,000 maidens out of nearly 25,000 overs. James Grundy was
nearly as accurate—'he kept dropping them on a cheese-plate'.
His batting, too, was on the steady side, and he once made 103

297

in 6½ hours. A little earlier was the giant John Jackson, fast round-arm, who caused many a batsman to trouble the square-leg umpire's corns, and was called 'The Foghorn' because he blew his nose loudly whenever he took a wicket. Wicket-keeper in these days was Charlie Brown, 'Mad Charlie', who was always talking cricket in business hours at the dyeworks, and, when excited by his own narrative, christened everything around him from the colour-tub.

So the years moved on to the impeccable Arthur Shrewsbury and the magnificent William Gunn, a partnership of dismay to all bowlers. It was Shrewsbury who in the days before the tea-interval used to say at lunch, 'A cup of tea, please, at half-past four'. Then, the next generation of Gunns, the workmanlike left-handed John, nothing to look at but a day's job to shift, and the quixotic genius George, who scored a century when he felt that way, and got out when he wanted to watch the others batting.

It was Nottingham that produced the brightest meteor in hitting, Edward Alletson, who, on a May day of 1911, cracked the Sussex bowlers for 189 in 90 minutes. He dawdled for 50 minutes over his first 47; then, between 2.15 and 2.55, scored 142, hitting Tim Killick for 56 in two overs.

And then came Larwood, greatest fast bowler of our day, maybe of any day; mighty in operation, unhappy in circumstance. Trent Bridge is the scene of each First Test. Worthily, for no ground is richer in heroic history.

Rabbit's Rights

In a Test match at Manchester, certain batsmen of lowly numerical position were taken to task by a critic for patting the pitch with their bats. 'What,' he asked, 'would Doctor W. G. Grace have said about tail-enders who patted pitches?'

Leaving the great Doctor aside for a moment, who with more wisdom and propriety should pat a pitch than the bowlers who bat so precariously upon it? In comparison with them, the star batsmen will soon be quite unimportant, nursing, at third-man or mid-on, wounds received from imperfect pitch-patting. But the bowler must bowl; he must be sound and unbruised in ribs and joints. Then, as to Doctor Grace. Why is this genial Titan always being adduced as an example of tyranny, a prototype of ogreish autocracy, frowning upon the rights and foibles of the lesser cricketers around him?

The Doctor may sometimes have persuaded an umpire to reconsider a decision or two. After all, the world came to see him bat, not to see him being given out. But, that he interfered with the private conduct and enterprise of other people's batting, is a false memory and an unjustified suggestion. I fancy he would have nodded approvingly at pitch-patting by tail-enders; unless they belonged to the other team, when, perhaps, he would have meditated opportunities of running them out in horticultural absence.

As one who has spent happy and exciting times at number ten and eleven, and all the while believed himself to have been a more accomplished player than at least three of those written down above him, I should like to say a few words, as the half-hour orators put it, on the task of lowly batsmen. Nor do I care if I have said them before. Repetition may lead to conviction, as the judge remarked to the first-offender.

The lowly batsman is, so to speak, outnumbered by three to one. First, the crowd don't believe he can bat. He must prove that he can, if he can. Secondly, as soon as he comes in, the principal bowlers clamour wolfishly for the removal of the change-bowlers. Thirdly, the umpires bethink them of light refreshment. Of these enemies, the first is the worst. Nothing is more abusing than the scornful and evident incredulity of an audience. How, for example, would Mr Heddle Nash get on if he were to appear at an Albert Hall which was full of people who believed him totally incapable of singing one note in tune, or, indeed, of singing at all?

This is the era of the trade union. So let the late batsmen form a union, and vote themselves a bill of rights:

(i) To be given guard with decent care, not with one derisory flick of the hand.

(ii) Not to be given out at the first opportunity.

(iii) To be believed when they score that boundary to very fine long-leg.

(iv) To be allowed to pat the pitch without having anyone asking what Dr Grace would have said about it.

Sir F. S. Jackson

F. S. Jackson, second son of the first Lord Allerton, was one of the greatest all-rounders that cricket has known; indeed, apart from W. G. Grace, who won almost total immunity from comparisons, it is arguable that no other cricketer of any country has equalled Jackson in the combined arts of batting, bowling, and captaincy. Yet the truth remains that, when cricketers discuss their past heroes, they say less, possibly because they have heard less, of Stanley Jackson than of Ranjitsinhji, Fry, and MacLaren. In like manner, when men speak of literature, they rarely mention John Milton; when of London, they are silent about St. Paul's.

'Ranji' lives on in talk and thought as the unapproachable standard of effective grace, as a still exciting and insoluble mystery from the East; as uncle and source of imitation to our own Duleepsinhji. MacLaren comes up, as the touch-stone of values in captaincy, as the very idea of controlled freedom in batsmanship. Fry is with us, nearly the last of those turn-of-the-century immortals, scholar-athlete, columnist, instructor of youth, ripostorial yet creative in wit and debate. But, around Jackson – much silence and not a little awe; which shows the world, not for the first time, as a fool, seeing what lies waiting to be said of so genial and sympathetic a man, who was perfect English, Yorkshire, in his clear equality to the strongest tasks of council and of the cricket field, in steadiness of nerve and temperament, in unshakable but unshowy confidence, and in that knightliness which was true as well as titular.

In 1887, at the age of sixteen, Francis Stanley Jackson first played for Harrow against Eton at Lord's, and accomplished little. Next year he scored 21 and 59, took 6 for 40 and 5 for 81; Harrow won; and won again in 1889, when Jackson, now captain, played an innings of 68 and took 5 for 81. At Cambridge where he received his Blue as a Freshman, his bowling as yet outshone his batting; his pace was a brisk medium, with difficult out-swerve varied by a well-concealed break-back. In his last two summers he was captain; in the second, 1893, he invited Ranjitsinhji to play against Oxford, and was himself chosen to play twice against Australia for England. His batting had now caught up with expectation. At Lord's he scored 91; at the Oval, 103, against such bowlers as C. T. B. Turner, H. Trumble, G. Giffen, and G. H. S. Trott. He would have played also at Manchester, but Yorkshire, by an arrangement then possible if not centrally approved, claimed his services against Sussex at Brighton.

During the next four Rubbers against Australia in England, Jackson played in every match. In 1899, he scored 118 at the Oval, in an opening partnership of 185 with Tom Hayward (137). In the tremendous struggle at Manchester in 1902, which Australia won by three runs, he made 128 in a total of 262. And so to 1905, the *annus mirabilissimus* of any one cricketer. Chosen as captain of England, he led them to victory in the rubber, headed the Test batting averages with 70, the bowling with 15 (13 wickets), and beat J. Darling all five times in the toss. At Leeds he scored 144 not out; at Manchester 113. His 13 wickets included M. A. Noble three times, C. Hill twice, J. Darling twice, S. E. Gregory, W. W. Armstrong, and Victor Trumper. But, far beyond the tale of figures, he had that last unnamed gift of the games-player; as batsman he could rise to the innings that mattered; as bowler, he could find the ball that counted. As to his captaincy, the gods did well to favour him.

For Yorkshire, he played many fine matches; but it was neither secret nor surprise that it was Test cricket, against Australia, which induced in him the highest performance and enjoyment. To the best, only the best brings fulfilment. The wisdom of circumstance withdrew him from such cricket at the climax of achievement. Such a man was, rightly, not to be a re-tracer of his steps down the mountain side, a mere subject of kindlier memory.

From cricket to politics and affairs he turned those same qualities of shrewdness, tact and constancy. He was Member of Parliament, Financial Secretary of the War Office, Chairman of the Conservative Party, a Privy Councillor, and Governor of

Bengal. Between whiles he found time to play golf from a handicap of plus one.

He had dignity without pomp; diplomacy with simplicity. He is a chapter in history. For the true amateur has almost passed from cricket; and the proconsul will soon be a story.

Frank Chester

Umpire Frank Chester signals a leg-bye with the Terpsichorean abandon of an Anton Dolin, and chucks up the stone for the first ball of the over as if he wished it were a cricket ball and he about to get amongst the first batsmen of summer 1914.

First-class umpiring is, as it should be, first-class; but the standard is set from Chester. He stands for weeks without a mistake of sight or hearing. He changed umpiring from an occupation to an art. It was he who first bent low and balanced his face almost on the bails, and so began a fashion which reached far down into club cricket and only stopped short of these rural matches in which the bowler's umpire must stand erect to save his kidneys and balance the bails. Only an umpire as nearly infallible as Chester could afford to adorn so formal a task with powers of idiosyncrasy.

Some years ago a suggestion was made that Chester should go over to Australia and help with the umpiring of the Tests with England. It was an agreeable idea, but, like the proposed offer of the Isle of Wight to our American allies, incapable of fruition.

Chester began to play for Worcestershire when he was only sixteen, in 1912. He took 19 wickets, including that of a certain E. Hendren, and, in a battle with Somerset, exchanged compliments with the master of the in-swinger, W. T. Greswell, each bowling the other for 0. His highest score was 27 not out. In the next year he grew to be an all-rounder of rich promise. He scored three centuries for his county, and, with G. N. Foster, put on 254 for the fourth wicket against Middlesex at Lord's, his own share being 148 not out.

In 1914 his batting left his bowling behind. His best score was 178 not out against Essex at Worcester. He seemed earmarked for England. Then there came the Kaiser's war. Chester, severely wounded, lost his hand, and that was the end of his own cricket.

Like all men whose job is done with artistry, Chester cares much for detail. In a Test between England and India at Manchester there was a considerable delay when the cricketers came out after lunch. Then it was noticed that Chester was checking the re-start to its exact time. A very little point, but typical of the man.

No Test match is quite the thing without Frank Chester. His presence crowns the occasion. And, if I may end with a personal touch, I always felt, when Chester was the bowler's umpire, that I must and would bowl my best. Anything less would be almost an insult.

All in the Game

Cricket Supper

Nothing has ever stopped England's cricket suppers; Hitler, nor snow, nor the Ministry of Fuel and Power. I have in front of me an invitation to one many miles from home, and the inviter, as is his way, offers no channel for refusal; only a little advice – 'Do not,' he writes, 'choose the port; we are not particularly famous for our wines.'

Cricketers, above all games-players, set store by antiquity; possibly because no one knows just how old cricket is. If someone gets up and says that he saw the Blackburn Rovers beat the something-or-others in 1891, he might just as well have stayed in his seat; but a man who saw W. G. Grace cracking them around at Bristol in that year has news-value and an audience. He may be a howling bore but he saw the Doctor in action. And so the speeches at cricket suppers are fond of secretaries who have been at the job for over fifty years, and of umpires who have stood for the village man and boy. Scorers under sixty are not quite to be trusted.

The songs also are old. Mr Brown, who has appeared for many years at square point, will oblige with 'Up and Down the Drapery', and, as an encore, will render 'The Four-horsed Charabanc', with that annually awaited line about high-class music being a little melancholy but always so refined. Last year, a talented guest played 'The Monlight Sonata', very spiritedly and well; but the applause was no more than discreet. He took us by surprise; and we aren't very good at surprises. But, if he comes again this winter, he will be expected to play the same piece over again. Chopin or Debussy would be a mistake. Then, at the height of the evening, the comedian comes on. Ours puts on a farmer's smock and carries a jar of water on a string. Without the jar he would be nothing. His jokes are neither new nor subtle, but they are expected. Our wit, like our secretaries and umpires, must be old.

Neighbouring cricket teams are represented. Their skill is extolled with affectionate exaggeration. We are willing to forget that only a few months before we drove away from their ground vowing that never again would we visit such a breeding-ground of dishonesty. And, for ten minutes before the dance, the conjurer, who has recently been elected a member of the Magic Circle, produces the nine of diamonds at exactly the right moment, and, flicking half-crowns from the treasurer's left ear, reminds us of that overdue subscription to the only Cricket Club that matters.

Day-Dreams

They are more easily controlled than those that visit us in the night. While asleep I have done great things at Wimbledon. After winning a rally of at least a hundred strokes, I have run forward to the net to shake my opponent's hand and found him changed into a goose, dressed in a small straw helmet, and walking up and down the base-line in an indeterminate but obstreperous manner. I have also been playing in a Test match at Lord's and, after a neat enough push past cover-point, have found myself running between the wickets without any progress at all, in spite of the exhortations of the Emperor of Abyssinia, who is standing square-leg umpire.

But, in the daytime, we can win as we like; without the interference of geese or emperors. Outside, the wind howls. It is the season of armchair golf. The afternoons draw in. But time and transport mean nothing. We settle down to our visionary triumphs. I remember an international golfer who never allowed his scholastic duties to interfere with his game. In the five minutes between lessons, while others were remarking angrily on the universal decay of puerile intelligence or feverishly studying the habits of scalene triangles, this supine pedagogue would close his eyes and go round Hoylake twice in under seventy, then get through another two rounds in the classroom.

Myself, I have a weakness for the Road Hole at St Andrews. I have played it in all weathers, but always in three. Sometimes in sunshine, with a light following breeze and a number two iron; sometimes into the wind, in the fourth round of the Open, with a 230 yard brassie shot that pitches two yards from the hole and stays there; then, with enviable nonchalance, I stagger the enormous crowd by putting bang into the middle of the hole. I never fail. For railway journeys I keep the old loved course of

Hindhead. Here, after tea in May, I play stroke for stroke with Harry Vardon himself, till, on the last green, his putt for a half in three slips past the hole; and all the passengers in the compartment can go to the deuce.

Cricket I reserve for the depths of winter and a roaring fire. Then I have a go at Don Bradman. The Australian champion takes guard and studies the field. But I have no need for slips or short-legs. No; I find just the ball I want: an in-swinger that straightens from middle-and-leg and sends the off-stump wheeling past the wicket-keeper. Then, greedy with triumph, I call back Victor Trumper himself from the years and bowl him with just such another. The east wind howls through the bare trees outside the windows; but inside, it is high summer, and the Test match is as good as won.

A Hundred Hundreds

Leonard Hutton's hundredth hundred in first-class cricket was in more than one sense well-timed. It came as a rounding-off to his wonderful performances in Australia in 1950–51, and as a numerical reminder of his supremacy in contemporary cricket. He reached it with a drive to the off-boundary, cricket's and Hutton's loveliest stroke; and he was batting at the Oval, scene of so many of his triumphs.

So, as thirteenth man, he joined the list of the mighty who have had the skill, the time, and the health to score a hundred a hundred times. A great feat. But, as we look at the list, we should remember also some of the very greatest who are not there: K. S. Ranjitsinhji and Victor Trumper, for two. In the judging of art, quantity is not of the first relevance; and, when we look up at the stars in the sky, it is not of their size that we are thinking.

Indeed, as we glance through this list of thirteen, let there be no nonsense about comparative merit. W. G. Grace and D. G. Bradman come seventh and eighth in the order. Let that be a warning to all arithmeticians. Far better to let the memory play around the differences of style and temperament which brought them all to the same triumph. F. E. Woolley and

C. P. Mead; alike only in being left-handed and great; Woolley, playing as if batsmanship were an exhibition of beauty, to be broken off at his, not the bowler's, will; Mead, conducting business on a pitch of which he had taken lease for this world and the next.

H. Sutcliffe and E. Hendren; Sutcliffe, the megalo-psychic; denying, by attitude, the existence of good luck, or, almost, of the bowlers themselves; Hendren, democratic, busily and gladly sharing the enjoyment and stresses of batting with spectators, umpires, scorers, and dogs. J. B. Hobbs and W. R. Hammond; alike in perfection of athletic balance and in judgment that flashes from brain to limb; different in that Hammond chose to go down the pitch to the spin bowling, whereas Hobbs liked more to play it in his crease.

Tom Hayward; I saw him far past his prime, but still with something magnificently military in his stance and moustache. Andrew Sandham and Ernest Tyldesley; both great; but both batting as it were under slight shadow; Sandham daily, under the shadow of Hobbs; Tyldesley, by retrospect and comparison, under the shadow of the immortal 'J. T.'

Apart from these stands L. E. G. Ames, the only wicket-keeper who has scored a hundred hundreds, and who kept, later than most, the gift of the quick foot and eye.

So to Grace and Bradman. No words can add to or subtract from their fame. And now L. Hutton joins the band. He is a worthy member.

Long Vacation

Success at games demands total freedom from care. I first learnt this truth at school when, soon after taking guard at the crease, I saw among the few spectators the unwelcome face of my schoolmaster, who had put me down for detention that sunny afternoon.

Nor is this truth invalidated by the desperate case of the illustrious England batsman who, they say, compiled his record aggregate of runs one summer almost entirely because he knew that there lay in wait, near the pavilion, the lady who, contrary to his expressed advice, had determined to marry him. He just had to bat on.

Freedom from care. The words are 'tolling me back' to the start of the Long Vacation at Oxford. Work, such as it was, is over. The mind is disburdened of the hideous complexities of that tortuous Teuton, Immanuel Kant. Let the Roman Empire rip. It is up to the examiners now. By the Porter's Lodge I meet my tutor, who has done his best. He is off to try out the wines of France and the architecture of Italy. Parting makes him polite; and he hopes, hesitating for the phrase, that we shall meet with the requisite measure of success at Lord's. As to us, we go off to Brighton, to try out the bowling of Maurice Tate, to fish from rowing-boats, and to shoot in the underground rifle-range on the Pier. We could also enter the Aquarium for 2d.

Meanwhile, some who said they must work, and others who had made no particular arrangements, stayed behind and played Long Vacation cricket. I fancy that they made more of these matches in the Victorian era. My old headmaster at school, on the long Sunday afternoon rambles of the Summer term, used to tell me of the heroic deeds performed by these Long Vacation cricketers when he was young.

The years had enlarged the stature of his early companions. All of them seemed only by some inexplicable mischance to have escaped the favourable notice of the University captain. They were the Blues of the Never-Land. Against heroes, too, they played. The Hon. Alfred Lyttelton detached himself from his Middlesex commitments to keep wicket against these Long Vacationers. Alfred Shaw, of Nottingham, for all his perfect length, could make no headway against young X of Keble College. W. G. Grace himself, in his giant prime, was clean bowled for 45 by the tearaway Z, and made kindly inquiries about his qualifications for a county. But Z went off to be a parson in the wilds of Cumberland, and the Doctor went back to Gloucestershire and forgot all about him.

What does it matter if it was all a legend? As the years lend enchantment to the days of youth, the runs and the wickets of the imagination are as good as any that illumine the pages of *Wisden*.

Goodbye, Larwood

Harold Larwood, with his wife and family, sailed for Australia in April 1950 on the same ship, I fancy, which carried him thither twenty-two years before with A. P. F. Chapman's England team. His welcome from that generous country was warm, this time in the less vernacular meaning of the epithet.

It is quite commonly thought that Larwood ceased from major cricket soon after his return from Australia with D. R. Jardine's team in 1933; but he played for Nottinghamshire through another six summers. The error is natural; his cricket for the county in these latter years was, in a sense, posthumous. It was successful enough; but he was suffering from an injury to his foot and, though he said little enough about it, to his feelings.

His fame is already legendary. Boys ask, 'How fast was Larwood? 100 miles an hour?' Just as they ask about Blériot's first flight across the English Channel, or the performance of the earliest De Dion Bouton motor-car. And the answer is, about as fast as a human being can bowl, and as straight.

His record in figures? As to them, they mean as little, or as much, as the candle-power of the moon. You didn't think of mathematics when you saw Larwood open the bowling; spectators thought of the poetry of rhythm and the *panache* of assault; batsmen thought of survival and, sometimes, of their wives and testamentary dispositions. There's been nothing like him since.

I met him just before he sailed, at a farewell party given by his former captain, Douglas Jardine. Larwood, who has the natural modesty of the great games-player, said, 'You know, I was never really fast in England.' At this statement, the hand of the illustrious Herbert Sutcliffe, that unflinching player of fast bowling, moved, almost involuntarily, to the region of the ribs.

They say that we have forgotten how to bowl fast in England. Maybe; maybe not. But we who saw him in action, that perfect action, or only read of him in books, we shall never forget Larwood.

'O Captain, My Captain'

When Sam Weller said of his master, then in some conjugal danger, 'Rum feller, the hemperor', he meant it more or less as a compliment. Hemperors, especially of Rome, China, or Goswell Street, tended to be rum. Rumminess came to be expected of them; and they rarely disappointed.

The same is true of the cricket captain. He stands out, in a rapidly self-levelling world, as one of the few unquestioned examples of absolute monarchy. Unquestioned, though not uncriticized. But, whereas his predecessor of classical story was apt to be criticized for what he did, the modern dictator of the cricket field is more often censured for what he fails to do.

Nero aroused comment by frequent attempts to poison his mother; Caligula, by appointing his favourite horse a Consul. The cricket Tyrant on the other hand, excites disagreement by neglecting to put on his slow leg-spinner at 3.30 p.m. or to place a fielder in the exact spot where he, apparently alone of 30,000 persons present, failed to foresee that the star batsman of the other side was predestined to offer the simplest of catches. But does he care? If he does, he is no cricket captain.

These reflections were in part induced by reading that the house where once lived that illustrious captain and batsman, Mr A. C. MacLaren, had come up for sale. Somehow the paragraph had a double, if melancholy, significance, for it was a reminder of the passing not only of a man but of an attitude.

As a Test captain, MacLaren lost at least as often as he won, yet, by the consent of informed contemporaries and now by unanswerable tradition, he stands with such as W. G. Grace and M. A. Noble, among the great captains. Why? Because his captaincy was a thing of romance as well as of science. His plans might be subtle enough, but they were expressed in the action of chivalry and daring. He did things as they occurred to him, by intuition or analytical observation. They might be wrong, but they were his own. In defeat or victory he pennons flew. He was the magnifico.

But MacLaren was, also, fortunate in his time. He lived in an age of limited publicity, before the interest of Test matches had risen, or sunk, from the athletic to the political. To the neo-Georgian, magnificence means nothing without results, and from International Sport the footsteps of Romance have receded. Today, MacLaren would never have got away with those Test defeats. And today we are in danger of asking one thing only from our captain, that he should win. That which was once heresy is now the orthodox doctrine. It is not too late to recant.

The Game of his Life

For thousands it is just the name of a sporting event rather than a cricket match, something that knocks about in the mind's box with the Derby, the National, and the Cup Final. For some, it is one more social event, when the men must dress, and the ladies look their best. But, for twenty-two young cricketers, it is the game of the year, perhaps of a life-time.

The fixture was always a 'natural'. Even in the days of horse transport Eton was not far from Harrow, and, for unreported years, the match was played at one or the other school. In 1818, indeed, they played each other twice, once at Easter. In 1805 George Gordon Lord Byron detached himself from poetical meditation on his favourite tombstone, and played cricket for Harrow, who were 'most confoundedly beat'; but the match was soon forgotten in celebrations, 'seven of us in a single hackney coach, four of Eton and three of Harrow'. Then, in 1822, to avoid the probable ban of Eton's somewhat ogreish headmaster, Dr Keate, the game was taken to Lord's and there, except for an odd year or so and two world wars, it has since remained.

Harrow won that first Lord's match, chiefly owing to the left-hand bowling of Charles Wordsworth, a nephew of the poet and later Bishop of St Andrews. There followed twenty-five years in which Eton predominated. Then came twenty years or so in which Eton could win only twice, though C. I. Thornton, of Eton, later to become *the* hitter of all time, did drive a ball clean over the old pavilion in 1868. Then, for a generation of men, affairs were tolerably level, till, in the latter years of Queen Victoria, the Dark Blue of Harrow more often than not won the day, and a temerarious letter-writer suggested that Eton should give up either rowing or cricket. But the tide, of cricket, turned in 1903, since when Harrow have won only four times.

Space forbids mention of more than a few individual heroes. But Harrow will never forget their E. M. Dowson, the left-hander who took thirty-five Eton wickets in five matches at the end of last century, and M. C. Bird, who hit two brilliant centuries in 1907, the year in which one Lionel Hallam Tennyson, played for his tearaway bowling, scored 1 and 1 at number Eleven for Eton.

But 1910 produced *the* match and *the* hero of the whole series. It was Eton's number 9 and 11. Manners and Boswell, who gave R. St L. Fowler his chance; and how he took it, bowling out Harrow with his off-spinners for 45 and winning the match by nine runs.

Time fails to tell of the deeds of the Crutchleys, the Crawleys, Enthoven, Tindall, and Pawle for Harrow, of Gibson, G. O. Allen, A. W. Allen, Akers-Douglas, and Hotchkin for Eton, and of many heroes besides. Yet none, however neutral, but has felt the spell at Lord's on the second afternoon of Eton *v.* Harrow, when the clock rushes or stops dead, according to taste, and the cheers and counter-cheers are on, and even beauty stands still to watch instead of being watched.

Last Man In

An eminent Number Eleven, than whom none made fewer runs in a stranger manner over a longer space of time, once told me that the mare which pulled the roller used to neigh when he walked out to bat. 'There was,' he said, 'welcome in that sound, and encouragement, and just that amount of sympathetic contempt with which one rabbit hails another across the rough on the golf-course.'

Horses are kinder than men. Any Number Eleven will tell you that. The trouble starts when, about the fall of the sixth wicket, he begins to fumble in his chaotic cricket-bag and Number One, who was out to a wonderful slip-catch, of course, watches his probably superfluous preparations with tolerant amusement. Our Number One sometimes used to ask me, 'Do you think your pads will be driving well today?'

The members, as he walks down the steps, eye him curiously, as if they are a little surprised, even disappointed, to find that he has human attributes, a couple of legs, a face, and the power of locomotion. The gateman, who has more of the roller-horse in him, smiles as the victim passes, and leaves the gate open with humorous prophecy. Yet, as he treads the green grass towards the wicket, he is happy. He has no care about which way the bowler spins the ball. All the bowling is the same to him; all easy; all impossible. He approaches the crease, and the fielders take rather longer than usual to rise, except the bowler, who has never sat down and waits in predatory attitude, thinking of an improvement in his analysis.

All this he can bear. But, soon, he makes a beautiful off-drive, a stroke worthy of Hobbs or Hammond, and – the spectators laugh at the evident mistake. He snicks one past slip, and – they laugh again. He can do no right, or wrong, He is beyond criticism, like a madman, or a cow.

Then, to crown all, his partner, some Number Six struggling for a mediocre fifty, starts to whisper gratuitous advice between the overs; his partner, who, under pretence of shielding him from the bowling, steals it for his own selfish ends. Then, this greedy and dictatorial run-stealer misses an off-break and is out; and gets the sympathy. No one cares that a few more balls would have seen Number Eleven move his score from 9 to 10. That's the truth of it, no one cares.

And does Number Eleven? Not he; not a row of rattling acorns.

Cricket Will Out

In Australia, I miss the games of cricket as seen, inconclusive but happy, from the window of an English railway train. This longing, *desiderium*, arises partly, perhaps, because there are sometimes and suddenly no trains to see from, and partly because in Australia there are no villages in the English sense and so no village cricketers.

It is not in the Australian character to play cricket haphazardly. No batsman emerges from under a green tree by a tavern, in belt and braces and one black pad, to the cheers, half-affectionate and half-derisive, of his fellow-revellers.

There is much cricket here of a minor, even of a very minor standard; and it is obvious that its players enjoy it in their own way to the full. It is a mistake to think that every Australian batsman is a Bradman in the bud, just as it is incorrect to imagine that American golf courses teem with Ben Hogan.

I have seen club matches in Australia where the inexactitude of the batting and bowling and fielding would make a visiting member of the Much-Grabham Wednesday Gasworks eleven raise a sympathetic eyebrow. But the cricket, however mildly or wildly incompetent, is serious. It sometimes smiles sardonically; but it seldom laughs aloud.

Then, late one Sunday afternoon, in the rain at Brisbane, I saw three boys at their game. The stumps were the trunk of a palm-tree, the bails were its foliage. There were no fielders. Two bowlers, one in his uncle's mackintosh, were trundling away, with abuse and laughter, at a batsman in bathing-trunks, who, like every boy the world over, did not regard being bowled, even twice running, as a legitimate cause of exit.

For a few minutes I was in England; except that in England this combat of three could hardly have been enacted; because they were playing their cricket in the precincts of a cathedral, a few yards from where we, the congregation, were coming out.

The Style is the Man

A former Australian Test cricketer told me how he once played for a team which contained everyone connected with death: a doctor, a solicitor, an undertaker, and a monumental mason.

The last-named, he said, fielded at cover-point and made jokes about the batsman's style. The undertaker, who often drove straight from the churchyard to the cricket field, kept wicket, and regarded each player as a prospective corpse. He never spoke except to appeal, which he did in hollow tones not expecting the answer 'no'.

Those of us who have been fortunate enough to play in English village cricket know that each profession begets its particular style of play. The most careful and correct batsmen are the parson and the schoolmaster. Both are instructors. One spends much time in improving the soul; the other in educating the mind. Both are concerned with showing an example. In each pursuit they are long used to only moderate success. So it is with their batting. They cling faithfully to orthodoxy. They play a 'shooter' with a perfectly straight bat held some nine inches above the ball. When caught at wicket off the hand they do not rub their left shoulder. They are, therefore, the most heroic and probably the least successful of village batsmen.

Professional gardeners make good medium-paced bowlers. I cannot tell you why, unless it be that they thrive on monotony and are not easily disappointed. Blacksmiths are popularly supposed to bowl fast and to hit colossally. But, in a varied village career in many countries. I've only met one playing blacksmith. He played back and crookedly to a half-volley first ball, and was not required to bowl.

Publicans, on the other hand, make very fair fast bowlers, when in training. They also bat well at about number six or seven. But, in a whole-day match, they should not be put in or not too soon after the luncheon interval.

Policemen, possibly because they like to get things exactly right and legal, appeal much and are apt to differ from the umpire's decision. Nor are they always as popular as they deserve to be with the crowd, which is apt to contain a few who cycle without rear-lights under the full moon.

Grocers, doubtless because of their close and exhausting acquaintance with invoices, are fond of hovering behind the scorer's shoulder and correcting him on a detail of the extras.

In the field, farm-hands are the most impervious to pain, and stop the fastest drives with their shins or hands indifferent. Caterers are very inattentive, because one eye is always waiting for the van that brings the tea. But a wise captain does not rebuke them.

For sheer hitting, give me the motor mechanic. He is muscular of arm and hand, and he doesn't give a hoot about results. But the best long-stops are house-painters. This cannot be explained.

Soon, after the long winter, all of them will be at it again; all over England; all stylists of their own immortal kind.

To Lord's Again

By foot, once again, is the way to approach Lord's, drinking the slow, deep draught of anticipation. The cigarette shop on the way had not changed. The proprietor and his wife emerged from behind their photographic gallery of film-stars, as ever readier for conversation than a sale. Business could wait. Life is too short for hurry. When the proprietor heard that I'd been to Australia, he looked at me as if to make sure of my identity. He knew someone, he said, who'd been over there, and he never came back.

Round the corner the street was as quiet as ever. The only change was that one more house had been taken over by the Government, for the Sanitary Inspector. But the other signs were reassuring. An errand-boy rode past on a bicycle far too large for him, whistling. A young navigator tested his new boat on a string in the Regent's Canal, to the obvious annoyance of the angler who had never had any luck.

Inside the W. G. Grace gates I saw the same spectator whom I always see on my first day at Lord's. He was waiting for his brother; who is always late. And there was the field itself. How green, after the huge, glaring, yellowy arenas of Australia.

But I missed the member with his telescope which he balances on the front rail of the pavilion, bending low to fix his eye on the footwork of the batsmen and the very texture of the pitch. He will surely arrive, when the sun is stronger, and he has finished cataloguing the ships at sea, or the stars in the May sky. He will, of course, bring his field-glasses as well, for double verification.

In the afternoon sun the Tavern grew more argumentative. On the grassy plot behind the Rover stand, one man sat with his back to the match, achieving that elusive triumph of thinking of absolutely nothing at all. Another spectator lay fast asleep, content with the mere fact of cricket and his own absence from the roar of traffic, from invoices, or the blare of his neighbour's radio. He would wake in an hour or so, and tell them, all wrong, all about the cricket, when he reached home. Near these two, a lady sat and took everything out of her handbag and put everything back in a slightly different order, as is the way of the ladies.

On the top of the grandstand Father Time, the weather-cock, fiddled eternally with the bails, and pointed his wind-arrow, hopefully, to the west. And, behind the scoreboard, the men in charge of the telegraph-numbers went agreeably mad, and said that Number Seven, long out, had made 173, then 29, then 46, then a pair of noughts.

Meanwhile, two attendants persuaded some fifty spectators who had emerged on to vacant benches in the sun to return to the cold shade of the covered seats. They would not have retired so obediently at Sydney.